CW01650516

BRITAIN IN OLD PHOTOGRAPHS

# STOWMARKET

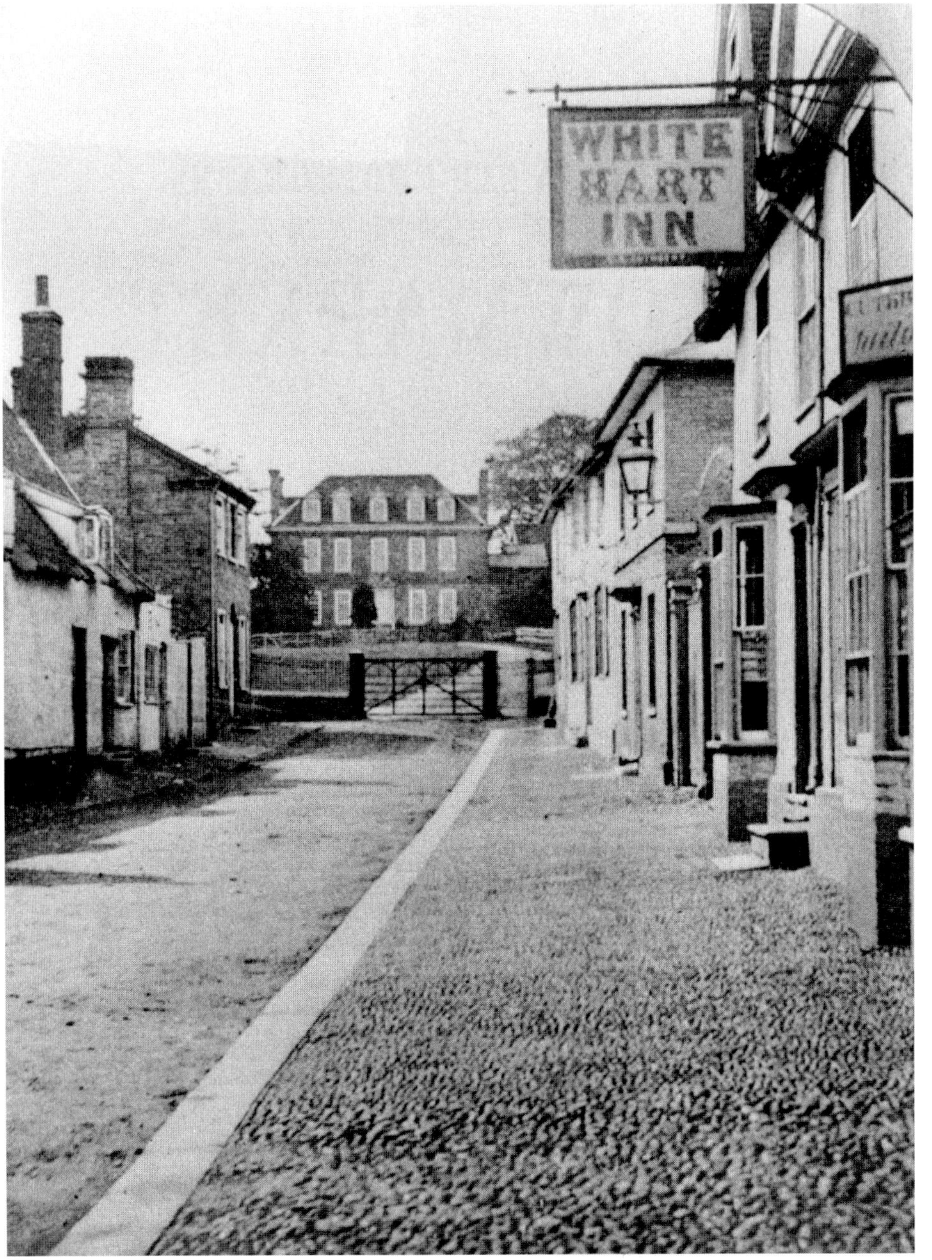


Victorian Stowmarket: Crowe Street and Abbot's Hall, seen in a photograph probably taken about 1875. The house and farm (the latter now the home of the Museum of East Anglian Life) took the name Abbot's Hall from the Abbots of St Osyth in Essex, owners of the manor until the time of the Dissolution. (Museum of East Anglian Life)

BRITAIN IN OLD PHOTOGRAPHS

# STOWMARKET

ROBERT MALSTER

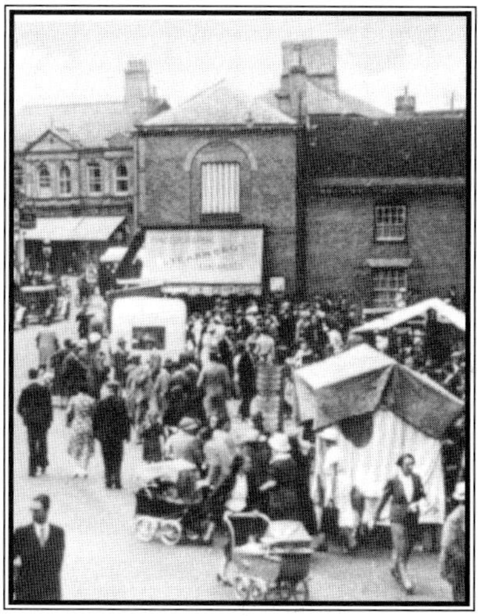

ALAN SUTTON PUBLISHING LIMITED

Alan Sutton Publishing Limited
Phoenix Mill · Far Thrupp · Stroud
Gloucestershire · GL5 2BU

Suffolk County Council

First published 1995



*Cover photographs*: (front) 'Wings for Victory' Week, June 1943; (back) Ipswich Street, 1950s.
*Title page*: Market day, 1930s. (Geoff Clarke)

**British Library Cataloguing in Publication Data.**
A catalogue record for this book is available from the British Library.

ISBN 0-7509-0897-1

Typeset in 9/10 Sabon.
Typesetting and origination by
Alan Sutton Publishing Limited.
Printed in Great Britain by
Hartnolls, Bodmin, Cornwall.

In memory of the Reverend A.G.H. Hollingsworth and Harry Double, historians of Stowmarket.

# *Contents*

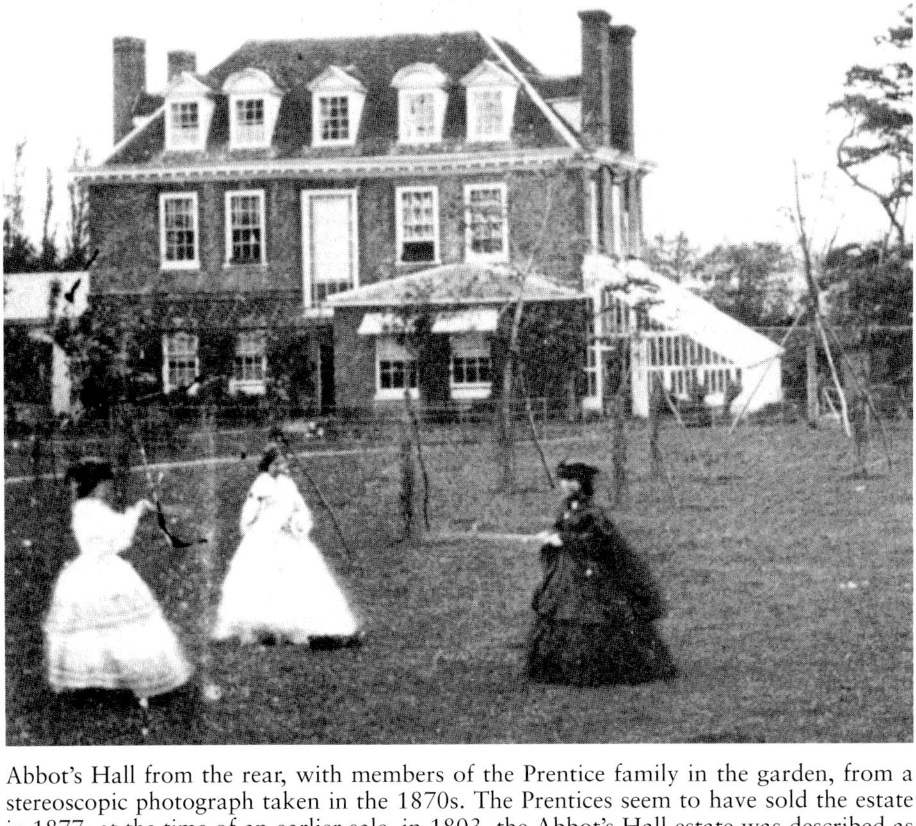

Abbot's Hall from the rear, with members of the Prentice family in the garden, from a stereoscopic photograph taken in the 1870s. The Prentices seem to have sold the estate in 1877; at the time of an earlier sale, in 1803, the Abbot's Hall estate was described as 'comprising an excellent brick built Mansion, coach-house, barn, stable, and suitable and convenient offices, a malt-house 40 coombs steep, gardens, an orchard, and 125 Acres of extremely rich and fertile arable, meadow, and pasture Lands and Hop Ground, in the highest state of cultivation'. (Museum of East Anglian Life)

# *Introduction*

Stowmarket is an example of an East Anglian phenomenon, a small market town that in the course of the 19th century became a centre of industry. In its setting amid the Suffolk cornfields it avoided the worst and grimiest manifestations of industrialisation, while the shattering catastrophe of 1871, when the local guncotton works exploded with devastating effect, ensured that the fact of that industrialisation was made plain even to those not directly involved.

My interest in this aspect of the town's immediate past was stirred when I led a course on industrial archaeology for the Stowmarket branch of the Workers' Educational Association some years ago. The effects of the chemical works, the explosives works and the iron foundry were not immediately apparent, except perhaps in the terraces of the little 19th-century suburb of Lime Tree Place, but they were to be found in the documents recording the growth of population from a mere 1,760 in 1801 to more than 3,300 half a century later.

The social effects of the economic changes must have been considerable. Stowmarket was always a lively little town, with a book club which at the beginning of this century had had an uninterrupted existence since 1796, a provident society established in 1832 and reorganised nine years later, and which in the 1850s had nearly 700 members paying monthly contributions, and a mechanics' institute established in 1845. From 1894 until 1974 the town had its own urban district council to organise its affairs, and was also the meeting place of Thedwastre and East Stow rural district councils, which at one time shared the services of Stowmarket solicitor Robert Wilkes as clerk.

In recording the town's history over the past century and a half in old photographs I have sought to concentrate to some extent on the trades and industries. The work has been the more pleasant for the willing help I have been given by a number of people; it is very true to say that without their generous and unstinting practical assistance this book could never have been produced.

Indeed, had it not been for the early encouragement of Geoff Clarke I would not have taken on the task of compiling such a record. Suffolk Local History Council recorder for Haughley and volunteer presenter for the East Anglian Film Archive, Geoff proved a very active assistant, producing pictures both from his own collection and from the negatives of the late George Wilden, which are now in his care.

At the Museum of East Anglian Life at Abbots Hall Lesley Colsell, David Birch and George Monger gave me much-needed support and produced

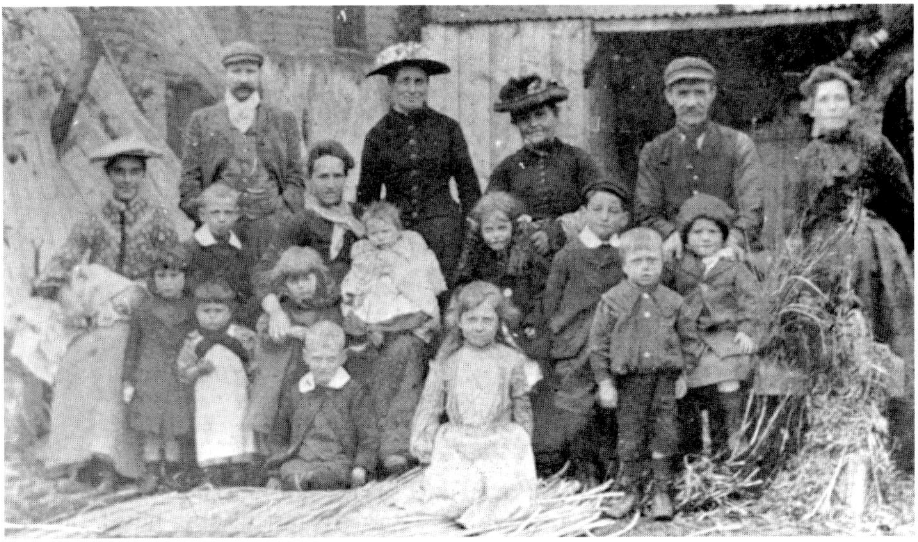

Along the Gipping were many osier beds, where willows were grown for basketmaking. The osier rods were peeled, or 'broken', before being supplied to the basketmakers. The local firm at the beginning of the century was Thomas Trigbuth Mullins & Son, wine flats, sieve and hamper manufacturers and osier and willow growers, of Wash Lane, Onehouse, and 70½ Lower Thames Street, London (a somewhat precise address!); later there were two, Robert Mullins in Wash Lane and George Mullins in Combs Lane, Great Finborough. This photograph of rod breakers in Duke Lane clearly belongs to the earlier period. (Ivan Codd)

pictures from the museum collection. Ron Pattle, too, went through his photographs in search of material for the book.

At the offices of Stowmarket Town Council Maurice Cansdale showed me the albums bequeathed to the council by the late Harry Double, who in his three books has set down so much of the recent history of the town. He also directed me towards Ivan Codd, who enthusiastically lent items from his collection of local photographs and supplied a great deal of information.

Ivan's enthusiasm was such that we spent a number of long sessions poring over his photograph albums and searching directories for information; Mrs Codd supplied us with tea and sandwiches as his evening meal spoilt in the oven. I owe them both a debt that cannot be repaid.

At Combs Tannery Nic Portway produced a wonderful store of old photographs, some dating back to the 1860s, telling of a family enterprise that linked industry and farming.

To all of them, my thanks. I must also express my gratitude to Simon Fletcher, of Alan Sutton Publishing, who suggested the subject of the book.

Robert Malster
Holbrook, 1995

## *Section One*

# THE VICTORIAN TOWN

Stowmarket was described in 1879 as a clean and healthy market town situated nearly in the middle of Suffolk. Its past had indeed been as a market town serving a wide area that was almost entirely agricultural, but in the third quarter of the 19th century Stowmarket was also an industrial town which was growing away from its old farming connections.

At one time the town had shared in the woollen trade, with a manufacture of worsteds, and also in the hempen cloth trade, but by 1850 there were only a sacking manufacturer and three manufacturers of horsehair seating.

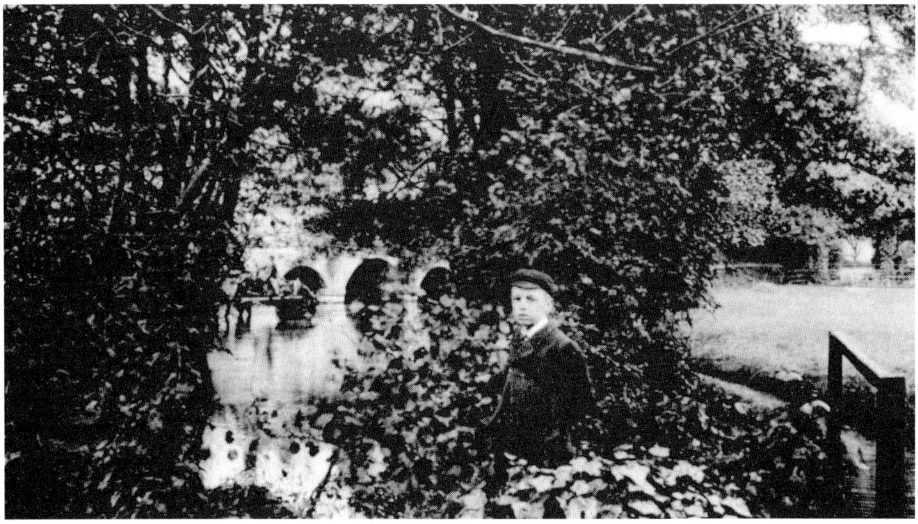

The Rattlesden river below Boulter's Bridge. There is a story that the stones for Bury Abbey were taken up this river to Rattlesden, but modern historians are sceptical of the authenticity of this. (John Wilton)

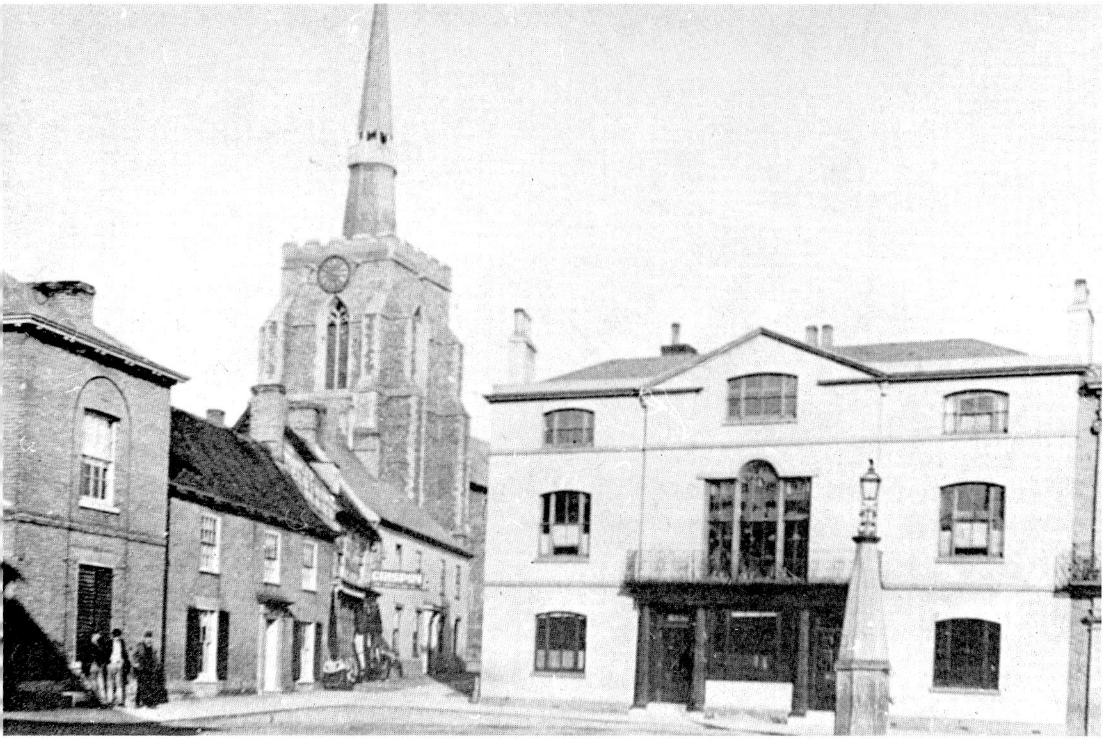

The parish church seen from the Market Place, *c.* 1868. In Cheapside, leading from the Market Place to Church Street, can be seen the shop of Thomas Crispin, pawnbroker and clothier. The battlemented top of the church tower was altered in 1876, when quite extensive repairs were done at a cost of £247 10s. (Geoff Clarke)

The construction of the Stowmarket Navigation in the 1790s stimulated the town's trade, and in 1830 Pigot's *National Commercial Directory* stated that 'a very considerable business is done in the corn, coal and timber trades . . . much business is done here in the malting trade: hops are cultivated to advantage in this vicinity, for which there is an annual fair'.

Between 1800 and 1850 the population of the town almost doubled, many country people being attracted into the town by the prospect of steady employment in its expanding industries, which received a further boost from the coming of the Ipswich and Bury Railway in 1846.

The railway sucked away the trade of the Gipping navigation, but it also seems to have promoted further expansion. Whereas the population of Stowmarket had been increasing at 250–300 a decade in the first half of the century, this rate of increase was almost doubled between 1861 and 1871. In that decade the number of people living in Stowmarket and Stowupland together increased by 645, and to meet the needs of the new arrivals seventy

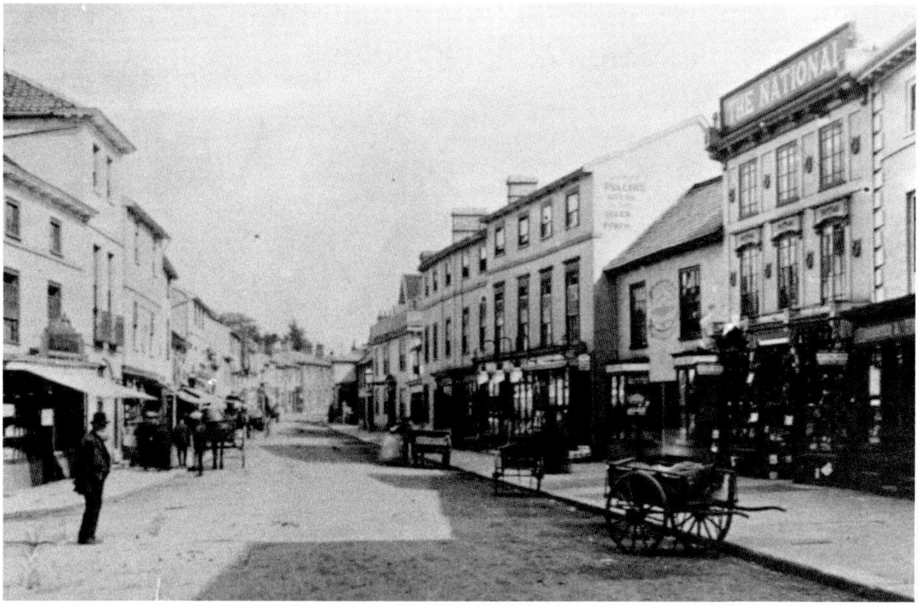


Ipswich Street from the Market Place, 1880s. The premises of Lankester & Wells, wine, spirit and cigar importers and bonders, are on the extreme right. Further along on the right-hand side is the shop of William Turner, family draper, dress and mantle maker, milliner, silk mercer, glover, hosier, carpet warehouseman and furnishing undertaker – and also agent for Pullars of Perth, the dyers. (Geoff Clarke)

new homes were built in Stowmarket. In spite of the builders' efforts there seems to have been a housing shortage in 1871, for the 833 inhabited houses were occupied by 983 families, indicating a considerable degree of multiple occupation. The position was eased by the building of another 97 houses in the next ten years, but after about 1880 the rate of house-building seems to have slowed down sharply.

When writing of Stowmarket and Stowupland it has to be borne in mind that the old boundary ran along the course of the River Gipping, so that the railway station and much of the town's industry was situated in Stowupland until boundary changes in this century extended the urban district to include parts of Stowupland and other neighbouring parishes. With the coming of the railway the course of the river above Stowupland Street was straightened to avoid the necessity of building bridges to carry the line, yet the boundary continued to follow the old course of the river for many more years.

The population of Stowmarket and Stowupland combined reached a peak of some 5,500 in 1891; that figure remained more or less stable for nearly 40 years, when there came a new wave of expansion which brought the Stowmarket population above 8,000, with almost another 2,000 in the village of Stowupland.

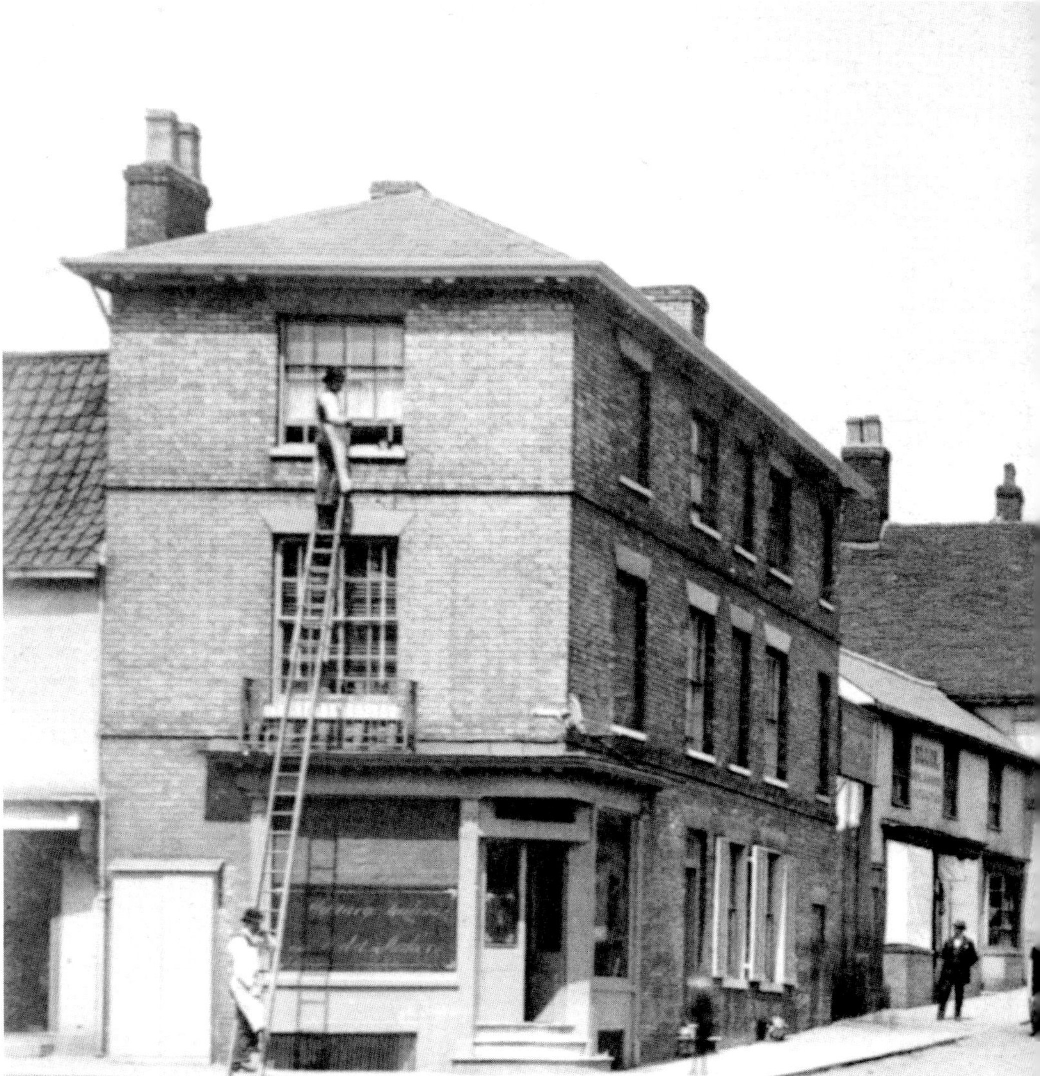

All eyes are on the photographer taking this picture of Bury Street at the junction with Station Road, on the right, and Tavern Street, left, *c.* 1890. Until about 1880 this part of Station Road was still known as Stowupland Street, Station Road being a new highway built in the 1840s to provide a direct link between the new railway station,

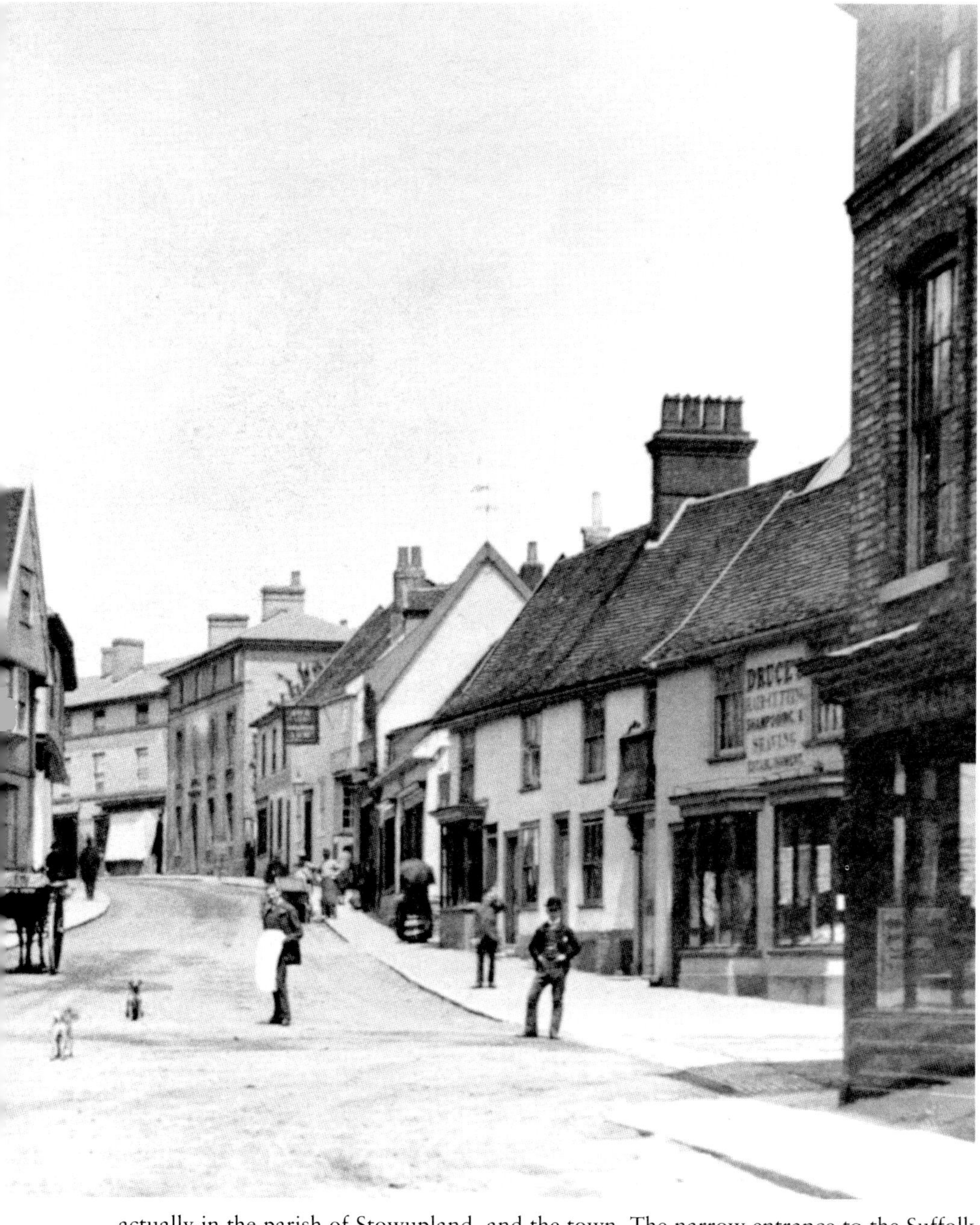

actually in the parish of Stowupland, and the town. The narrow entrance to the Suffolk Iron Works of Woods & Co. can be seen on the left of Bury Street, next to the shop of William Ellis, harness maker, who has put up the blinds to keep out the glare. (Geoff Clarke)

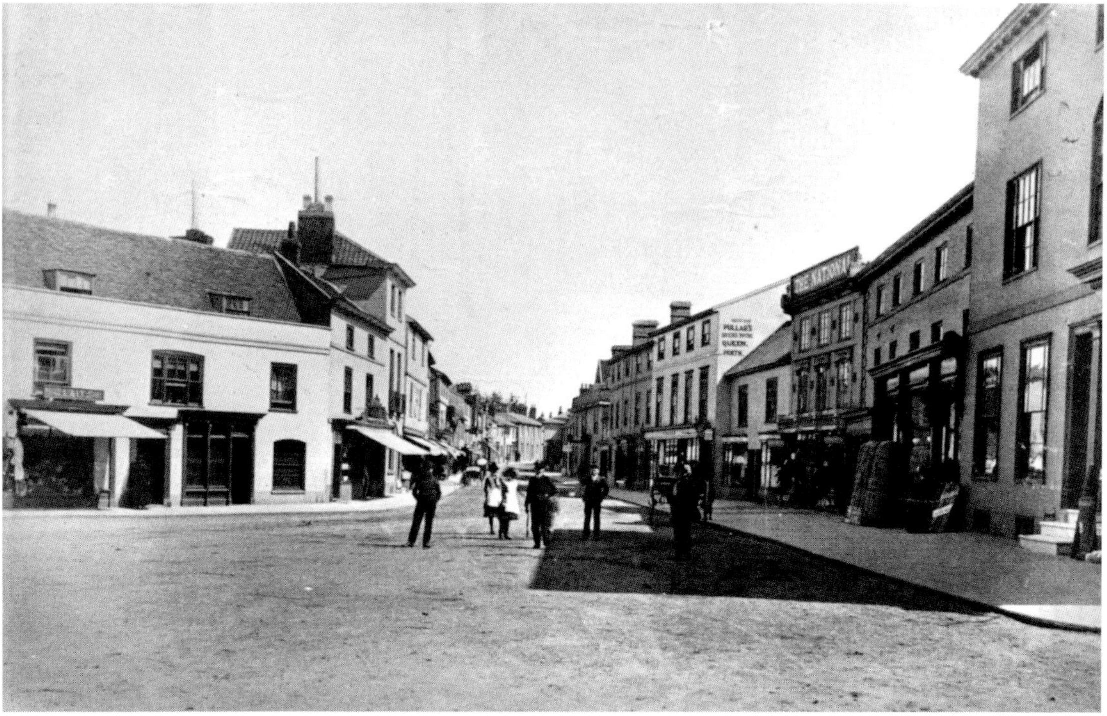

A view of the Market Place and Ipswich Street, *c.* 1890. With hardly any traffic, a few inhabitants stand idly in the middle of the road to watch the photographer going about his work, and to provide him with a small nucleus of human interest in an otherwise deserted street. (Geoff Clarke)

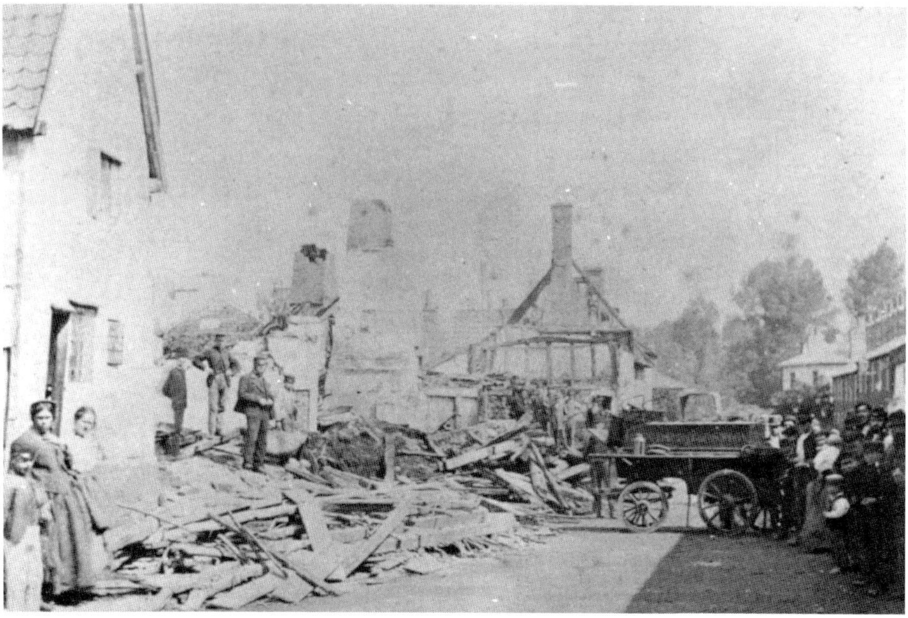

A catastrophic fire destroyed 18 houses and a beerhouse called the Carpenters' Arms in Bury Street on a Sunday morning in July 1868, making 81 people homeless. The flames were fanned by a strong wind and spread rapidly along the row of mainly timber-framed houses, in spite of the efforts of firemen from the town brigade and a number of other brigades in the area. The manual fire engine in the picture above is marked 'Hundred of Stow'. (Ivan Codd)

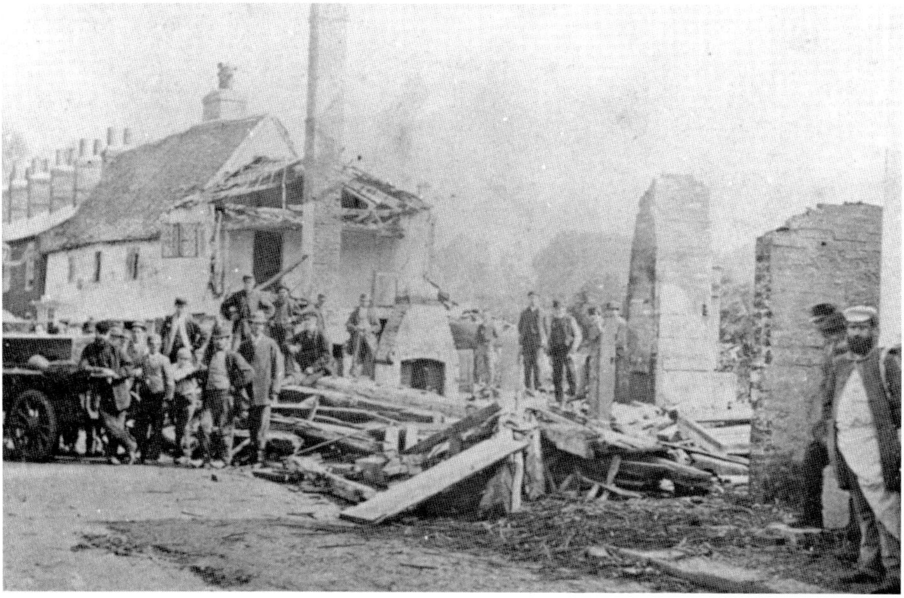

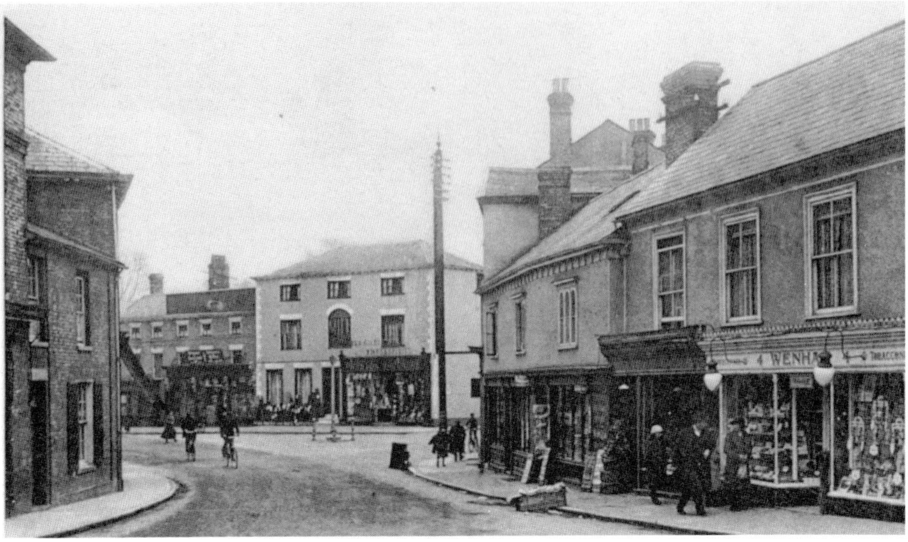

Miss Lily Wenham's confectioner's and tobacconist's shop at 4 Market Place can be seen on the right of this view of the Market Place, taken from near the junction with Station Road and Tavern Street, probably *c.* 1912. Below is the same view from the opposite direction, looking up Bury Street. Prominent in both pictures is the massive pole bearing telephone wires outside the post office, which housed the first exchange. Both views, and those on the next page, are from postcards issued by Miss Wenham. (RM)

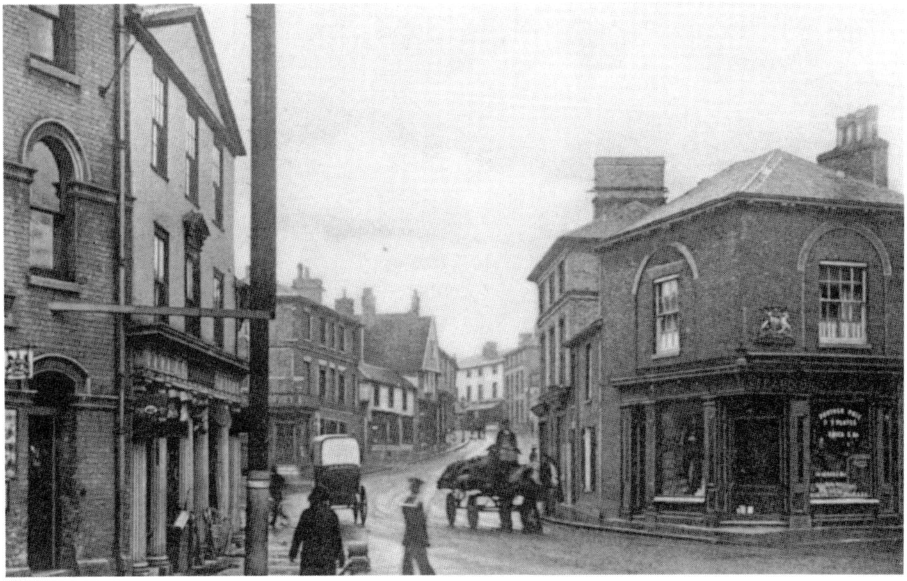

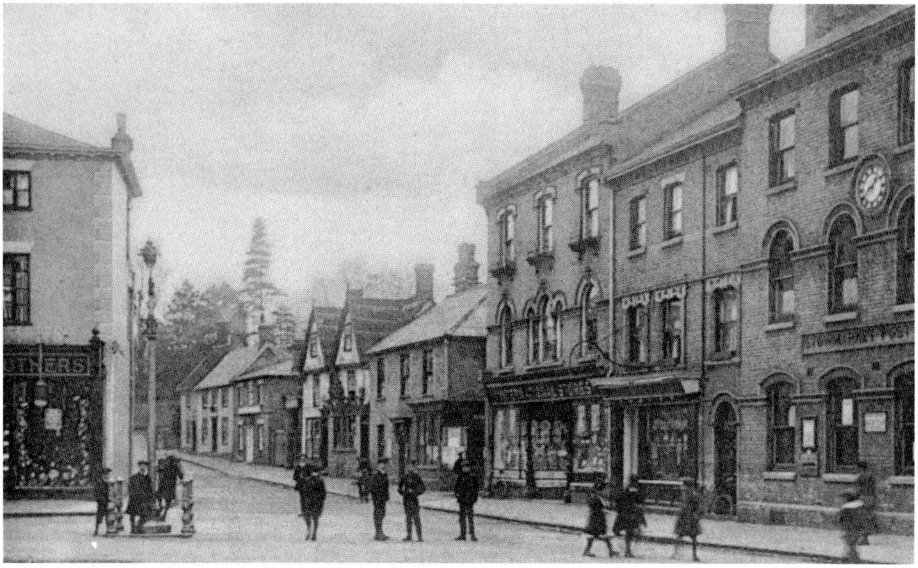

Looking up Crowe Street, *c.* 1912, with the post office, Herbert Arnold's butcher's shop and the International Stores on the right. Further up is the White Hart, with its two gables, and on the left is the shop of Preston Brothers, drapers and grocers. Below is Ipswich Road, with some of the sturdy houses built in the latter part of Queen Victoria's reign to house newcomers to the town; in the background the road climbs slightly over Boulter's Bridge. (RM)

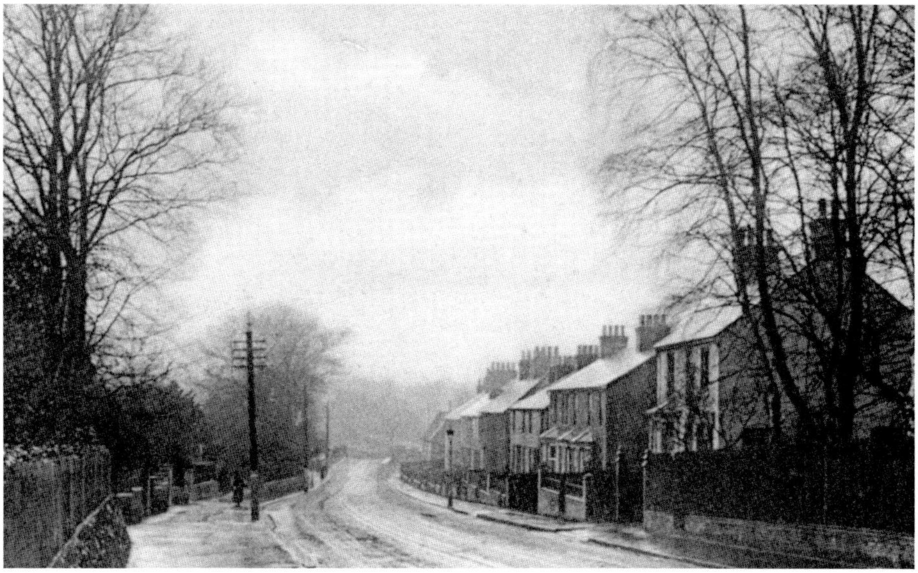

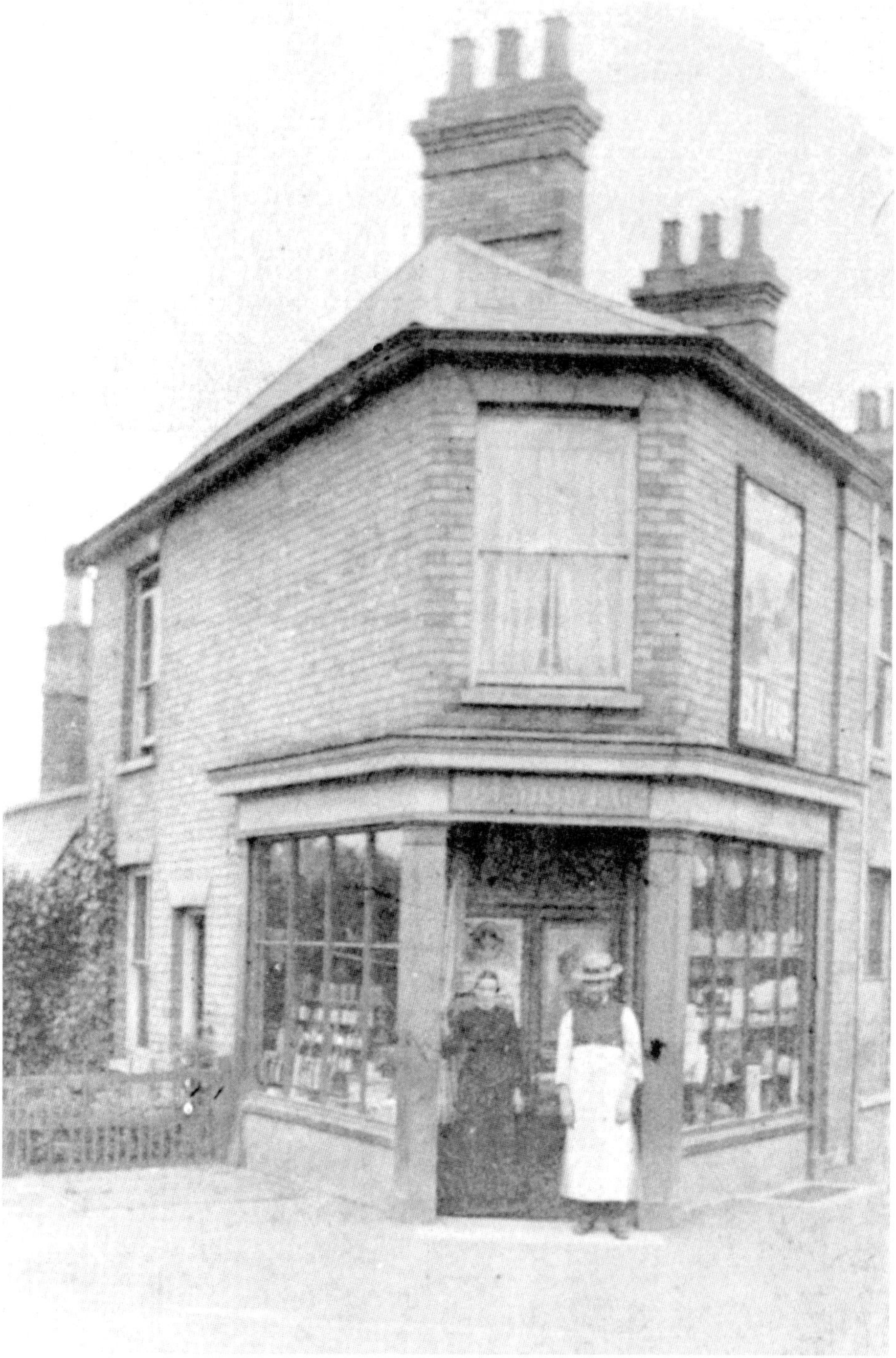

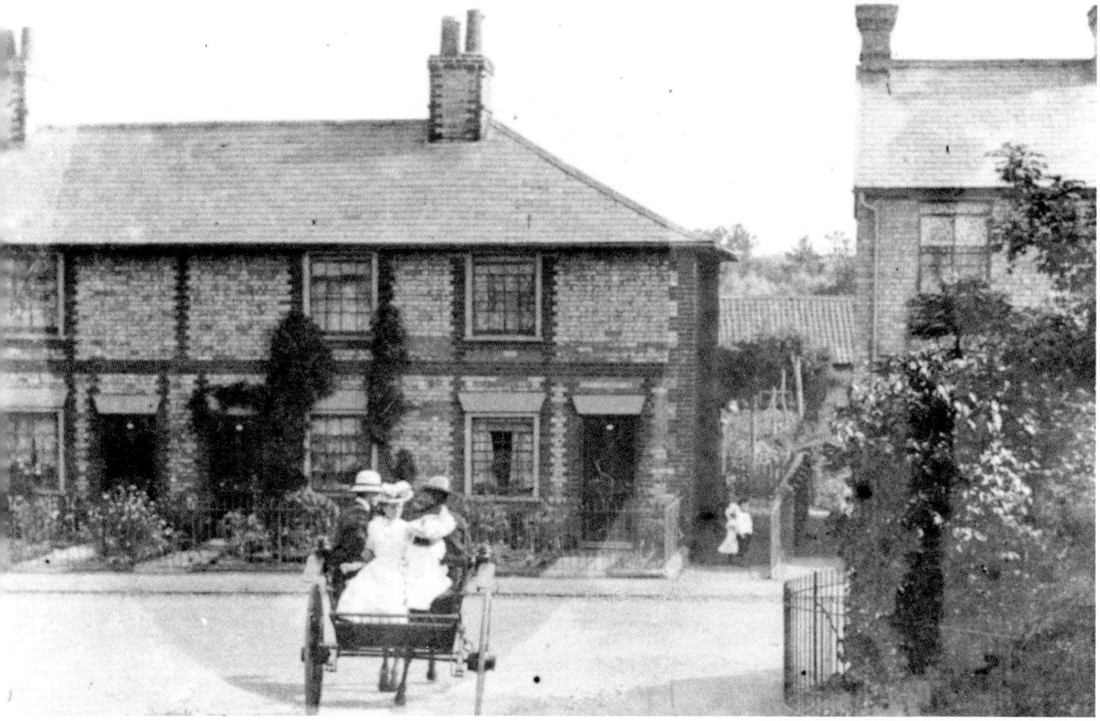

Off Ipswich Road was the little mid-19th-century suburb known as California, a name which almost certainly reflects the fact that the first houses were being built there at about the time of the California gold rush of 1849. These small houses with their mixture of red and white bricks are at the junction of Lime Tree Place and Bridge Street. (Ivan Codd)

*Opposite:* John Mower and Mrs Mower stand in the doorway of their corner shop in Lime Tree Place. John Mower was a grocer and provision merchant here in the 1880s and 1890s. (Ivan Codd)

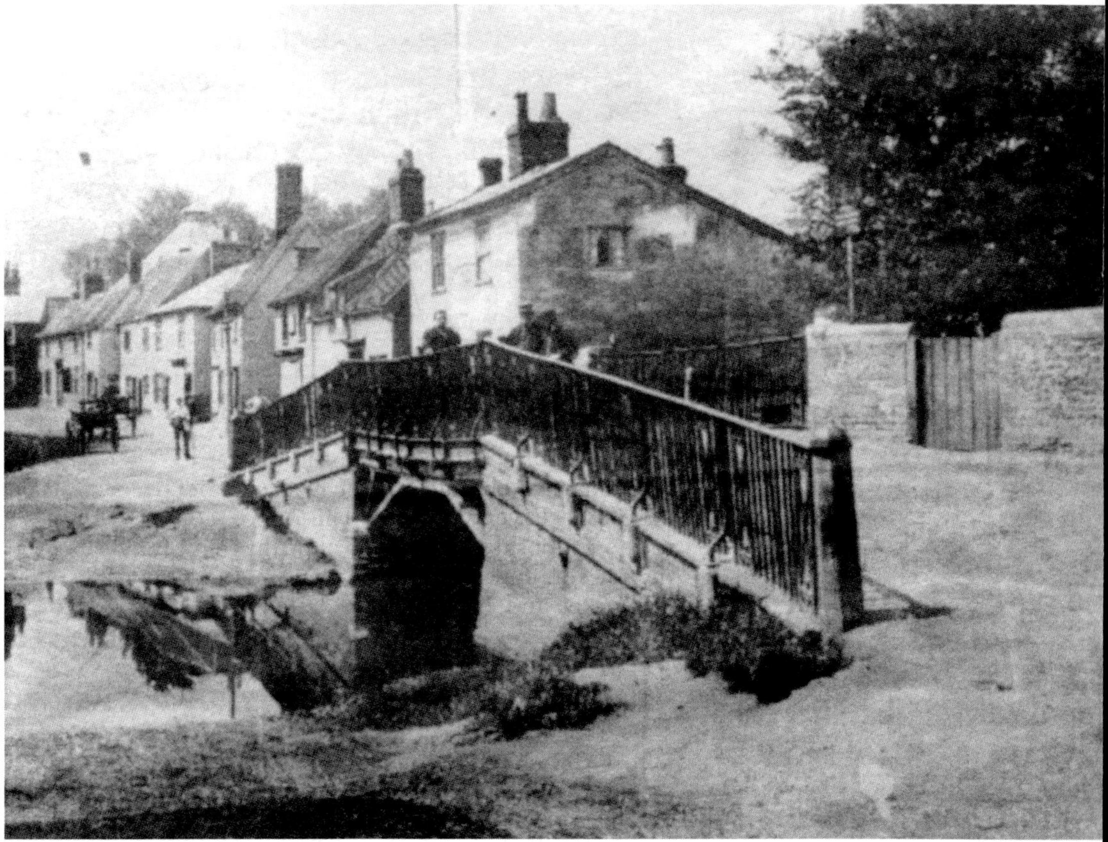

Although the print on the opposite page shows that in 1838 there was only a ford and a footbridge across the Gipping in Stowupland Street, an iron bridge was erected in the 1840s. By the time this photograph was taken later in the 19th century the bridge was sagging in the middle, and it was replaced by a brick arch bridge which was widened in 1972. The bridge is often known as Pickerel Bridge, from the long-established hostelry on the Stowupland side. (Ivan Codd)

*Section Two*

# THE NAVIGATION

Even at the beginning of the 18th century there had been suggestions that Stowmarket's trade, largely agricultural though it then was, would benefit greatly from the canalisation of the River Gipping. The opposition of the Corporation of Ipswich led to the proposal being dropped at that time, and it was not until 1790 that 'An Act for making and maintaining a navigable Communication between Stowmarket and Ipswich, in the County of Suffolk' was passed by Parliament.

The 17-mile navigation was opened throughout in 1793, and as a result the town's commercial progress was stimulated to a considerable extent.

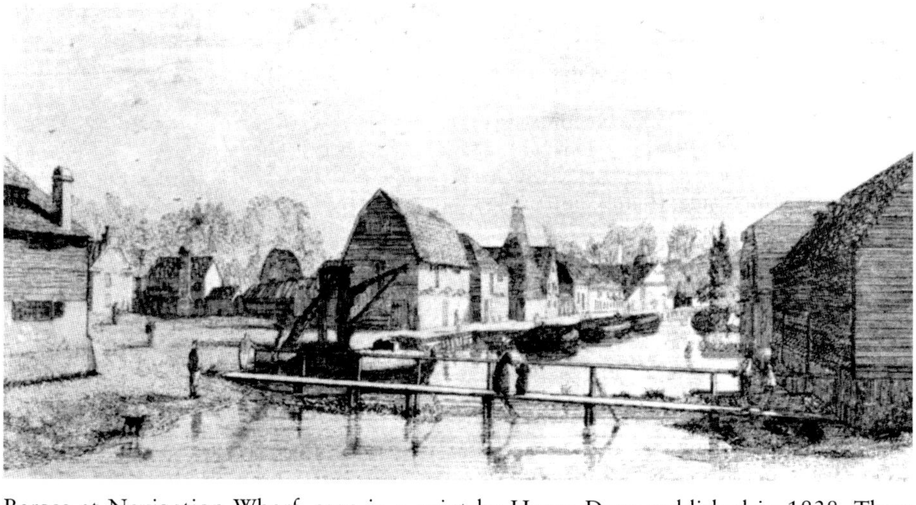

Barges at Navigation Wharf, seen in a print by Henry Davy published in 1838. There was only a footbridge in Stowupland Street, and waggons had to ford the river at this point. The maltings alongside the river can also be seen in the photograph on page 39. (Ivan Codd)

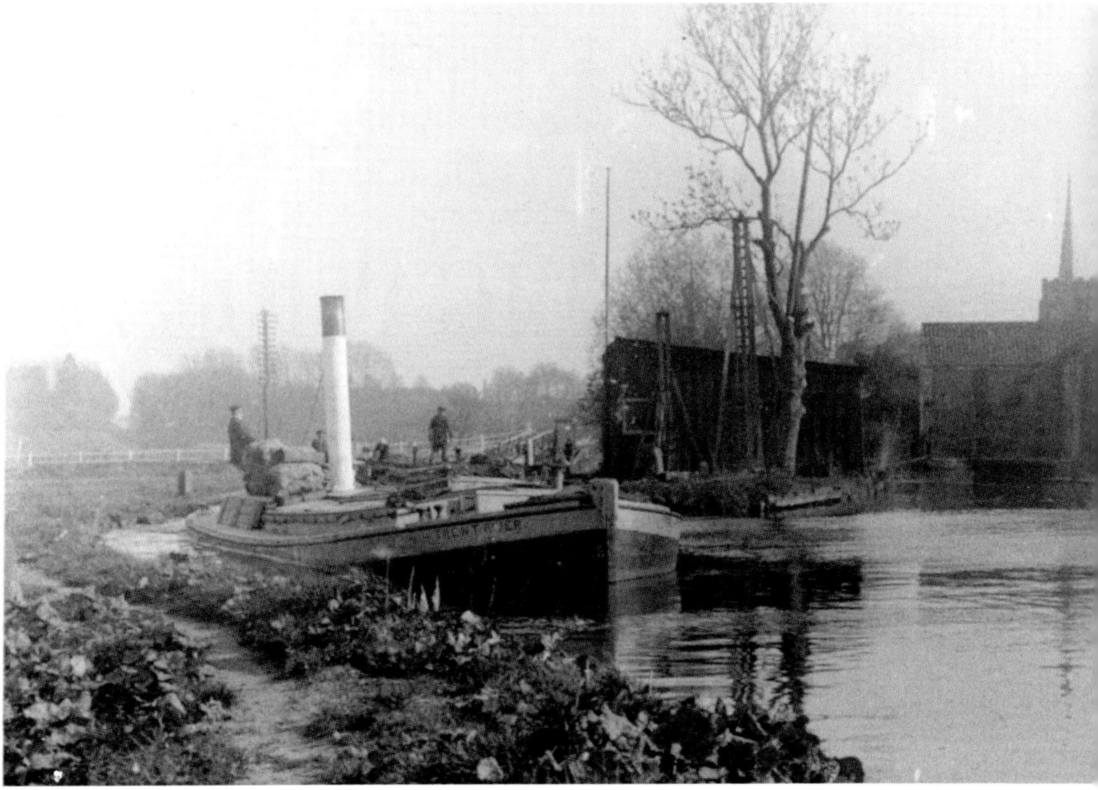

Packard's steam barge *Trent River* on its way upriver with two barges in tow. Sadly, there was insufficient depth for it to proceed beyond Bramford, and after about 1914 the barges no longer came up to Stowmarket. (John Wilton)

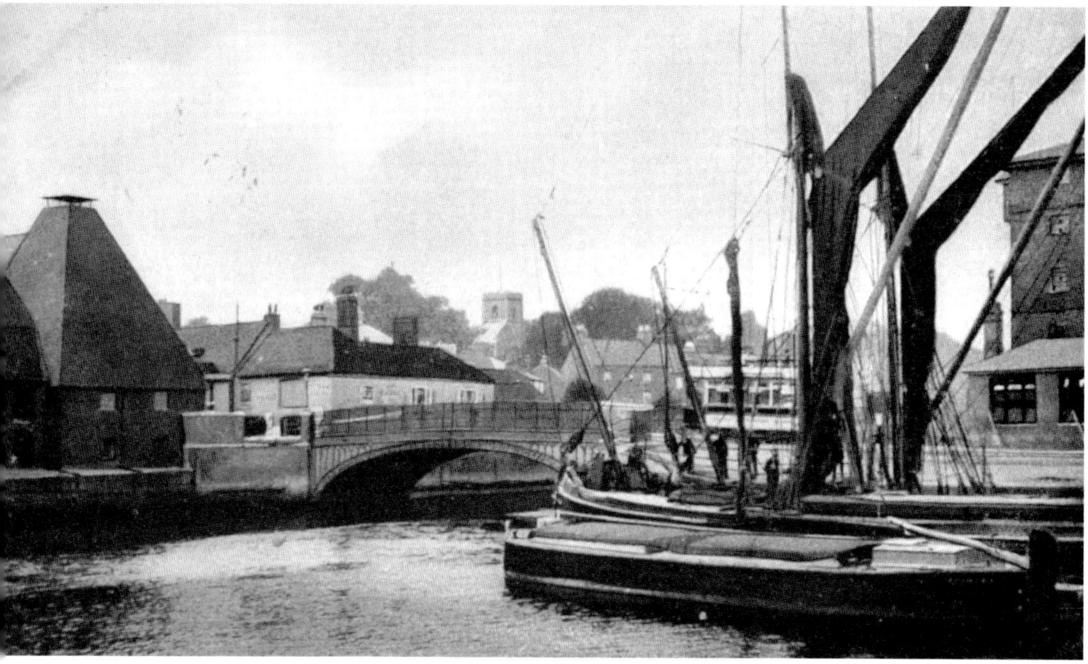

A Gipping barge lying alongside two spritsail coasting barges at St Peter's Dock, Ipswich. On the right can be seen part of Eastern Union Mills, built by Joseph Fison when he moved from Stowmarket to Ipswich to set up in business as a manufacturer of chemical fertilisers, a corn miller and seed crusher. Thomas Prentice & Co. of Stowmarket had premises not far away at Neptune Wharf, and later at Flint Wharf. (John Wilton)

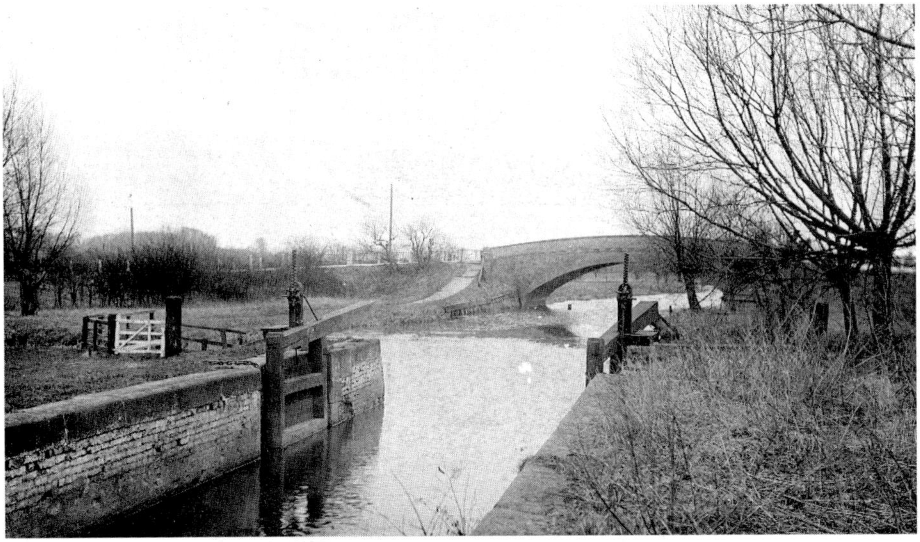

The lower gates of the lock at Claydon stand open ready to receive a barge bound up to Stowmarket, *c.* 1908. By this time traffic to Stowmarket had declined to no more than the occasional barge to Prentice's manure works or the explosives works. No barges are to be seen in the view below of the river at Stowmarket in about 1910. On the right are the buildings of the gasworks, with the kiln of one of the Prentice Road maltings rising above the rooftops. (John Wilton)

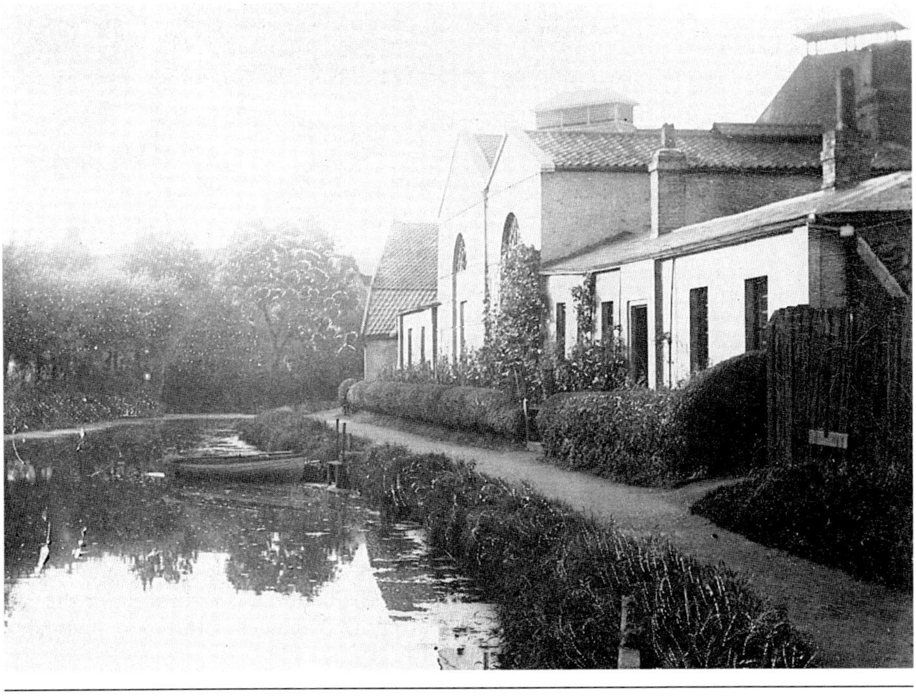

*Section Three*

# THE RAILWAY

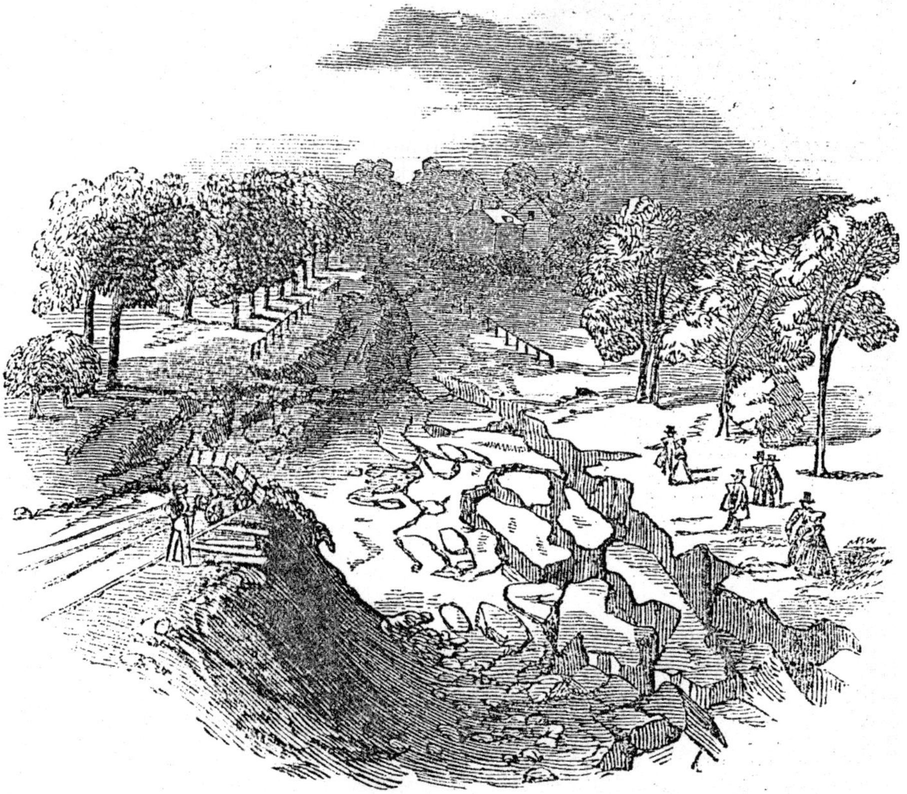

'For many weeks past the efforts of the contractor and labourers employed on the Ipswich and Bury Railway at Stowmarket, have been completely baffled by the rapid subsidence of the embankment at that place and the continued absorption of the earth thrown down since the occurrence,' says the report that goes with this contemporary engraving, published in 1846. (Ivan Codd)

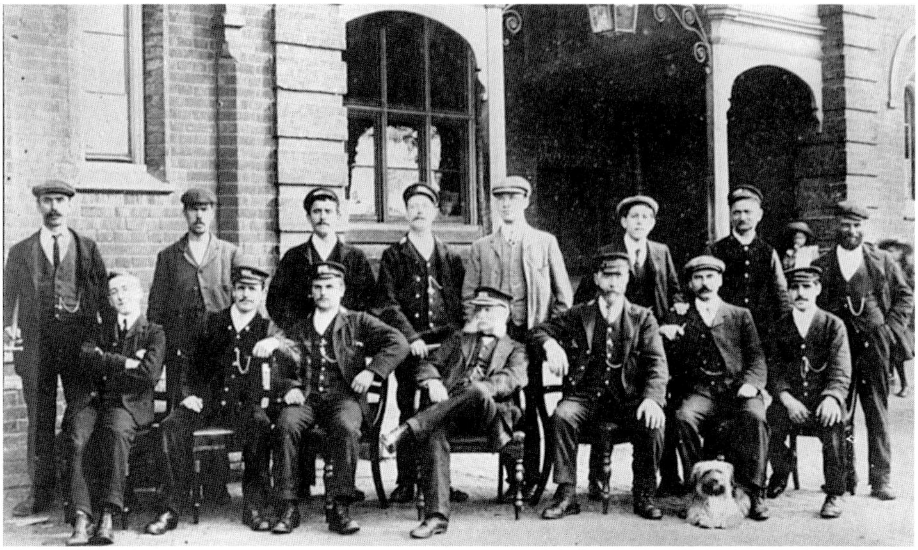

In Great Eastern Railway days (before the grouping of 1923) Stowmarket station had a considerable staff, here lined up for the photographer. The stationmaster takes his ease in his armchair in the middle, with his chief clerk on his left and others, porters, clerks, cleaners, lined up beside and behind him. On the extreme left is the carriage and wagon examiner, with his wheel-tapping hammer carried with military precision under his right arm. (Ivan Codd)

The Ipswich and Bury Railway arrived in Stowmarket in 1846 and further boosted the town's trade, albeit at the expense of the navigation. Building of the line up the Gipping valley proved difficult because of the boggy ground on the Ipswich side of the site of Stowmarket station, and after the prepared trackbed and rails had disappeared into the mire the engineer, Peter Bruff, decided to employ the same stratagem used by George Stephenson to cross Chat Moss, on the Liverpool and Manchester Railway; the line was floated across the bog on a raft of brushwood. The Stowmarket bog turned out to be twice as deep as the notorious Chat Moss.

The fine station was designed by Frederick Barnes, an Ipswich architect who also designed the Congregational church in Ipswich Street, destroyed in an air raid in 1941. There were complaints by the railway shareholders at the expense of these stations, but it does seem that the people of Stowmarket were determined to have a station which they deemed suitable for a town with such pretensions as theirs. Not only did the parish authorities make a low-interest loan of £3,000 to the railway company to finance the building work, but they contributed £1,000 towards the cost of building a new road from the town to the station.

The wide embankment on the Ipswich side of the station soon carried goods sidings from which branch sidings crossed the river to reach commercial premises on the town side.

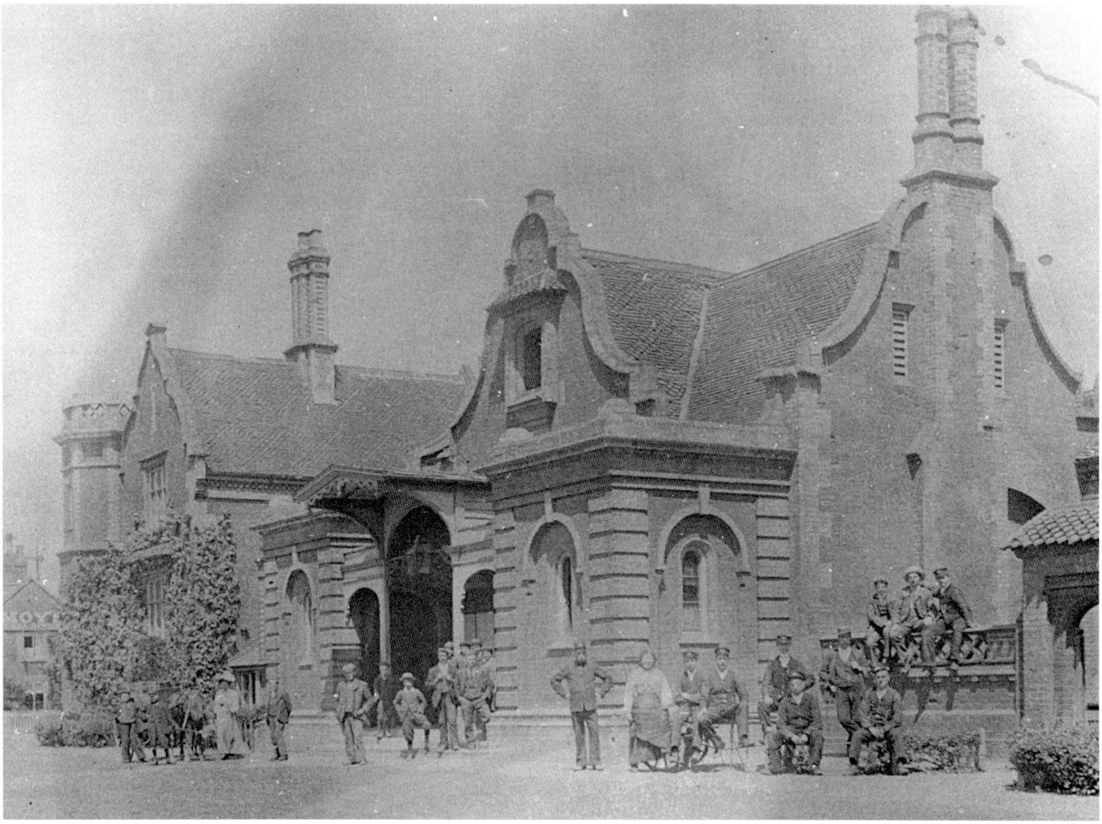

Stowmarket station was Frederick Barnes' masterpiece, 'one of the handsomest in the county', according to White's 1855 directory. The local authorities had contributed to the cost so as to ensure that it was a building fitting to a community of such pretensions, but the *Norwich Mercury* criticised the railway company for erecting such a lavish station: 'This station is one of a series upon the expensive erection of which considerable blame has been cast by the Shareholders on the Directors, and it is wanting in taste as well as economy.' The station staff have been joined by a postman, standing with hands on hips, and a number of others in this photograph from the early years of this century. (Ivan Codd)

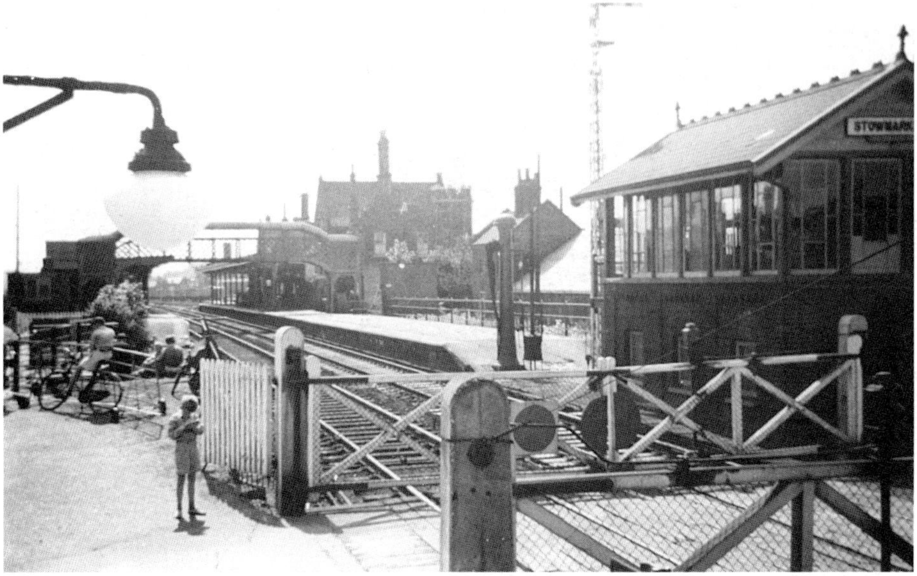

The level crossing gates at the station, operated by the signalman in the adjacent box. Other features in the view are the iron footbridge, the water crane for filling the tanks of engines using the station, and the tall lattice signal post at the end of the down platform. Below is signalman Alf Spall, turning the large wheel which operated the crossing gates. (Both Ivan Codd)

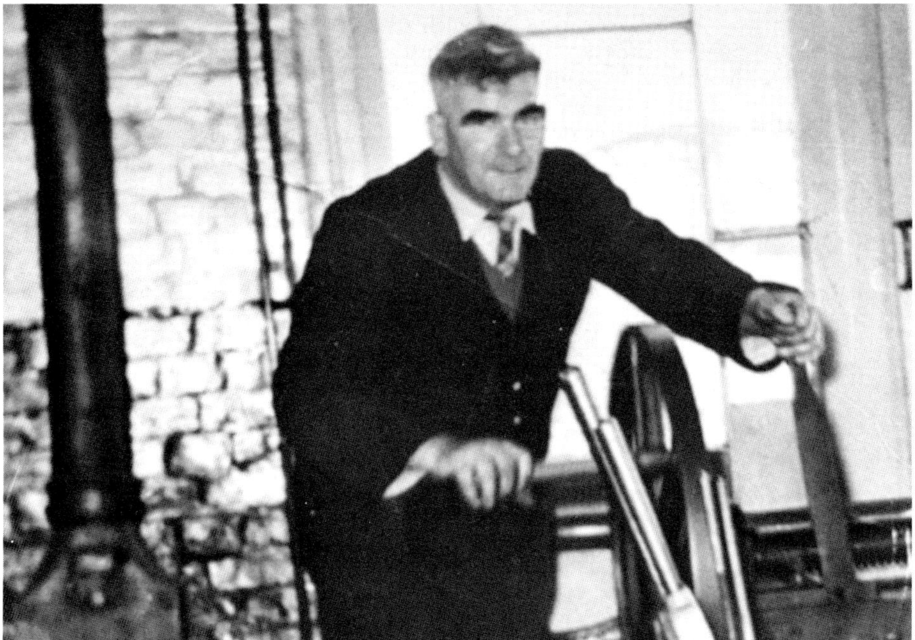

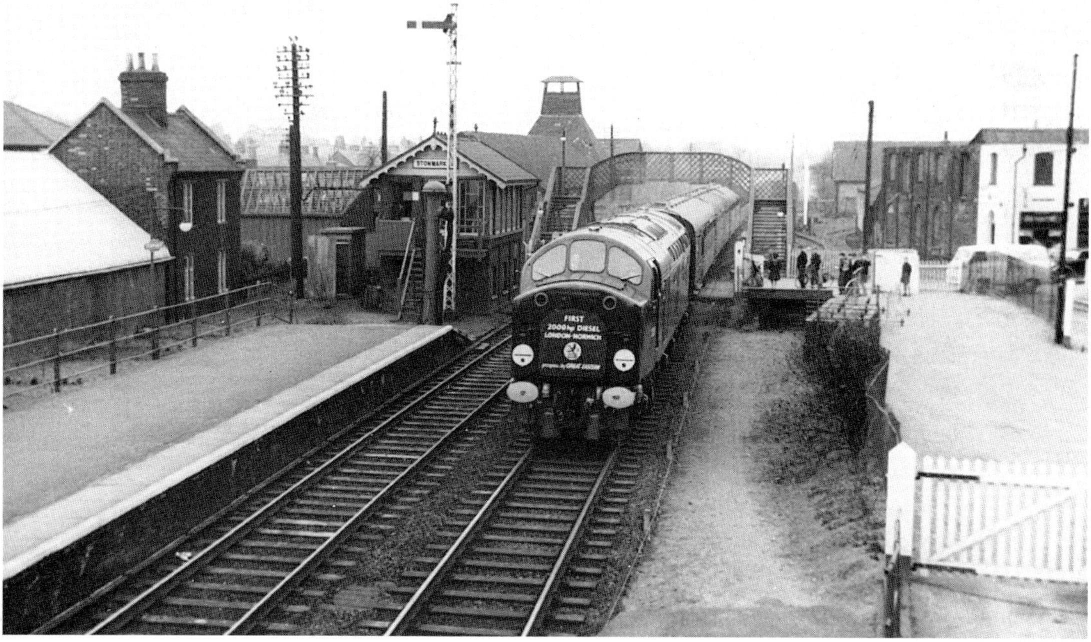


The first passenger train hauled by one of the Class 40 diesel locomotives passing through the station on its way from Norwich to Liverpool Street, 18 April 1958. A siding used to branch off the up main line just to the north of the crossing and run along the roadway on the extreme right of the picture, rejoining the main line near Prentice Brothers' fertiliser factory. About 1897 a goods train was being shunted when the engine derailed, blocking the down road; a breakdown crane was sent from Ipswich, but that derailed on the same set of points, blocking the up road. Within a quarter of an hour of this happening the up Manchester boat train arrived at Stowmarket, full of passengers travelling to the Continent; it was brought to a stand. Quick thinking on the part of a young railwayman, George Welham, resulted in a decision to set the boat train back, clip the points and bring the train through the siding, thus avoiding the blockage on the main line. This is the only known instance of a passenger train passing Stowmarket in this way. (Ivan Codd)

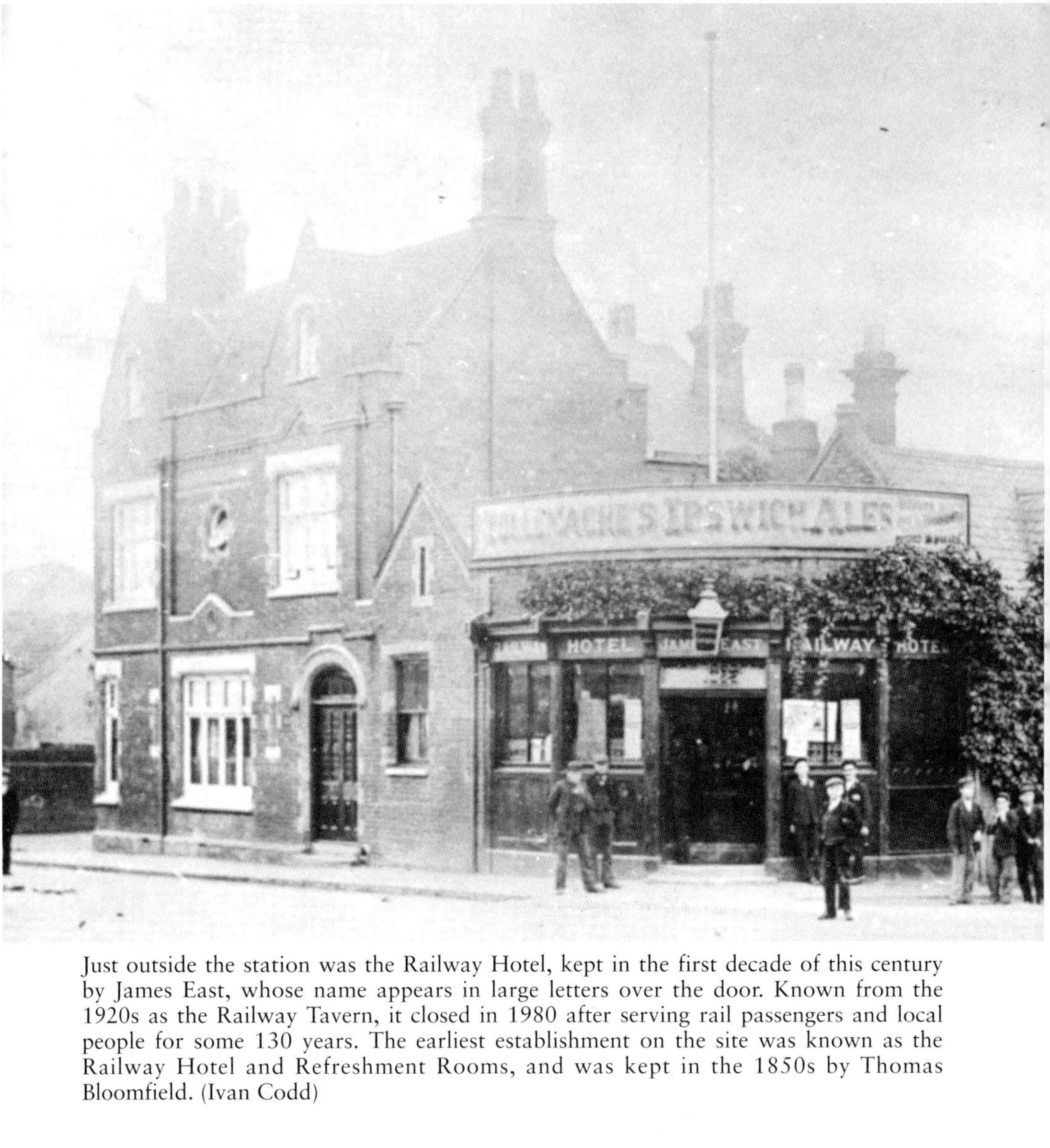


Just outside the station was the Railway Hotel, kept in the first decade of this century by James East, whose name appears in large letters over the door. Known from the 1920s as the Railway Tavern, it closed in 1980 after serving rail passengers and local people for some 130 years. The earliest establishment on the site was known as the Railway Hotel and Refreshment Rooms, and was kept in the 1850s by Thomas Bloomfield. (Ivan Codd)

*Section Four*

# CORN, MALT AND BEER

A number of Stowmarket tradesmen combined the occupations of miller and maltster, while a few not only combined those trades but had a hand in a number of others as well.

Down at Combs Ford, where the first mill is said to have been built in 1540, William Boulter was throughout the 1830s and 1840s operating the old timber-framed water mill that took its power from the Rattlesden river. By 1880 the miller there was Ebenezer Cooper, and later still Samuel Southgate took over, but the mill was still known as Boulter's Mill right up to the time of its demolition. From about 1910 onwards Abram Southgate, the last miller to operate on the site, had steam as well as water power, but the mill ceased work in the 1920s; it

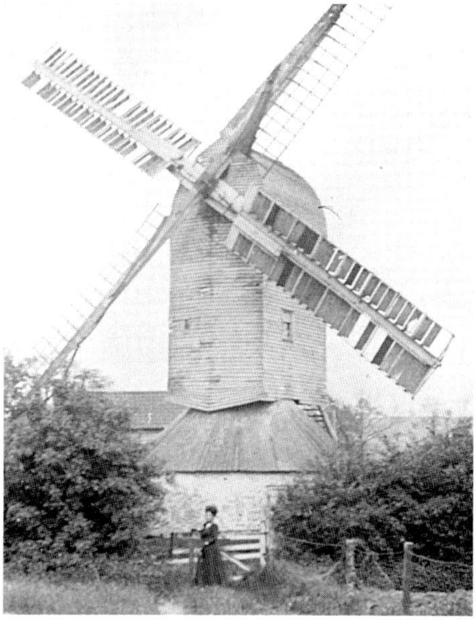

This post windmill, fitted with a combination of two spring sails and two canvas-covered common sails, stood at the Bury Road end of what is now Violet Hill Road, close to where Cherry Tree Road is today. (Ivan Codd)

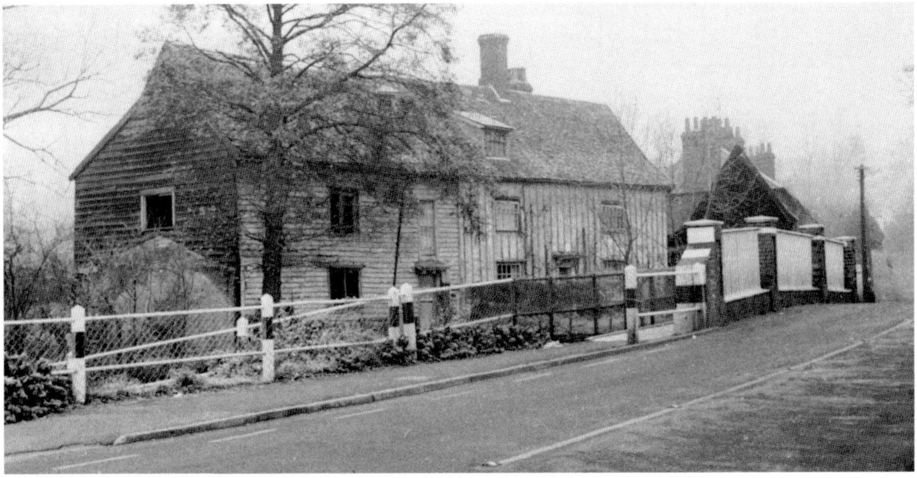

Boulter's Mill at Combs Ford is derelict in this photograph, which was taken not very long before the building was demolished. William Boulter had been the miller throughout the 1830s and 1840s, and it was his name that was used to describe the mill ever thereafter. (Geoff Clarke)

was demolished in about 1959. Oddly enough another Southgate, Herbert, operated Alton Mill at Stutton, which has been re-erected at the Museum of East Anglian Life at Abbot's Hall.

The other early mills in Stowmarket, and those at Combs and Stowupland, were windmills. Joseph Fison's windmill was on the site in Finborough Road on which a steam mill was later built, while the other three Stowmarket mills were all close to the junction of Violet Hill Road and Bury Street; the southernmost of the trio disappeared when the cemetery was laid out, for it had stood in the corner of the field that became the cemetery.

By the 1870s, however, several of the local millers had invested in steam engines to drive their mills, and while some regarded the new source of power as an auxiliary for use when the wind dropped, others had fine new mills erected of brick and timber.

William Hewitt, maltster and miller, corn, coal and hop merchant, had the Victoria Mills built on a site beside the railway line close to the Stowupland Street level crossing, and the Albert Mills was erected on the corner of Bond Street and Crown Street.

In about 1840 there were seven maltsters working in the town, and a decade later there were nine, some of them clearly operating a number of the local malthouses. Indeed, several of those listed in directories at this period were in a very extensive way of business, with interests that extended far beyond malting; because of its seasonal nature malting tended to be a trade that was run in conjunction with others.

Not all the malt made in the town's maltings went down the navigation to Ipswich and London breweries, for there was a large brewery in Stowupland

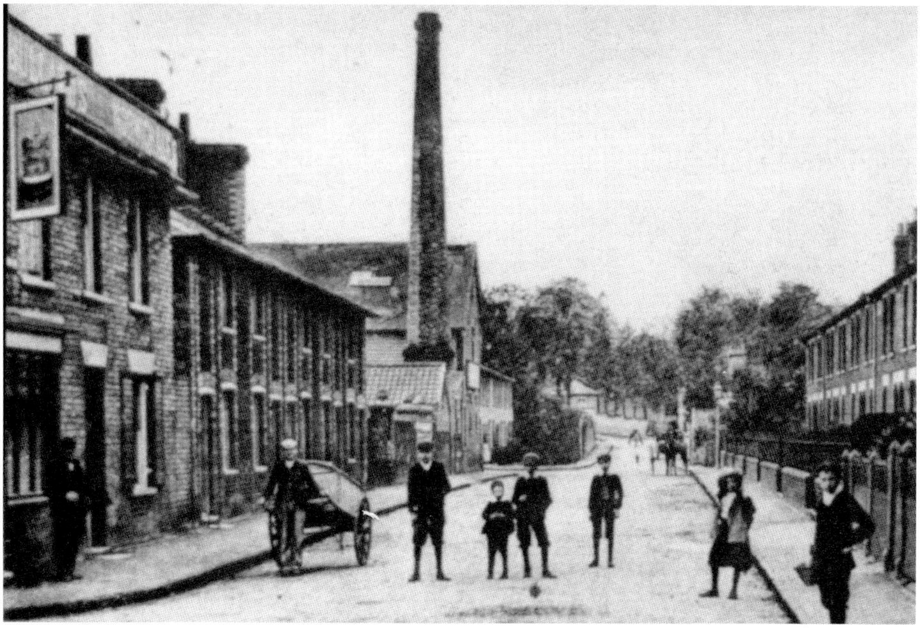

Crown Street in the early years of the present century, with the Crown on the left and Thomas James Smith's Albert Mills on the corner of New Bond Street, as it was then known, in the middle of the picture. By the time this photograph was taken the mills had passed to Walter James Smith, who was also a hop merchant as well as a flour miller, as seen in the view below of Stowupland Street close to the Pickerel Bridge; the Hop Pole Tavern can be seen in the background. (Both Ivan Codd)

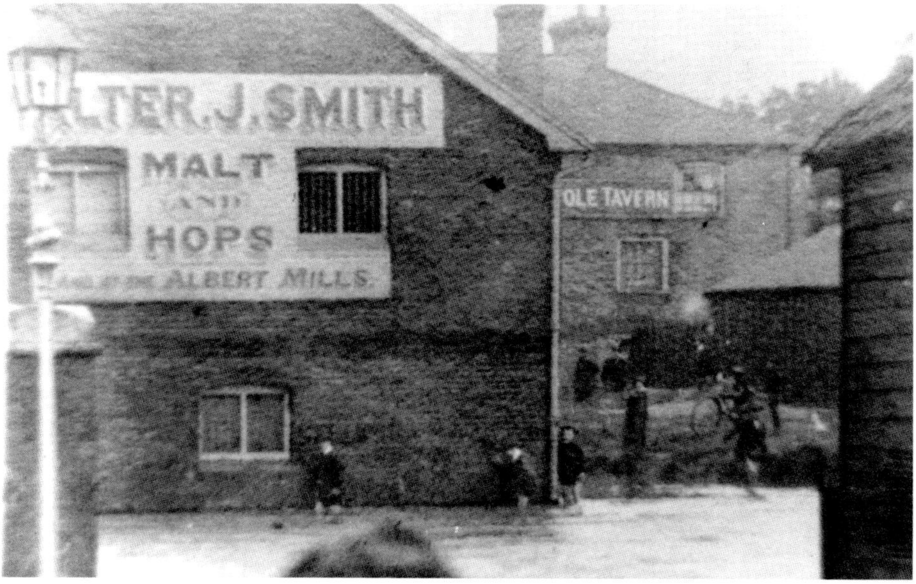

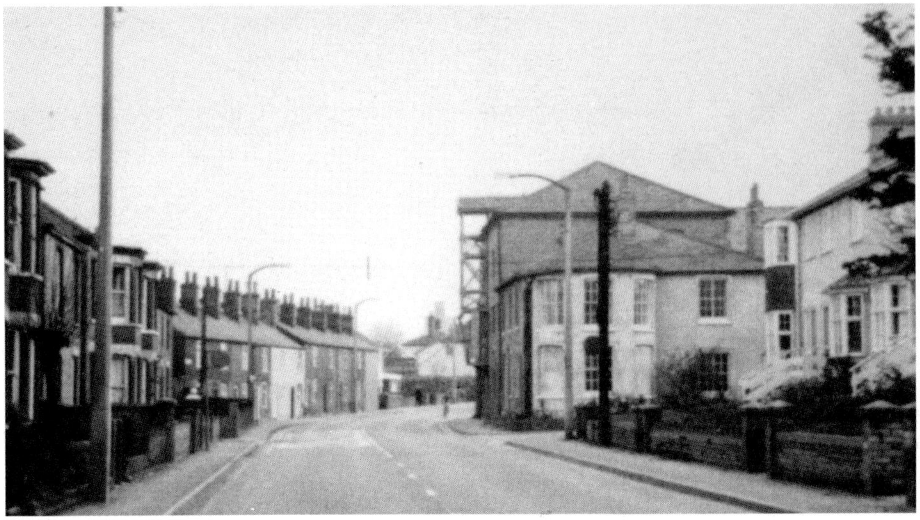

This malting in Bury Street eventually became the works of Husky's, makers of insulated clothing. The gantry projecting over the pavement was used for hoisting sacks of barley brought in from local farms to be turned into malt on the malting floor. The houses on the left were built at about the turn of the century, extending the town northwards. Below are the Victoria Mills, built by William Hewitt, maltster and miller, corn, coal and hop merchant, beside the railway line close to the Stowupland Street level crossing. The mill has gone, but the lower walls have been incorporated into the existing garage which occupies the site. (Ivan Codd)

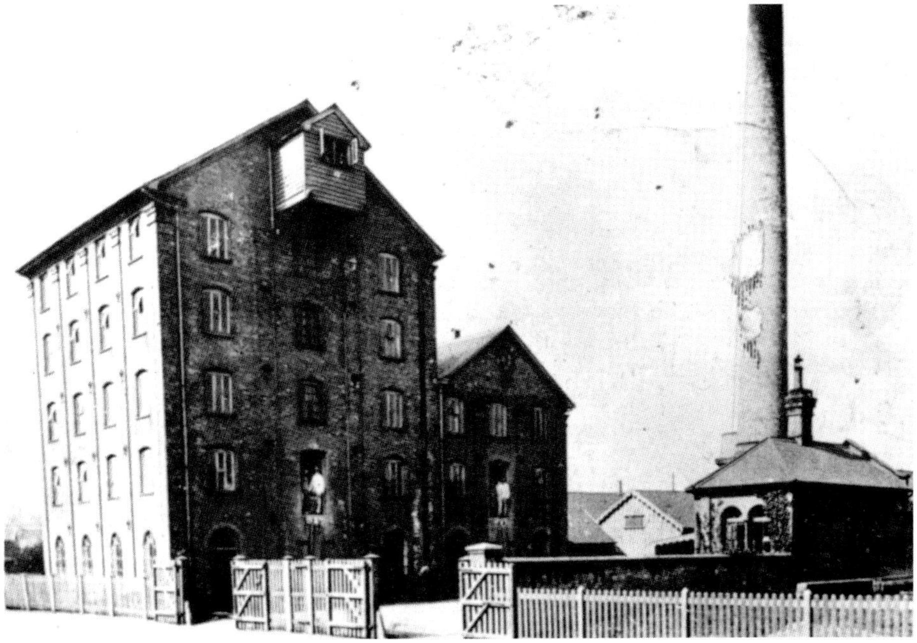

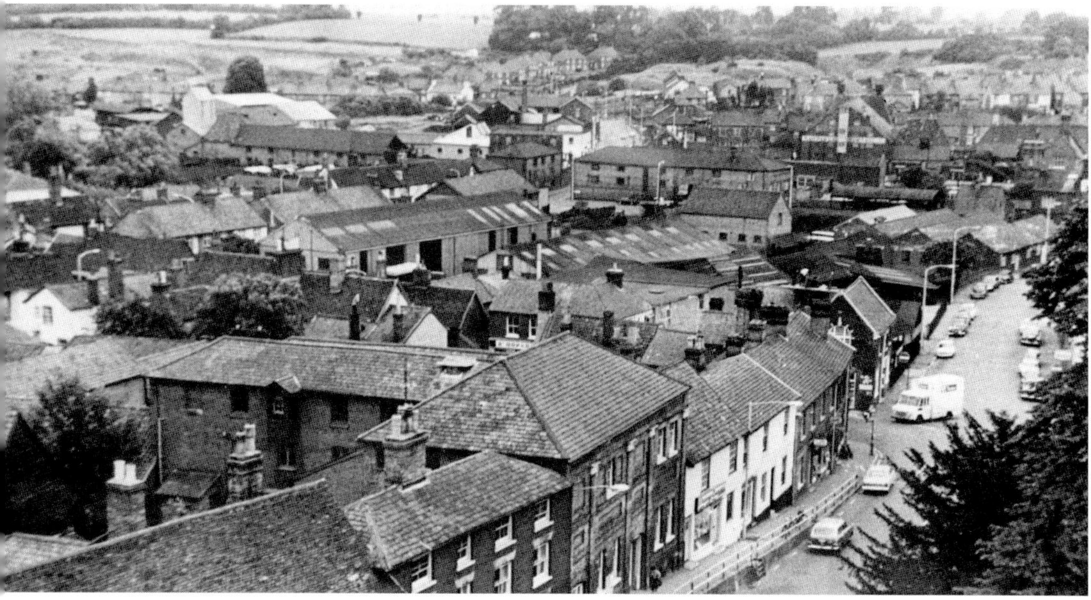

Looking down from the church tower on the former brewery and waterworks buildings in Station Road, 1960s. Beyond is Woodward & Woodward's saleyard, and further out are the former Lankester & Wells bonded store and some of the industrial premises around the railway station, which itself is just visible at upper right. (Ivan Codd)

Street operated by George Stevens and John Wells Stevens in the 1840s. The Rev. A.G.H. Hollingsworth records in his *History of Stowmarket* that India pale ale was being sent down the river in iron barges for export; these barges, built in an Ipswich shipyard, were early 'ironpots' that were able to raise mast and sail and continue coastwise to London after being towed down the Gipping by horse.

An artesian well sunk to provide water for brewing proved so productive that the Stevenses were able to provide the town with a piped water supply, some time before much bigger towns than Stowmarket had such amenities. The bore was 330 ft deep and yielded as much as 200 or 300 gallons a minute.

In the 1870s Alexander Clutterbuck had the Stowmarket Brewery, but in 1883 it was acquired, along with 35 public houses and the Stowmarket Water Company, by the Bury brewers E. King & Sons, later to become Greene, King & Sons. The Bury firm continued to supply water to the town as well as beer, laying new mains and constructing a reservoir capable of holding 200,000 gallons in 1887, later adding an expensive water softening plant. After running the waterworks for well over 30 years Greene, King sold them in 1920–1 to Stowmarket Urban District Council for £10,000.

There was another brewery in Violet Hill, and Thomas Prentice & Co. are also said to have included brewing among their many interests towards the end of the last century.

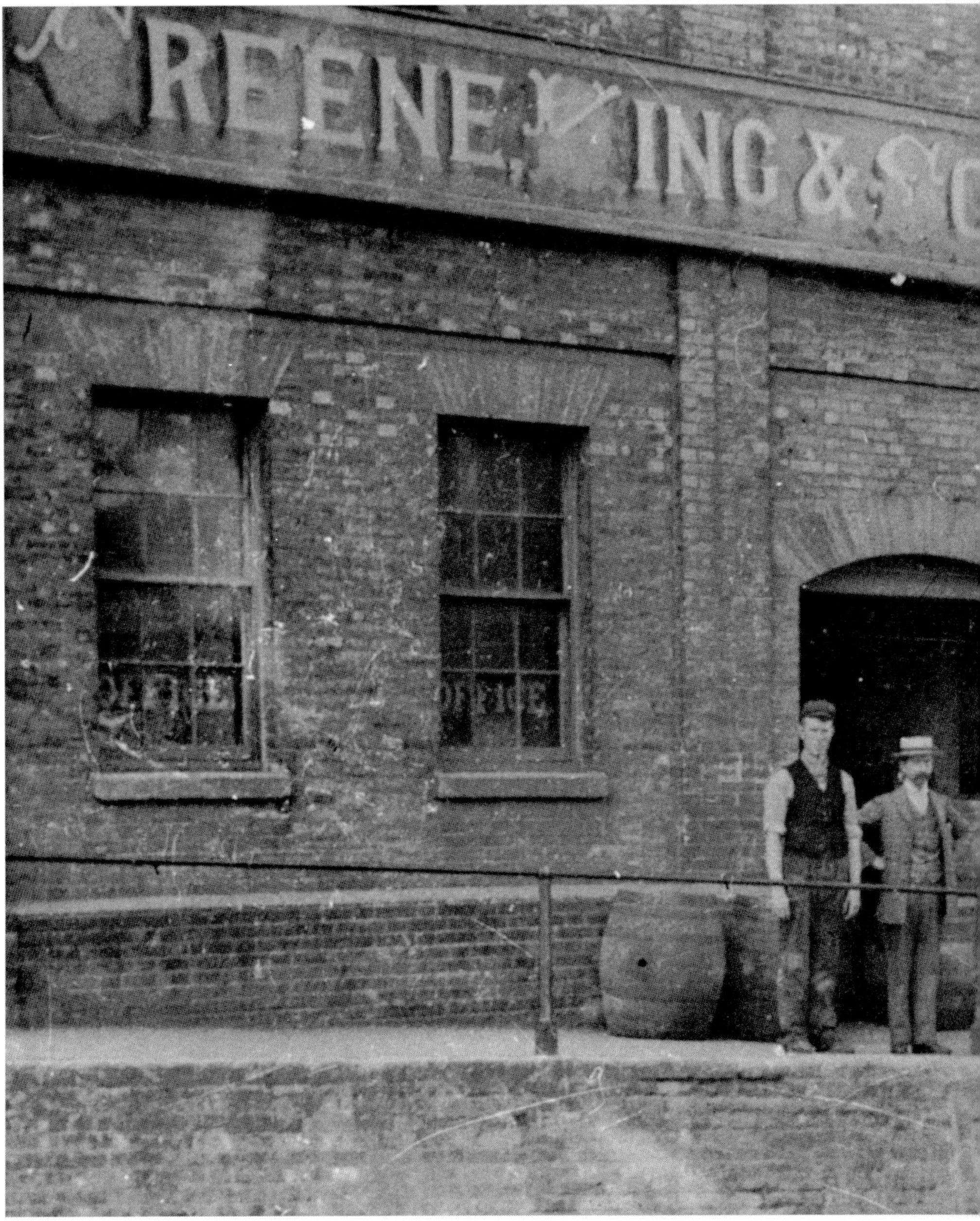


A Greene, King dray loading outside the Stowmarket Brewery, which had been bought by Edward Greene in 1883. With the merger of 1887 of E. Greene & Son and F.W. King & Son the brewery became a bottling store for Greene, King & Sons, which it continued to be until 1920. Next door is the shop of Cracknell & Son, basketmakers and rod merchants (that is, they sold the willow rods used in basketmaking). George

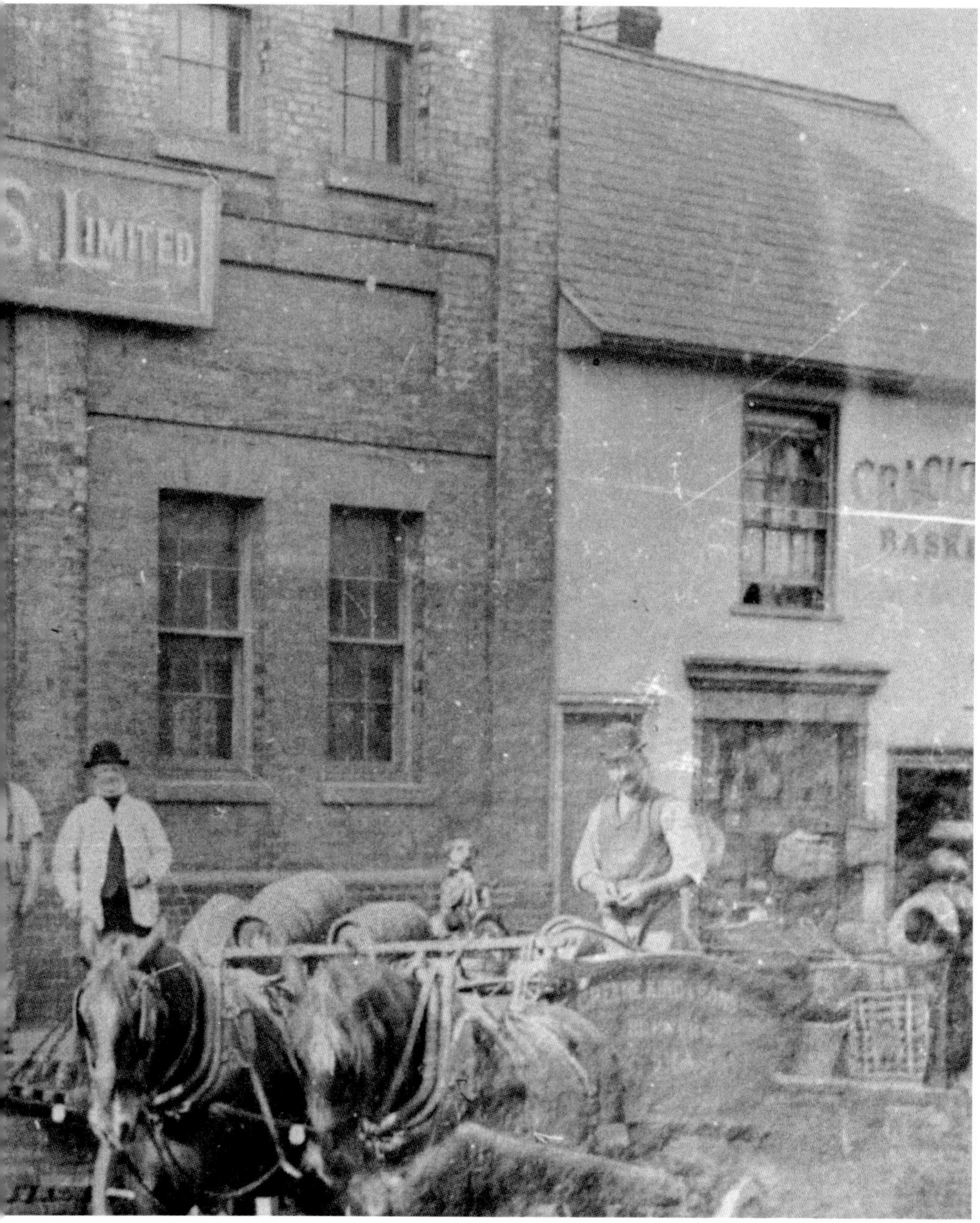


Cracknell had been a cooper and basketmaker back in the 1870s, and his executors were basketmakers and rod merchants in the 1890s; the business then became Cracknell & Son, and Arthur Cracknell seems to have taken over in the opening decade of the present century. In 1912 he was one of four basketmakers in and near the town; by the 1920s he had gone and there was only one. (Ivan Codd)

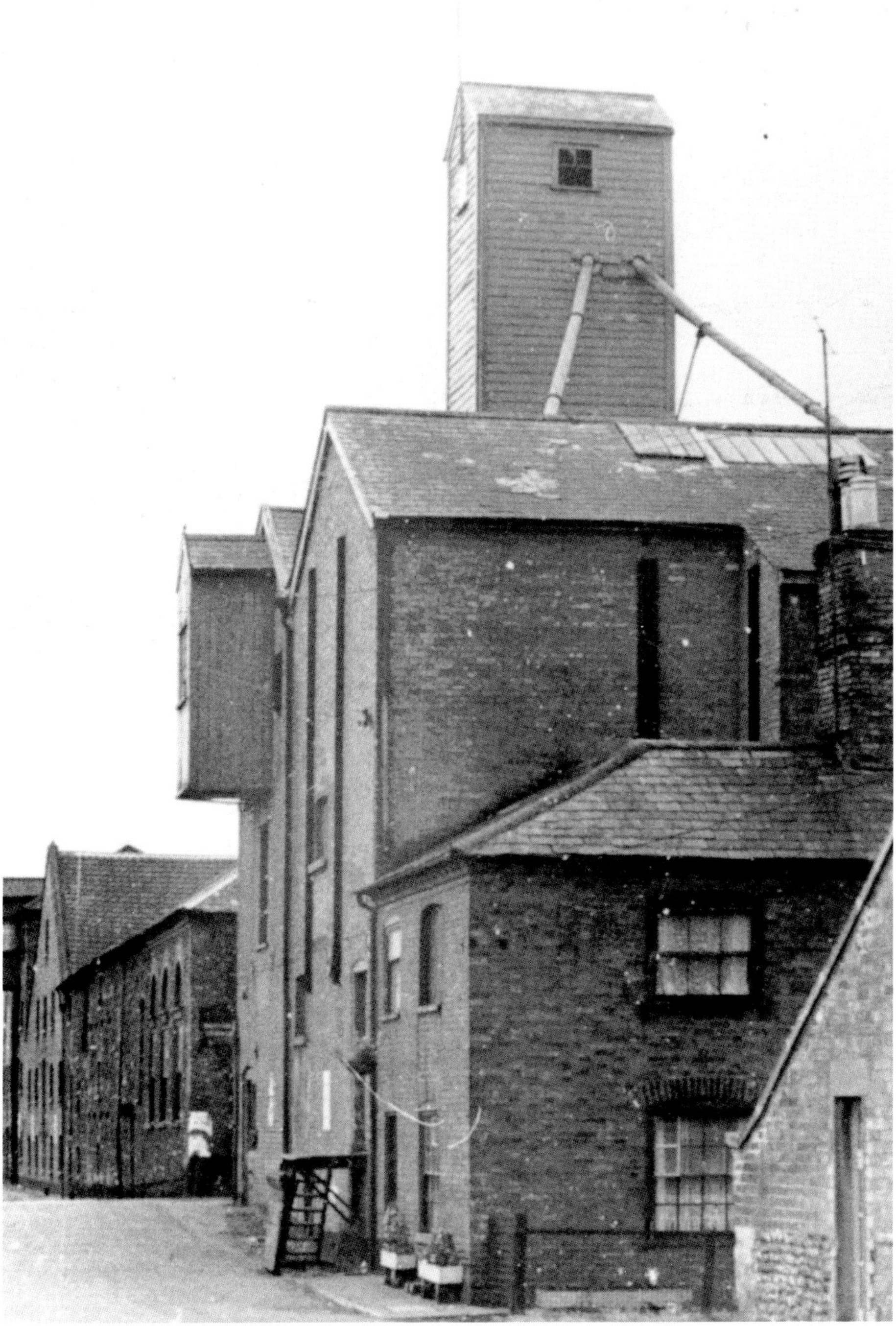

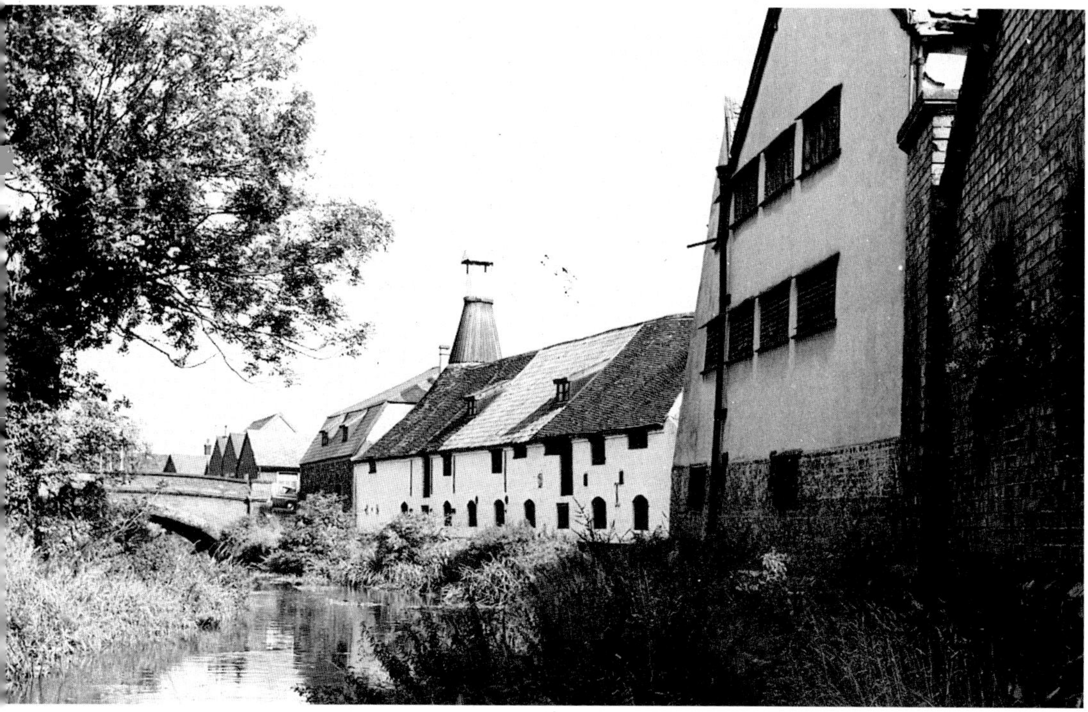

Riverside maltings and the Station Road bridge. These maltings were all in existence when Davy made his etching of the Navigation Wharf in 1838, but the bridge was a product of the railway age, erected as part of a new road to the railway station in the 1840s. The nearer maltings were burnt down, and those nearer the bridge have become a night club and restaurant. (Ivan Codd)

*Opposite:* Maltings in Prentice Street, all now demolished. The wooden tower on the nearest malting houses was an elevator that brought the barley up to the garner floor and to the steeps in which it was soaked at the beginning of the malting process. The hump in the road (which still exists) marks the site of a level crossing for a siding, which crossed the river by a bridge to reach Thomas Prentice's yard and maltings on the town side. (Ivan Codd)

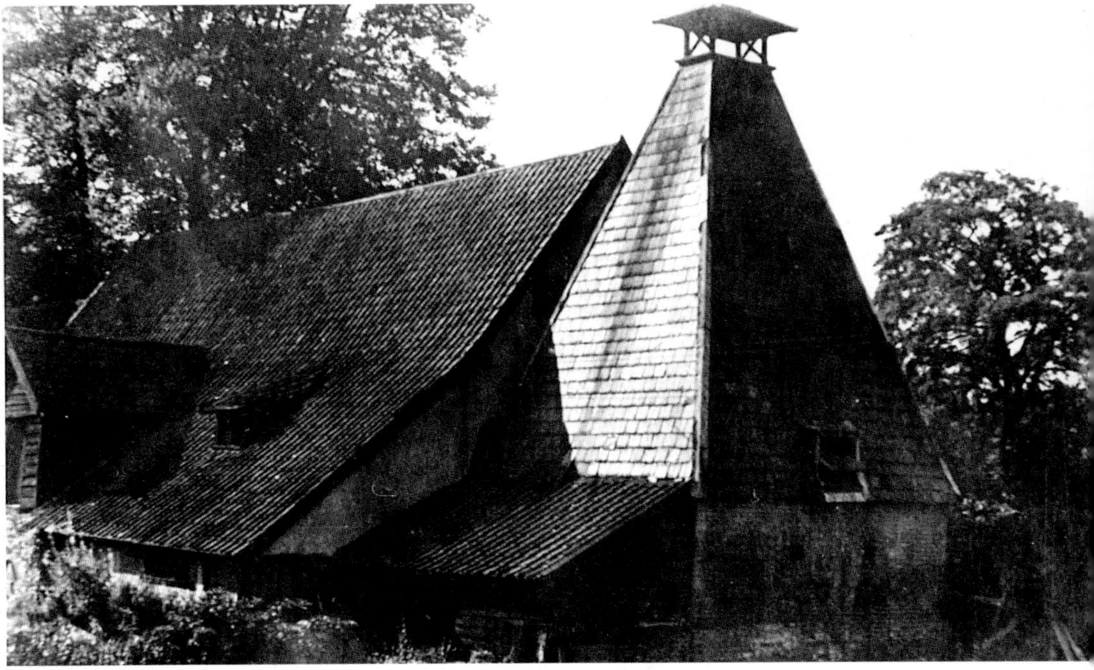

Malting received a considerable boost when the Stowmarket Navigation was completed in 1793. This little malting in Duke Lane (later known as Duke Street) was converted from a barn, probably at about the time barges began trading to the town; a navigable cut from the Gipping brought them right up to the malting. The malting floor was clearly an insertion, and the kiln in which the green malt was dried was simply built on to the end; the old barn doors were retained, and can be seen at the extreme left. This building was converted into a house in the 1980s. (Ivan Codd)

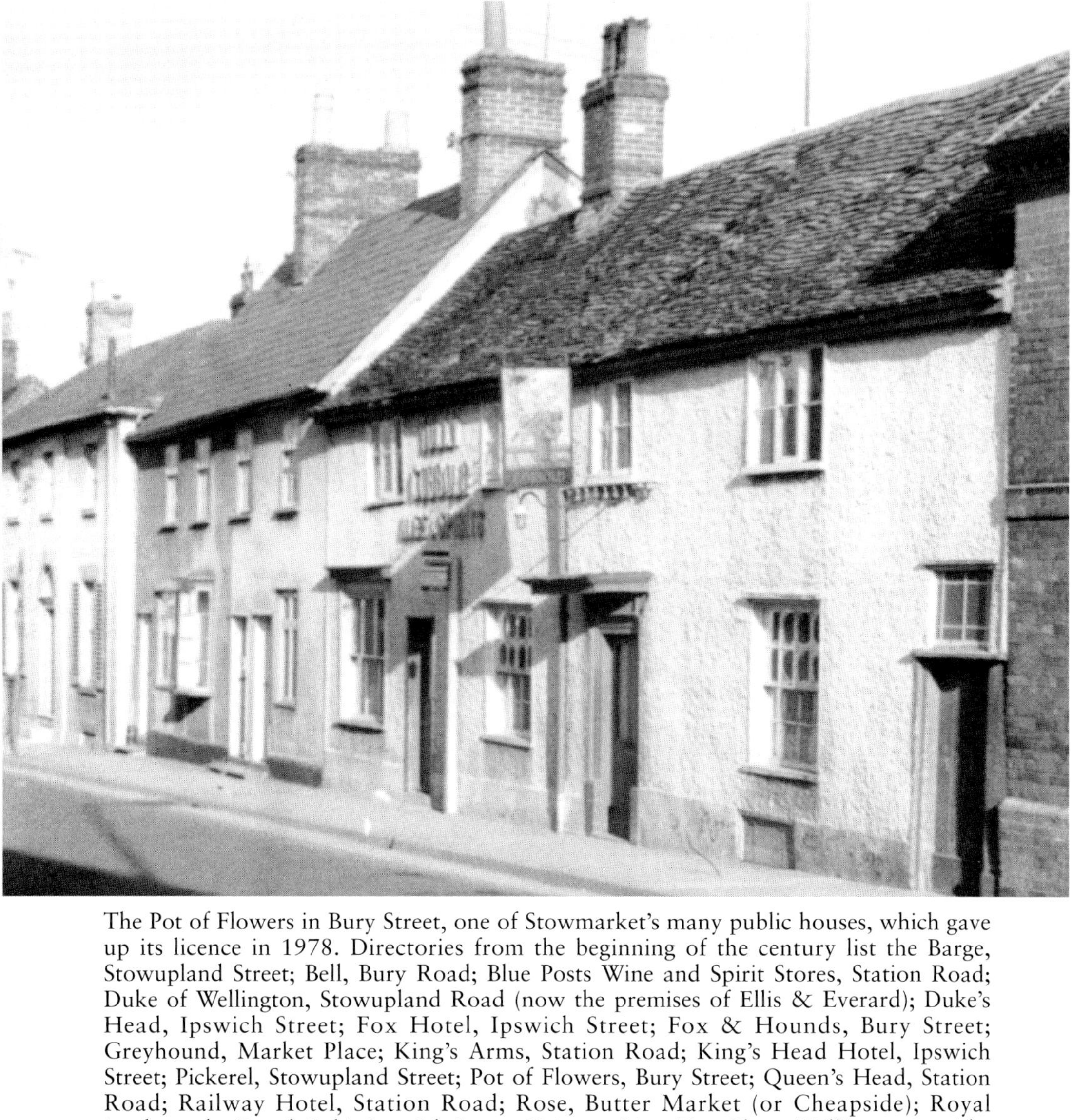

The Pot of Flowers in Bury Street, one of Stowmarket's many public houses, which gave up its licence in 1978. Directories from the beginning of the century list the Barge, Stowupland Street; Bell, Bury Road; Blue Posts Wine and Spirit Stores, Station Road; Duke of Wellington, Stowupland Road (now the premises of Ellis & Everard); Duke's Head, Ipswich Street; Fox Hotel, Ipswich Street; Fox & Hounds, Bury Street; Greyhound, Market Place; King's Arms, Station Road; King's Head Hotel, Ipswich Street; Pickerel, Stowupland Street; Pot of Flowers, Bury Street; Queen's Head, Station Road; Railway Hotel, Station Road; Rose, Butter Market (or Cheapside); Royal (perhaps the Royal Oak), Ipswich Street; Unicorn, Lime Tree Place; Wellington Inn (the Little Wellington), Stowupland Road; and White Hart, Crowe Street. There were also a number of beer houses, which possibly accounts for such missing names as the Crown in Crown Street and the Hop Pole Tavern. (Ivan Codd)

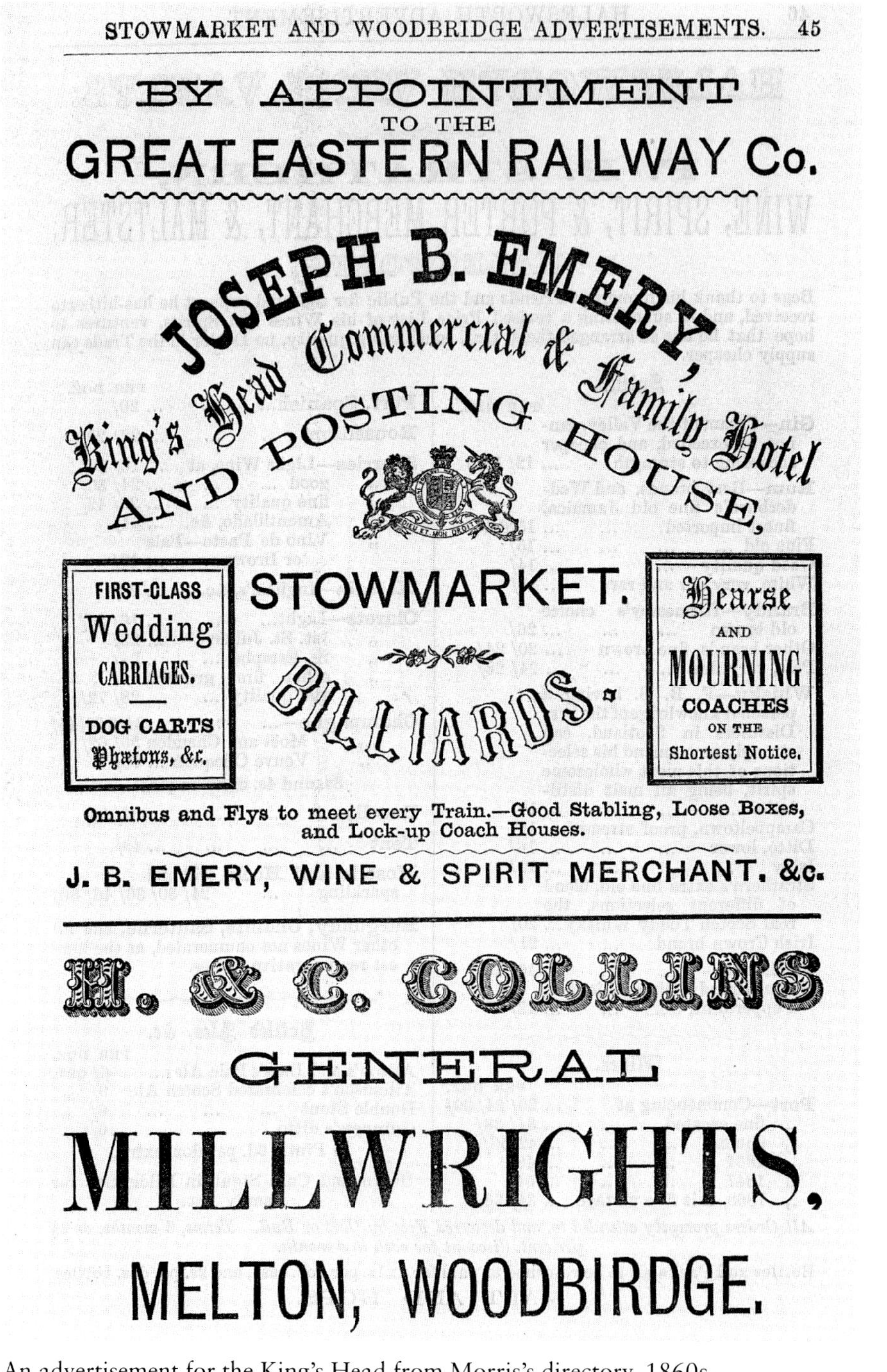

STOWMARKET AND WOODBRIDGE ADVERTISEMENTS. 45

BY APPOINTMENT
TO THE
GREAT EASTERN RAILWAY Co.

JOSEPH B. EMERY,
King's Head Commercial & Family Hotel
AND POSTING HOUSE,

FIRST-CLASS
Wedding
CARRIAGES.
DOG CARTS
Phætons, &c.

STOWMARKET.

BILLIARDS.

Hearse
AND
MOURNING
COACHES
ON THE
Shortest Notice.

Omnibus and Flys to meet every Train.—Good Stabling, Loose Boxes, and Lock-up Coach Houses.

J. B. EMERY, WINE & SPIRIT MERCHANT, &c.

H. & C. COLLINS
GENERAL
MILLWRIGHTS,
MELTON, WOODBIRDGE.

An advertisement for the King's Head from Morris's directory, 1860s.

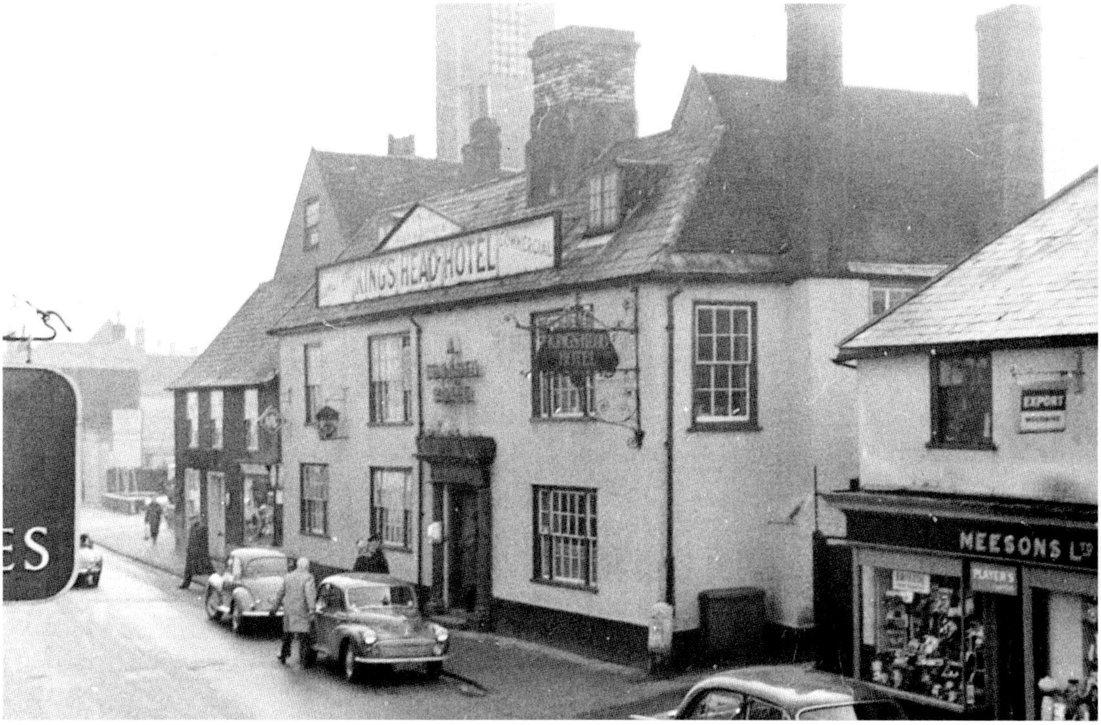


The King's Head Hotel seen from the other side of Ipswich Street, 1950s. Two Morris Minor 1000s are parked outside. At the corner of the building stands an old milestone showing that it was 12 miles to Ipswich – by the old road through Needham Market and Claydon. In the 19th century the King's Head was advertised as a family and commercial hotel and posting house; that is, travellers could obtain a change of horses at the King's Head stables. An omnibus, horse drawn, was driven down to the station to meet all trains. (Ivan Codd)

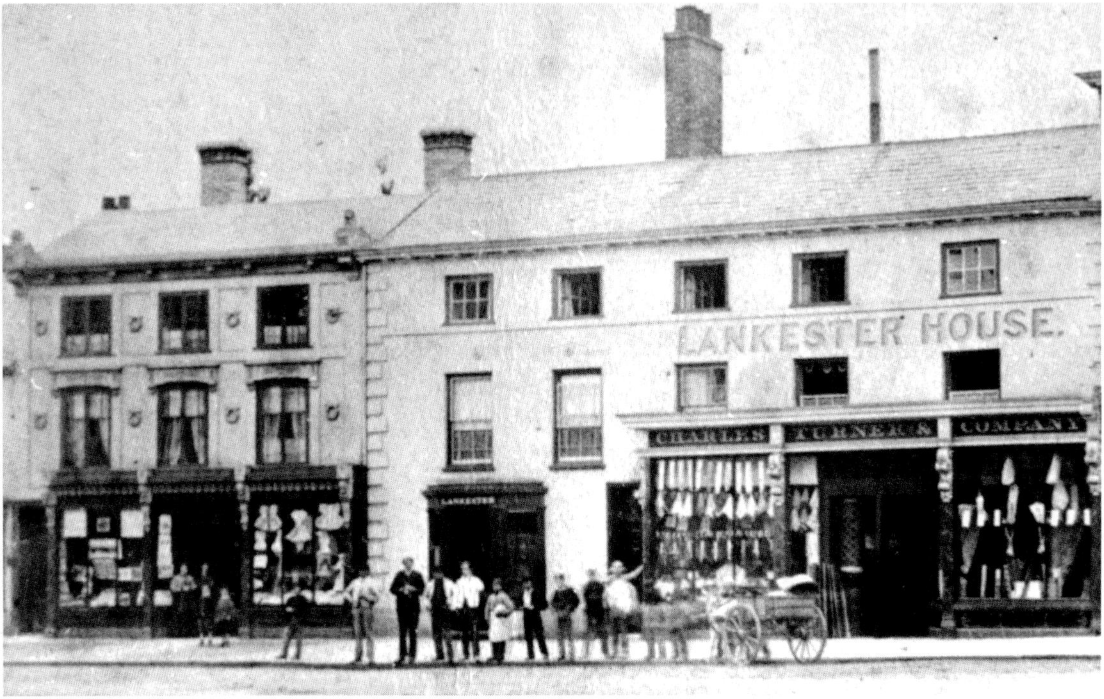


Lankester House was the site of Lankester & Wells' wine vaults, which extended under the Market Place roadway. The firm had extensive interests both in Stowmarket and elsewhere, at one time having premises in Nottingham. (Ivan Codd)

*Opposite:* A full-page advertisement in the *Post Office Directory* of 1879 for Lankester & Wells, later to become Lankester, Wells & Bartlett Ltd. This firm, said to have been founded in 1785, had a large bonded warehouse near the railway station, and later expanded to other places well outside Suffolk. The Lankester family had connections by marriage with the Webbs, of Combs Tannery. (RM)

# SPECIAL ANNOUNCEMENT.

# LANKESTER & WELLS,

## WINE, SPIRIT AND LIQUEUR IMPORTERS

(ESTABLISHED 1785),

PROPRIETORS OF THE

## GOVERNMENT BONDED STORES, STOWMARKET.

L. & W. have the pleasure to invite attention to their bonded Stores at Stowmarket, the first warehouse under the Excise opened in the Eastern Counties, and at the same time beg to suggest the especial advantages they can thereby offer to the consumers of wine. In the first place, the consumers are enabled to purchase wine in bond at its original cost equally well as if bought in the wine producing districts, adding only the cost in transit; and next, they may keep the wine for years on the premises at Stowmarket, under the immediate supervision of the Excise, and remove it at their convenience on paying the usual duties, with the certainty that the wine has improved in the wood, and will sooner develop into character when bottled. Upon removal from bond, L. & W. would bottle the wines, if desired, merely charging cost of labour, bottles and corks, and would deliver the wines free of charge to their destination.

Their stock of duty-paid wines in bottle, in the Market Place Vaults, embraces the finest vintages of wines shipped from Portugal for many years past, and a large and varied selection of Pure Sherry, Old Madeira, Fine Claret and high-class wines of every description. L. & W. respectfully solicit a personal inspection of their old established vaults, and would have pleasure in submitting samples of any of their wines on application.

### THE NEW SPARKLING WINE,

## RHINEGAU CHAMPAGNE.

This delicious wine is produced from the finest Champagne Grapes, grown in the most favoured district of Germany, and within three miles of the celebrated *Johannisberg Castle.* It is of delicate flavour and high bouquet, and being very moderate in price, can be recommended as the

## CHEAPEST CHAMPAGNE EVER OFFERED TO THE PUBLIC.

**PRICES—First Quality, rich or dry - 42s. per dozen bottles.**
**Extra Quality „ 46s. „ „**
**4s. additional per 24 half bottles.**

## PICK-ME-UP,

**The new UNRIVALLED LIQUEUR.—Pick-me-up for Luncheon. Pick-me-up with Soda, Potass and Seltzer Waters for Summer Drink. Pick-me-up for the Sporting Flask. LANKESTER & WELLS (the proprietors) supply the above in 1, 2, or 3 dozen cases at 42s. per dozen bottles, 4s. additional per 24 half bottles.**

### THE OBAN BLEND

## PURE OLD HIGHLAND MALT WHISKY.

For years we have found difficulty in obtaining a PURE MALT WHISKY direct from the Highlands of Scotland, naturally and thoroughly matured. We have consequently felt it necessary to visit the district and arrange for a direct supply of old Whisky, both in Bond and Duty Paid. The latter arrangement will enable us to send SMALL CASKS TO OUR CUSTOMERS from the Bond direct.

**THE OBAN BLEND** is the produce of FOUR HIGHLAND STILLS BLENDED TOGETHER, and well matured by age—for, be it understood, that no artificial process of mellowing, nor any system of double distillation can give to Whisky the characteristics that are developed by time. The oils of the Malt contained in this Whisky are highly nutritious, and when decomposed by age, form those delicate and fragrant ethers which distinguish pure Malt Whisky from the coarse grain spirit generally sold as Scotch Whisky.

**The Oban Blend, 42s. per dozen, 21s. per gallon.**

Average age 5 years. Packages to be returned or paid for.

**CARRIAGE PAID TO ALL RAILWAY STATIONS FOR ORDERS OF £2 AND ABOVE.**

## OFFICES:—MARKET PLACE, STOWMARKET.

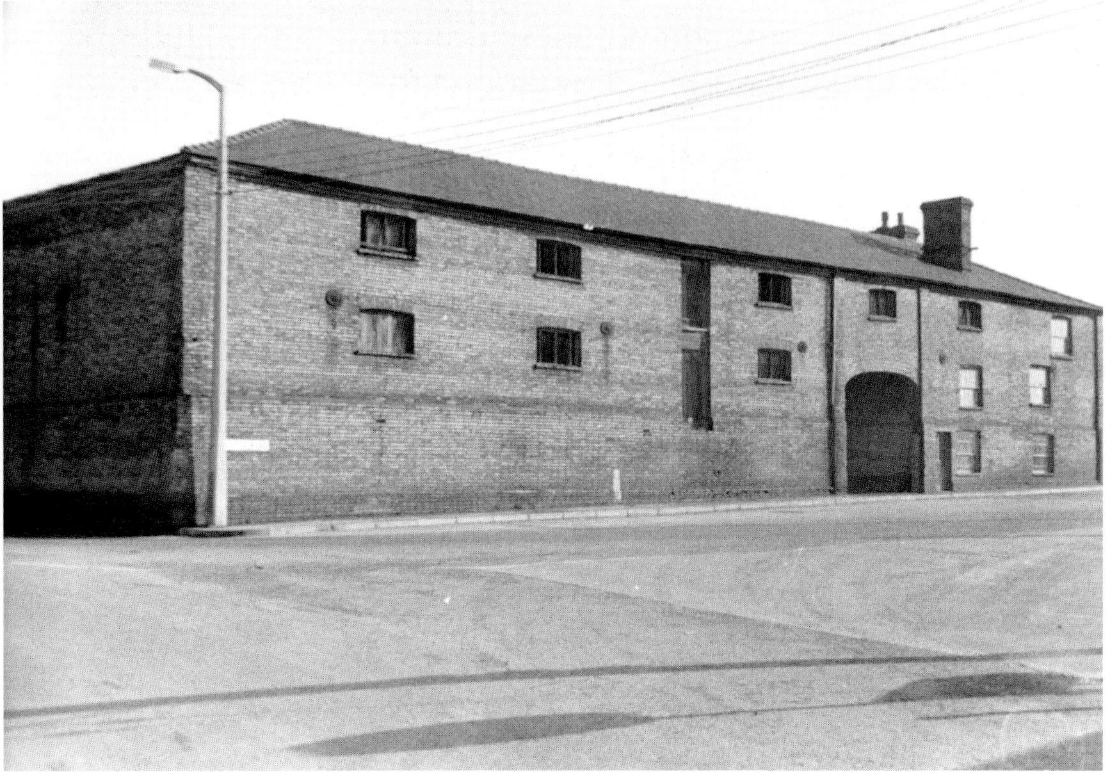

This building at the corner of Prentice Road and Stowupland Street housed Lankester & Wells' bonded warehouse and, at the far end, the Hop Pole Tavern, otherwise known as 'The Poor Man's Hotel'; working people living in the countryside beyond walking distance and employed in Stowmarket would stay there during the week, returning home for the weekend. A railway siding passed through the arch, across Prentice Street and over a bridge to reach commercial premises on the town side of the river. The whole building was demolished in about 1972; its disappearance made possible the development of a new road system, but it has not added to the character of this part of the town. (Ivan Codd)

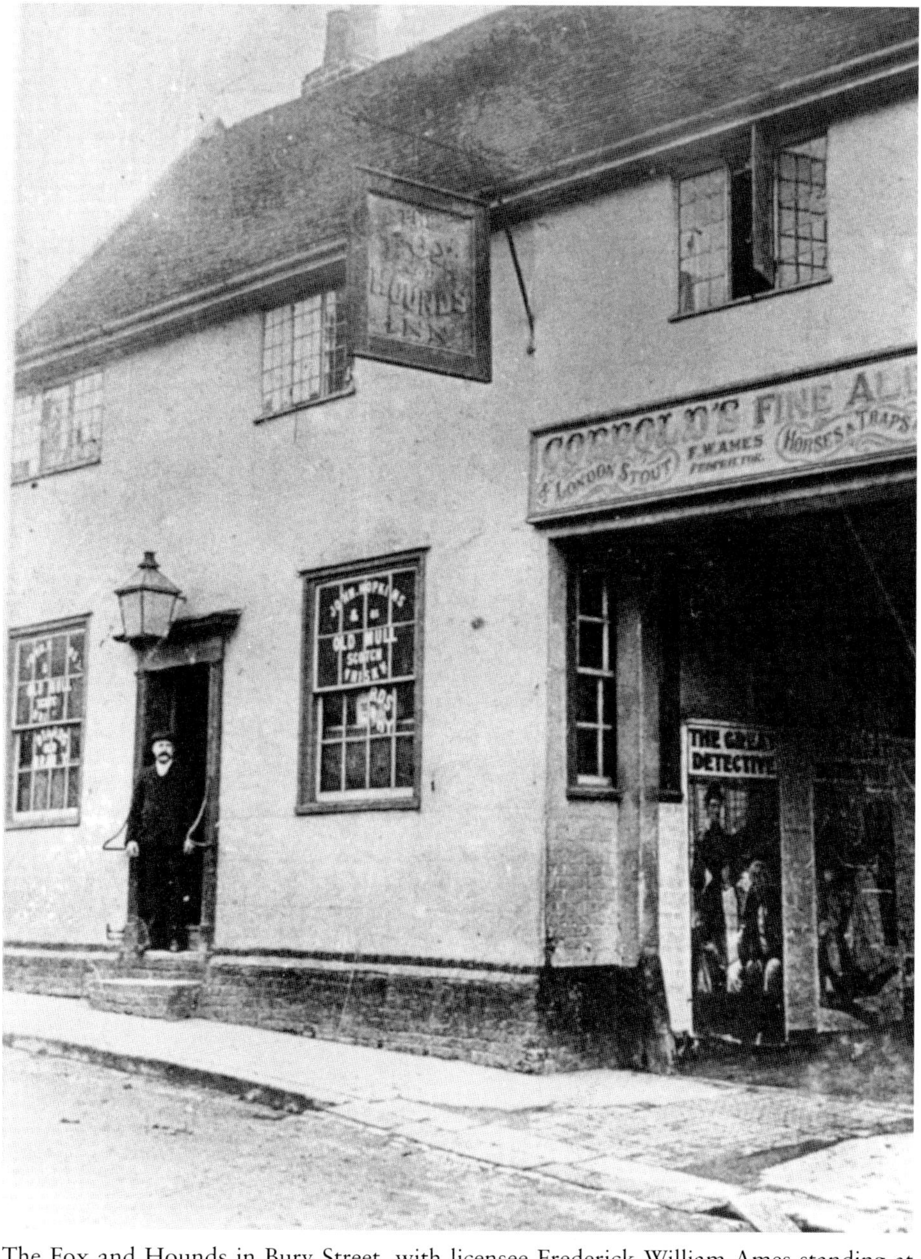


The Fox and Hounds in Bury Street, with licensee Frederick William Ames standing at the door. As can be seen from the sign over the yard entrance, he also had horses and traps to let. In the 1920s an extension to the Stowmarket Co-operative Society store was built on the site. (Ivan Codd)

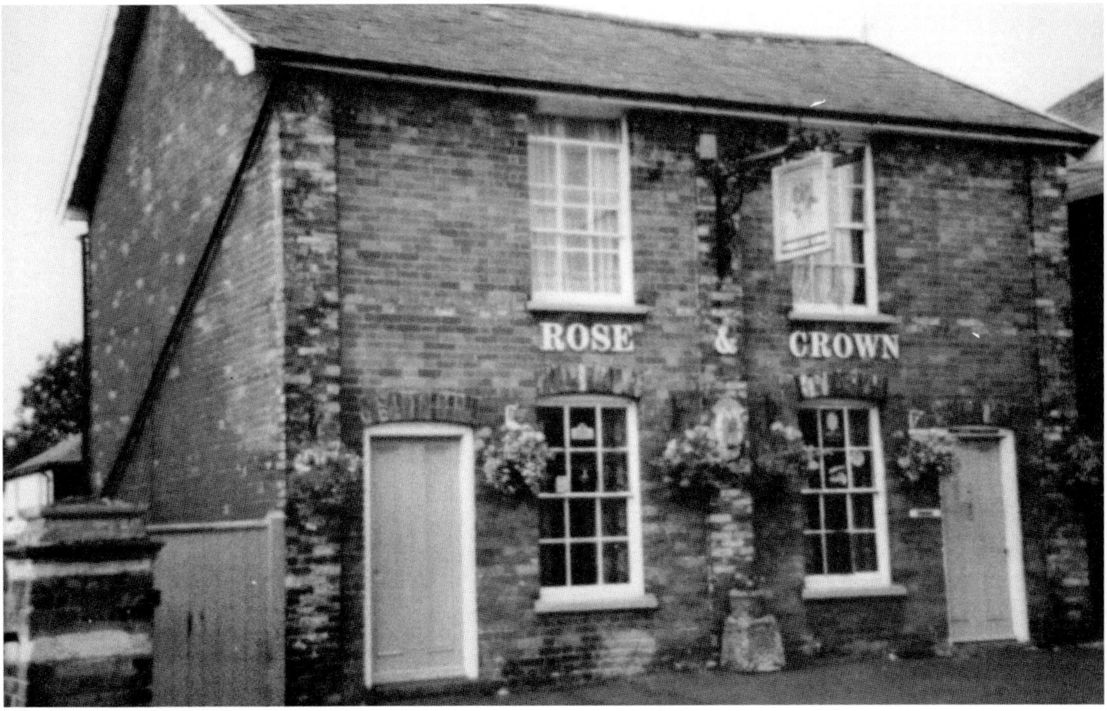


The Rose & Crown in Bridge Street served the California area of the town, a 19th-century suburb occupied largely by workers in the town's new industries. In the 1890s George Diaper was operating the Crown Brewery here, and for many years the Rose & Crown was a beerhouse, as distinct from a public house – which sold wines and spirits as well as beer.

*Section Five*

# CHEMICALS

Soon after the middle of the 19th century two industries became established in the town which were to have a great impact on local life, the manufacture of chemical fertilisers and the making of explosives. Both owed their existence to members of the Prentice family.

Manning Prentice (1759–1836) moved to Stowmarket from the Bungay area in 1799, becoming a pillar of the local Congregational church, of which he was the first deacon, jointly with a J.B. Tailer (who no doubt gave his name to Tailer's Lane). His grandsons Thomas and Manning Prentice and Joseph

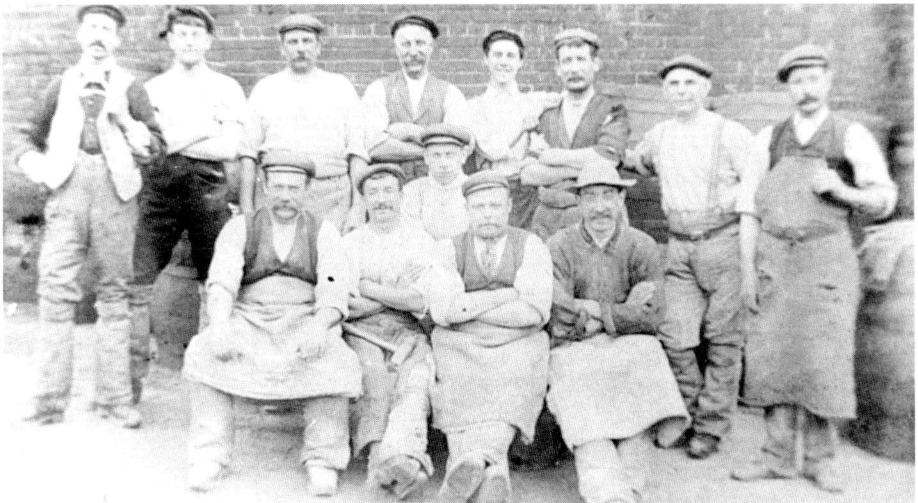

Employees of Sutton & Phillips, brewers' chemists, of Stowupland Road, *c.* 1900. Sutton & Phillips set up in Stowmarket during the 1880s as competitors to Prentice Brothers, who among all their other trades listed themselves as brewers' chemists; earlier Charles William Sutton had been in business as Suffolk's only brewers' chemist at Earl Stonham. (Ivan Codd)

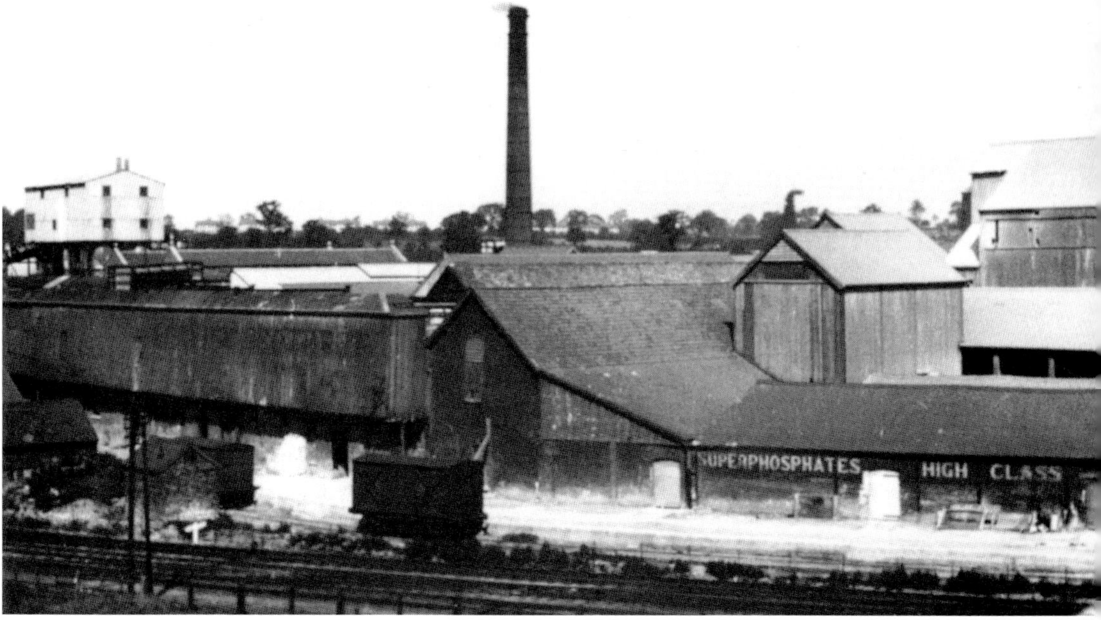


Part of the Prentice Brothers fertiliser works, which had its beginnings in 1856 when artificial manure was being produced from coprolites. Built by Thomas Prentice & Co., it was taken over in 1868 by a new company, Prentice Brothers, formed by Eustace and Edward Prentice. They were joined a little later by Manning Prentice. (Ivan Codd)

Fison were at school in Essex with David Livingstone, the famous missionary, and there were plans for Thomas and Manning to join him in Africa. In the event they went into business in Stowmarket and, in spite of some tart comments over their 'defection', Livingstone corresponded with the three over a long period. The three men married three sisters: Manning Prentice married Susanna Ridley, Thomas Prentice Catherine and Joseph Fison Anne.

Thomas Prentice and Company were corn and coal merchants at Navigation Wharf, just below Stowupland Street, in 1844, with Prentice & Hewitt operating a sawmill and trading as timber and slate merchants as well as ironmongers in Stowupland Street. Both these firms were operating some of the town's maltings. Thomas Prentice and Company, with Thomas's son Manning Prentice as its principal, later extended its activities by leasing the gasworks in Prentice Street from the company of shareholders which had run it since it had been built in 1835–6.

Even later the same firm expanded into the manufacture of asphalt floors and pavements, and also opened an agricultural chemical works for the manufacture of artificial manure. The trade in 'artificials' depended on coprolites, the phosphatic nodules quarried in the coastal areas of Suffolk and

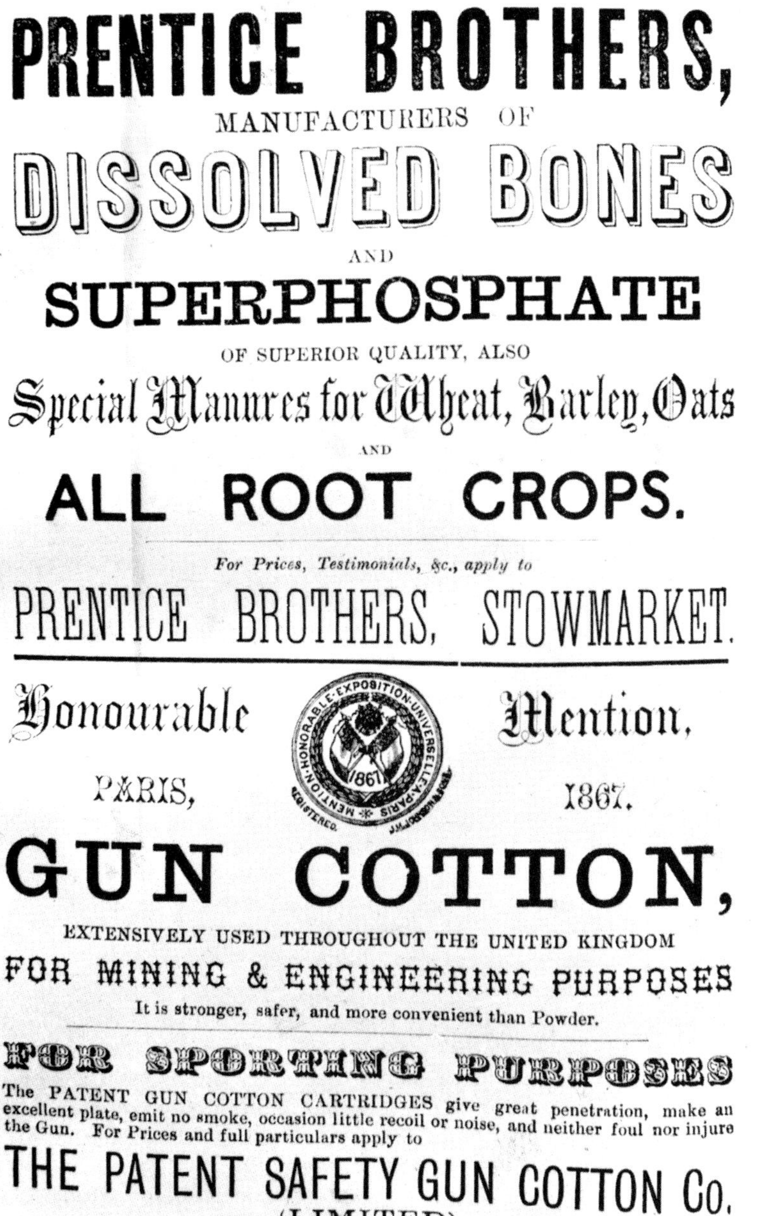


An advertisement from the late 1860s for Prentice Brothers and the Patent Safety Gun Cotton Co. Ltd. (Ivan Codd)

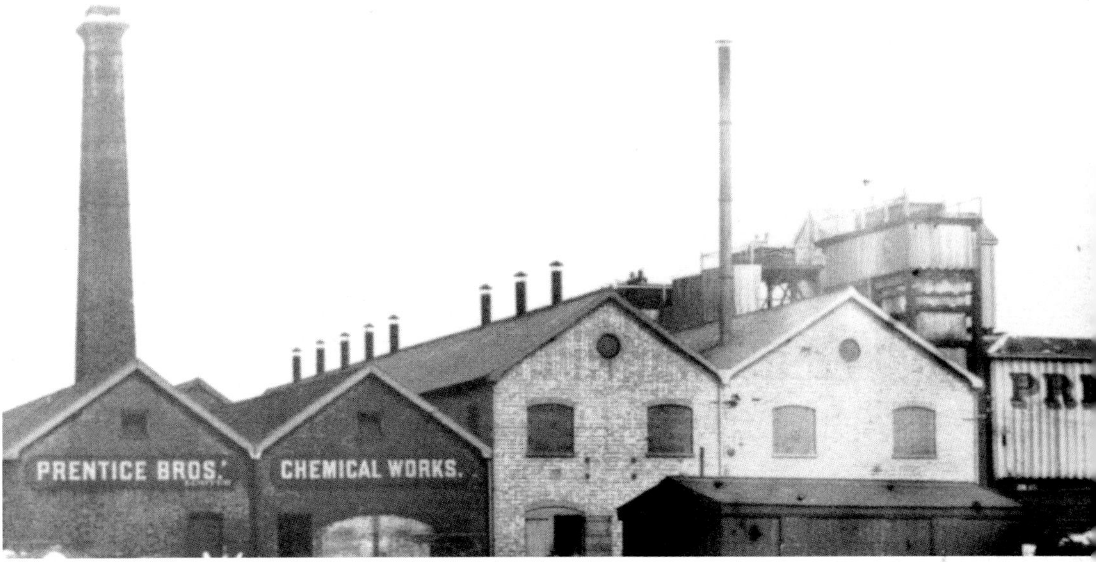


Another part of the Prentice Brothers factory, on the east side of the railway line a little more than a quarter of a mile on the Ipswich side of Stowmarket station. (Ivan Codd)

in Cambridgeshire, which were almost certainly brought up the navigation; these were first crushed and then dissolved in sulphuric acid in 'dens' to produce a fertiliser that could be easily assimilated by plants.

The sulphuric acid and superphosphate works built in 1856 were taken over in 1868 by a new company, Prentice Brothers, formed by Eustace and Edward Prentice. They were joined a little later by Manning Prentice (a later generation than the one mentioned above), an outstanding chemical scholar who became well known as the inventor of a process for concentrating sulphuric acid in a platinum pan. He also developed a continuous still for the production of nitric acid.

Manning Prentice took over responsibility for most of the company's operations when Edward Prentice was killed in the 1871 explosion and in 1891, seven years after the death of the second brother Eustace, he converted the business into a limited company, of which he became managing director.

Prentice Brothers suffered a severe setback in 1922 when the works was devastated by a serious fire. The 1920s was a difficult period for fertiliser manufacturers generally, with falling demand exacerbated by imports from abroad, forcing British companies to reduce both prices and output.

In 1929 Prentice Brothers amalgamated with Packards and James Fison (Thetford) Ltd, and Joseph Fison and Co. Ltd of Ipswich, to form Fison, Packard and Prentice Ltd. The object of the amalgamation was to ensure that the resources of the three companies were pooled to provide a better and more

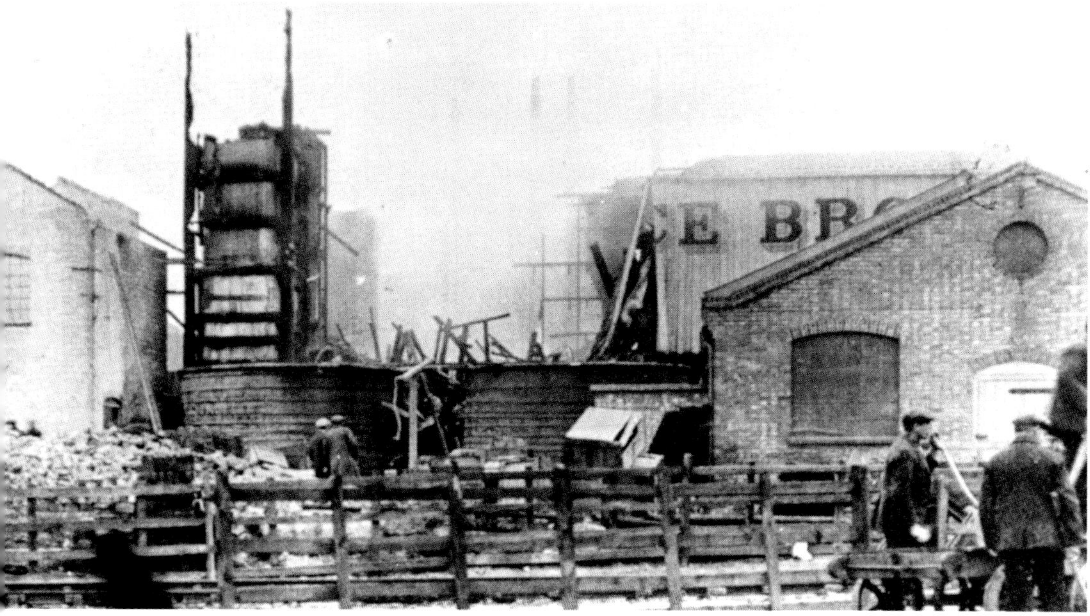


The same part of the works after the disastrous fire of 1922. (Ivan Codd)

economical service to agriculture and to strengthen the company position. The company became Fisons Ltd in 1942.

As part of its other activities the firm of Thomas Prentice produced its own sulphuric acid. Some years earlier, in the 1840s, an Austrian scientist had produced an explosive by the action of a mixture of nitric and sulphuric acid on cellulose, and in the 1860s experiments were carried out at Stowmarket into the production of this explosive, guncotton.

The first factory at Stowmarket for the manufacture of guncotton, to a design by Professor F.A. (later Sir Frederick) Abel, was built in the early sixties. At this time the basis of manufacture was long staple cotton in the form of yarn, which was dipped in a mixture of acids. The nitrated cotton was put into wire baskets, placed in running water and left, sometimes for several weeks, until sufficient of the free acids had been washed away. As it is probable that water from the Gipping was used for this washing process and was afterwards returned to the river, the effect on water quality downstream of the works can be imagined.

The manufacturing process was far from safe, and in 1864, only a year after the works went into production, two women employees died in an explosion there.

As chemist to the War Department Professor Abel spent some time at Stowmarket while researching more efficient methods of production. In 1865 he patented a guncotton pulping and compressing process by which explosive

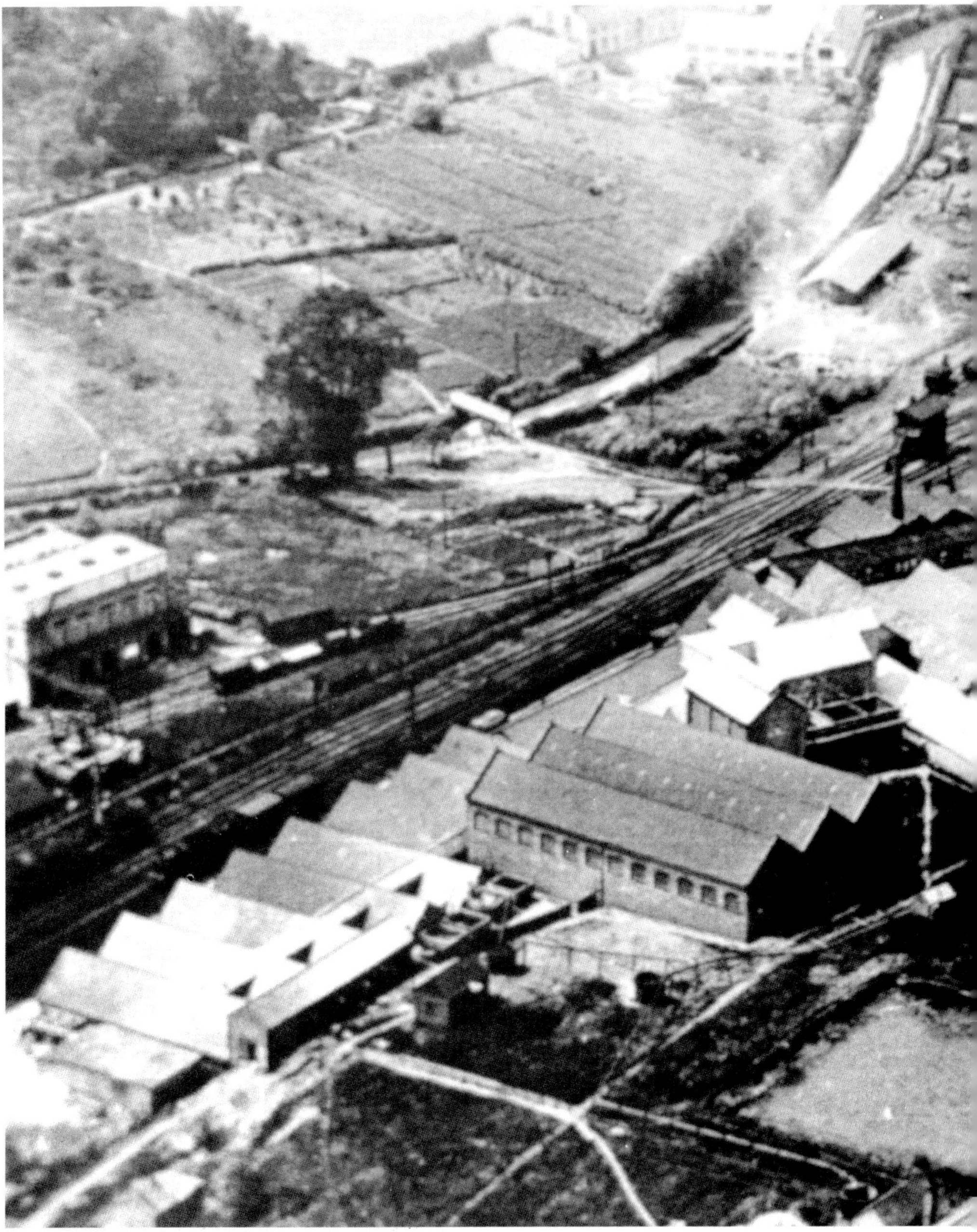

An aerial view of Prentice Brothers' works, *c.* 1925. By this time the buildings destroyed by the fire had been replaced. The River Gipping can be seen curving across the top left-hand corner of the picture, and prominent are the extensive goods sidings which once existed on the Ipswich side of the station. (Ivan Codd)

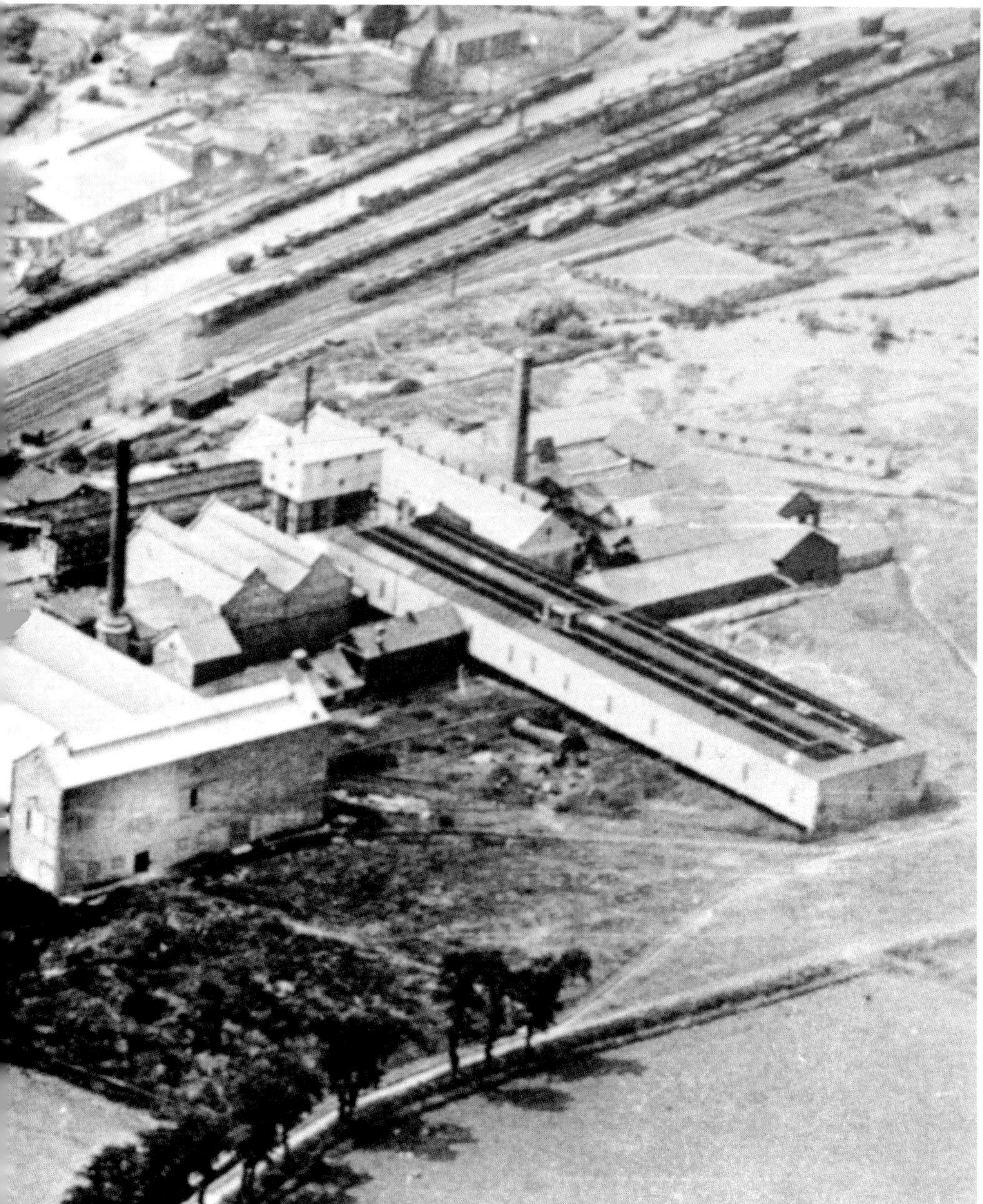

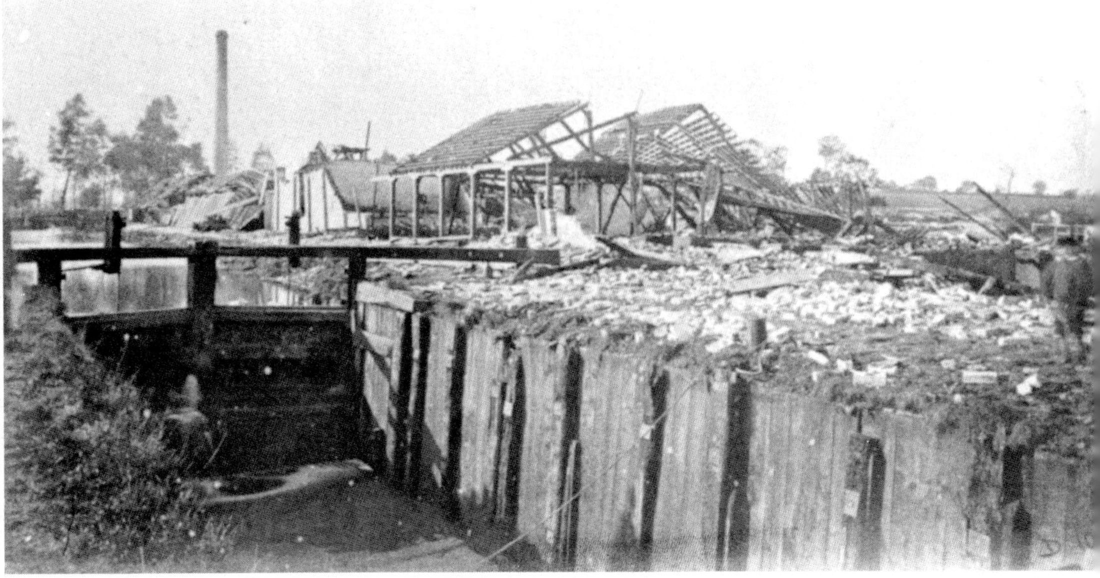

The Patent Safety Gun Cotton Co. Ltd was not many years old when on 11 August 1871 a series of disastrous explosions devastated the works and killed 24 people, including Edward Prentice and his nephew William. This photograph shows the wreckage of the guncotton works, seen from the last lock on the Stowmarket Navigation. The river not only served to carry away the products of the works but also provided water for washing the guncotton, part of the manufacturing process. (Ivan Codd)

of a density and purity hitherto unattainable could be made from cheap cotton waste. The Stowmarket works immediately took up the new process, and in 1870 a new factory was licensed for the manufacture of explosives. At the same time the Patent Safety Gun Cotton Co. Ltd was formed to take over the business. Eustace Prentice became managing director of the new company.

The title of the new company was belied by the events of Friday 11 August 1871. 'Stowmarket is a wreck,' announced the *Suffolk Mercury* the following day. 'At five minutes past two o'clock yesterday afternoon an explosion occurred at the Gun Cotton Works of Messrs. Prentice and Co., which has involved an awful, but hitherto unascertained, loss of life, and has left the town almost as great a wreck as if it had been bombarded by an enemy's guns.'

Three magazines filled with 14 tons of guncotton had exploded, killing a dozen workers and injuring many more. Some workers were trapped in blazing buildings as fire spread through the works.

The managing director, Eustace Prentice, was on holiday in Switzerland, but another director, Edward Prentice, with his nephew William (who had just arrived home from Heidelberg, where he was at university) and all four Stowmarket doctors, hurried to the works. Edward and William were engaged in rescue work when a second explosion blew them both to pieces. A third

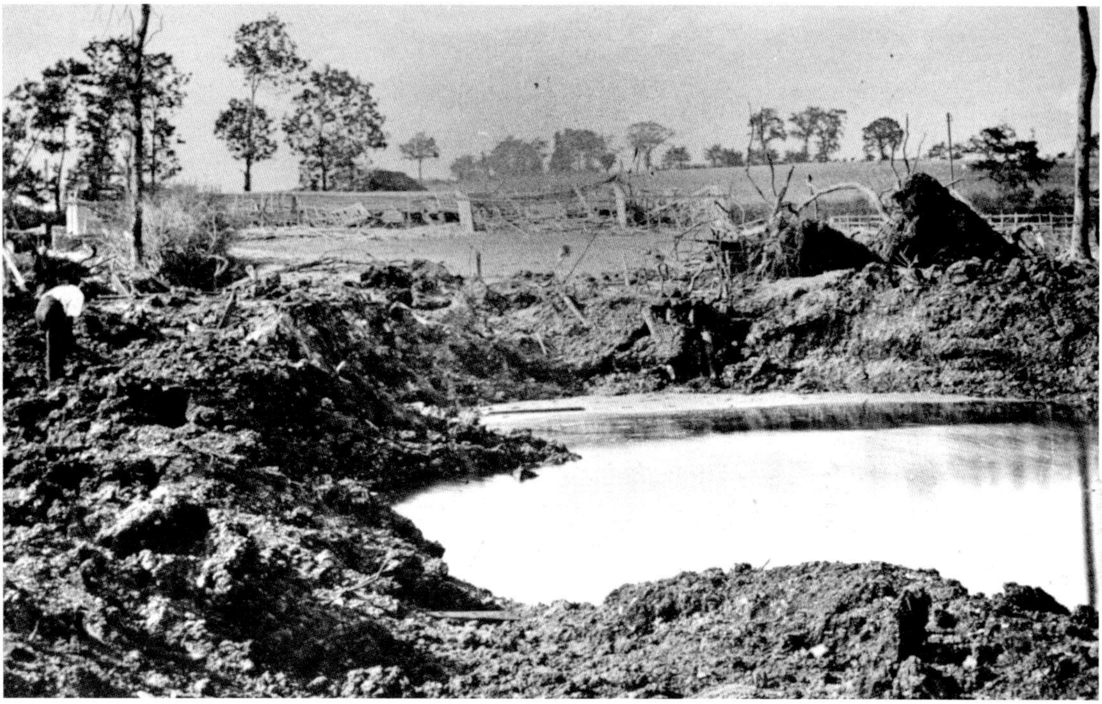

This crater was the site of one of the magazines which exploded that day. (Ivan Codd)

explosion later fortunately caused no further casualties. Altogether 24 people died, half of them boys and girls under 17. At least one of the workers who died was only 12.

The inquest into the deaths of all 24 people lasted for three and a half weeks. At the end the jury brought in a verdict that did nothing to remove the air of mystery over the cause of the disaster: 'We find the explosion causing the death of the persons on whom this inquest is held was produced by some person or persons unknown adding sulphuric acid to the guncotton subsequent to its passing all the tests required by Government.'

An appeal raised £3,472, almost a third of which provided immediate relief for the sufferers, and Manning Prentice paid out £1,500 to three trustees to reimburse those who had suffered loss or damage.

Before the end of the year work was in progress on the rebuilding of the works on an enlarged and improved plan. The company wisely dropped the word 'safety' from its title and was known simply as The Stowmarket Guncotton Co. Ltd until 1881, when it was renamed The Explosives Co. Ltd. In 1885 it became The New Explosives Co. Ltd.

The works produced a range of products including blasting charges and explosives for military use, and in 1898 the company embarked on the manufacture of cordite. Much of the production was sent downriver by barge,

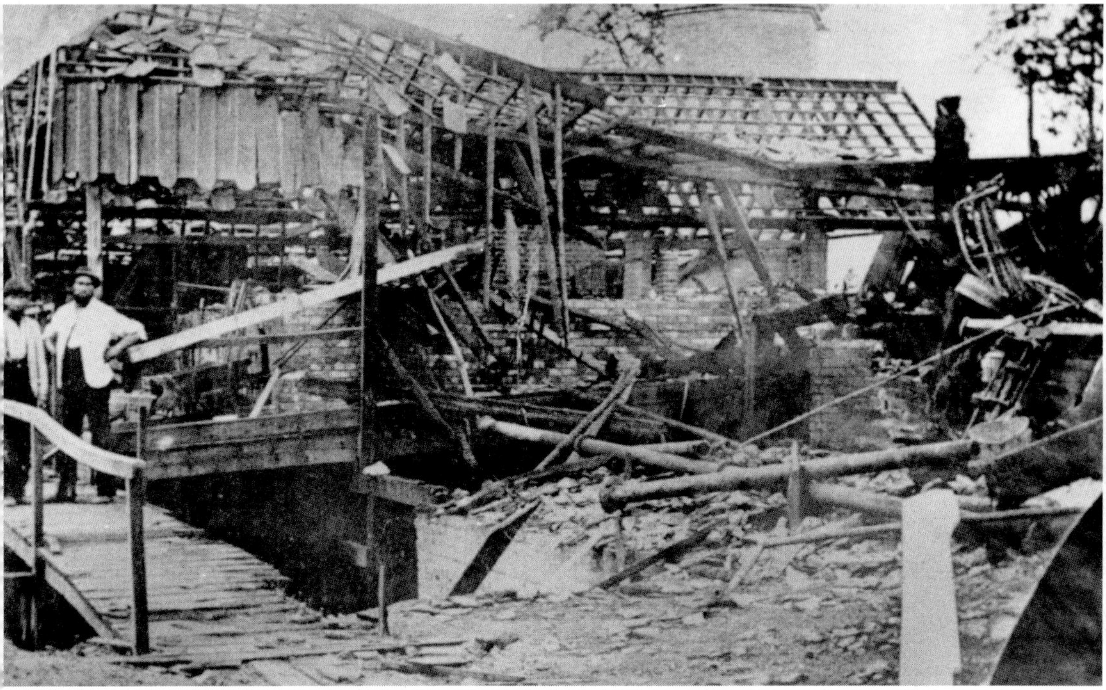

Enormous damage was caused in the town as well as in the guncotton works itself by the explosions. Above is all that remained of one of the sheds in the works.

to be loaded into seagoing vessels at Ipswich, but the state of the navigation prevented barges reaching Stowmarket after 1910, by which time the railway was carrying the major share of the company's production.

During the First World War the output of guncotton was quadrupled. The workforce was increased from about 500 to upwards of 2,000 and work went on day and night, shift workers being brought in from Ipswich and Bury St Edmunds on special trains to augment the locally recruited labour, and a big new manufacturing building was erected.

Possibly it was the bringing in of so many new and untrained workers that was responsible for two accidents which occurred, the first of them not long after the outbreak of war. Happily there were no casualties when the building in which raw cotton was 'pulled', sorted and dried caught fire in October 1914, but four workers died when a cordite magazine exploded in May 1915.

During the war the factory added the manufacture of aircraft dopes to its other activities, thus setting a pattern for the future. Production of explosives ceased soon after the end of the First World War, when the company's name was changed to Necol Industrial Collodions Ltd, indicating its new role in producing cellulose coatings mainly for the car and furniture industries. In the 1920s the company became Nobel Chemical Finishes Ltd.

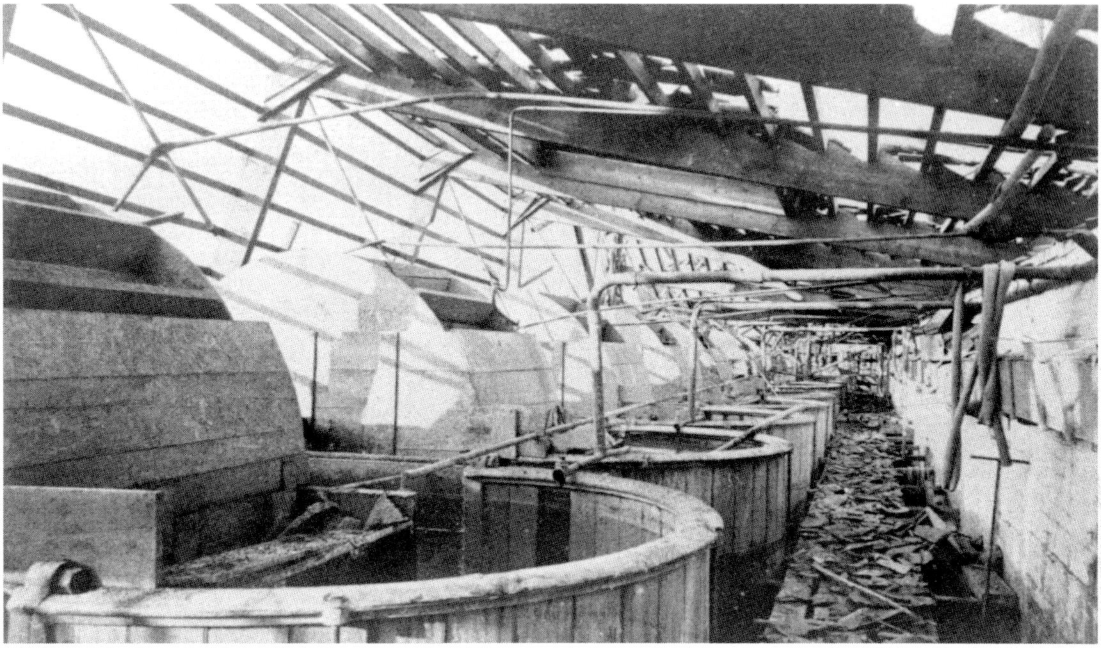

The inside of one of the processing buildings. (Ivan Codd)

Colonel Vivian D. Majendie, who was called in to investigate the explosion, came to the conclusion that the initial explosion had been due to the spontaneous decomposition of impure guncotton. The impurity, in the form of sulphuric acid, had been wilfully added to the guncotton after it had passed through the process of manufacture and testing, he said. There is no record of the evidence on which Colonel Majendie based his conclusion. A reward of £100 was offered by the Government to anyone who would provide information, but nobody ever came forward to claim it; perhaps anyone who knew the real cause had died in the explosion. (Ivan Codd)

**GUN-COTTON EXPLOSION**

**STOWMARKET.**

**V. R.**

**£100 REWARD.**

WHEREAS the Jury at the Inquest lately held at Stowmarket returned a verdict to the effect "That the Explosion was the result of some Person or Persons unknown having added Sulphuric Acid to the Cotton Pulp after it had passed all the tests required by Government," the above Reward (of £100) will be paid by Her Majesty's Government to any person who shall give such information as shall lead to the Discovery and Conviction of the Perpetrator or Perpetrators of this Outrage; and a FREE PARDON will be granted to any Accomplice, not being the actual Offender, who shall give such information as shall lead to a like result.

By Order,
CLEMENT HEIGHAM,
Chief Constable of Suffolk.

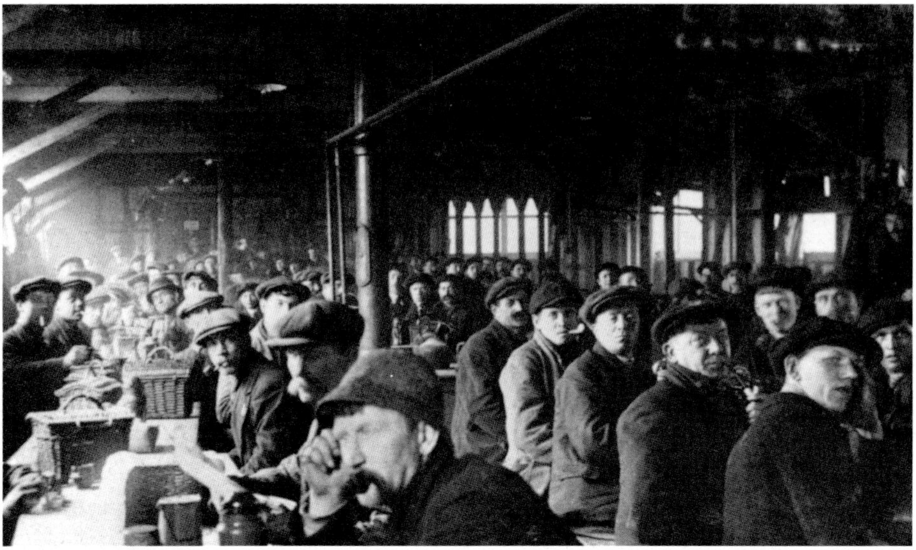

It must have been a relief for many to take a dinner break in the canteen, where as well as having their 'bait', carried in their baskets, they could enjoy a smoke. The canteen was provided not by the company but by the Church of England Temperance Society, as an alternative to the licensed premises normally frequented by workmen. Below, men coming on shift line up to be searched for cigarettes, matches and anything that might contribute to causing an explosion. Hobnailed boots were, of course, prohibited, and those working in hazardous places were even banned from wearing belts with buckles; instead their belts were laced with leather thongs. (Both Ivan Codd)

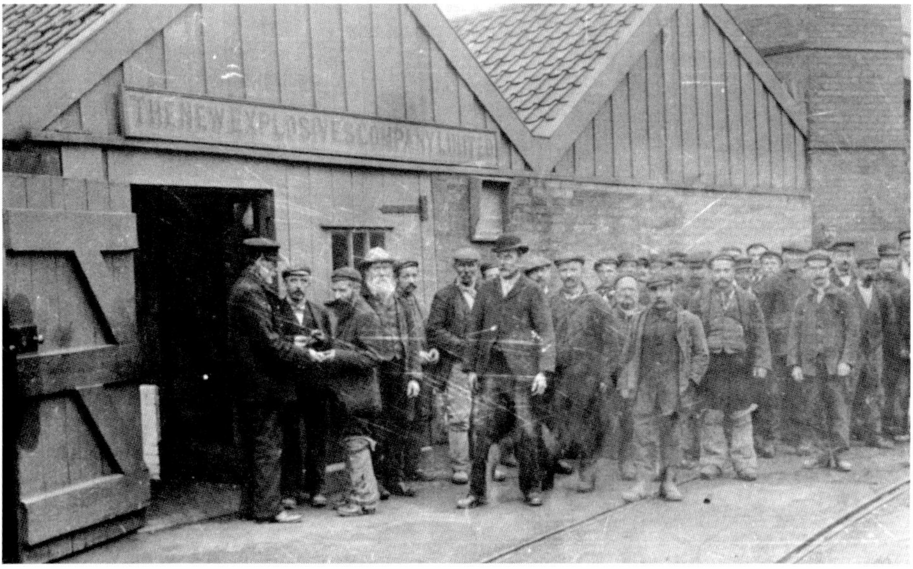

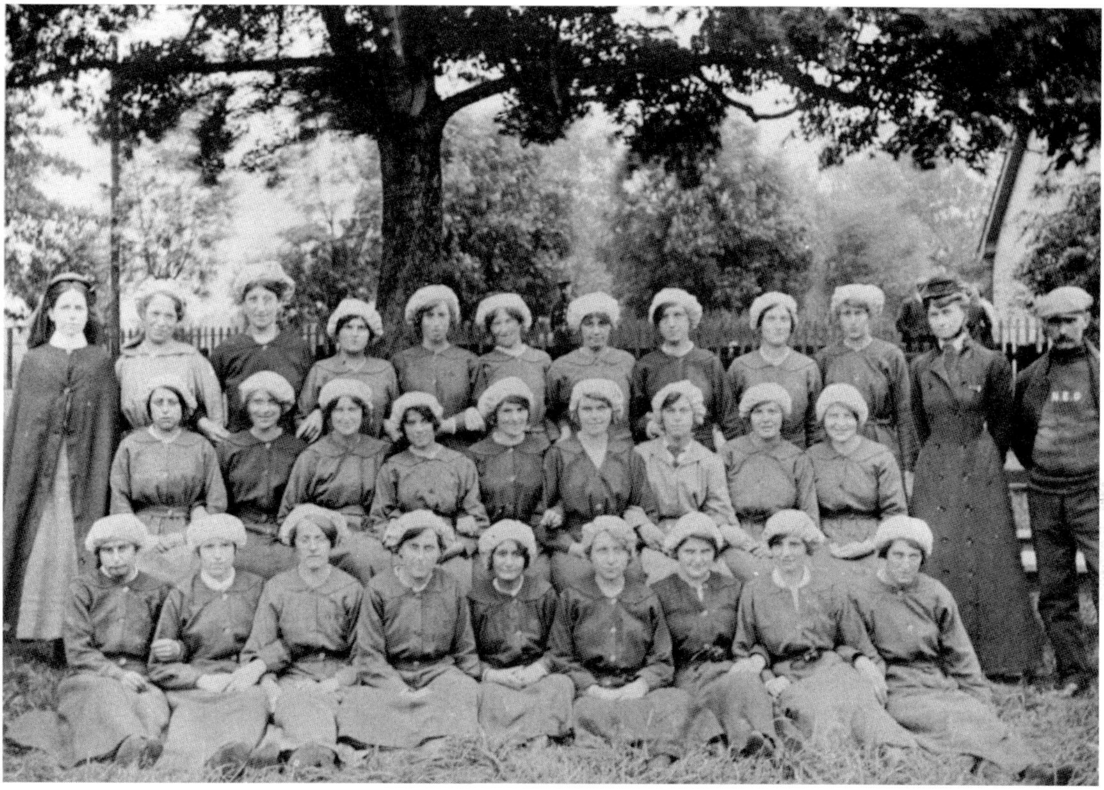

Women workers at the New Explosives Co. Ltd in the early years of this century. They all wore a uniform, as did the male employees; the solitary man on the right wears his uniform 'gansey' with the letters NEC on it (some workers also had numbers on theirs). Next to him is the works nurse. (Ivan Codd)

Eventually the works became part of the Paints Division of Imperial Chemical Industries (ICI). Since then a wide range of paint products has been added, such as aircraft finishes, paper lacquers, base solutions for leather and nail varnishes, and acrylic lacquer for the car industry.

With the commissioning in 1972 of the 90 ft high Big Batch Plant, with its attendant row of giant silos, and the commissioning in 1978 of the Acrylic Resin Plant, which stands where the original paint-making building of the works used to be, the Stowmarket site has grown into one of the most modern and best-equipped paint factories in the world.

It is interesting that the explosives industry should have spawned a paint-making plant, for as far back as 1879 Henry Parker Hayhoe & Co. were operating as patent paint solvent manufacturers in Bury Street.

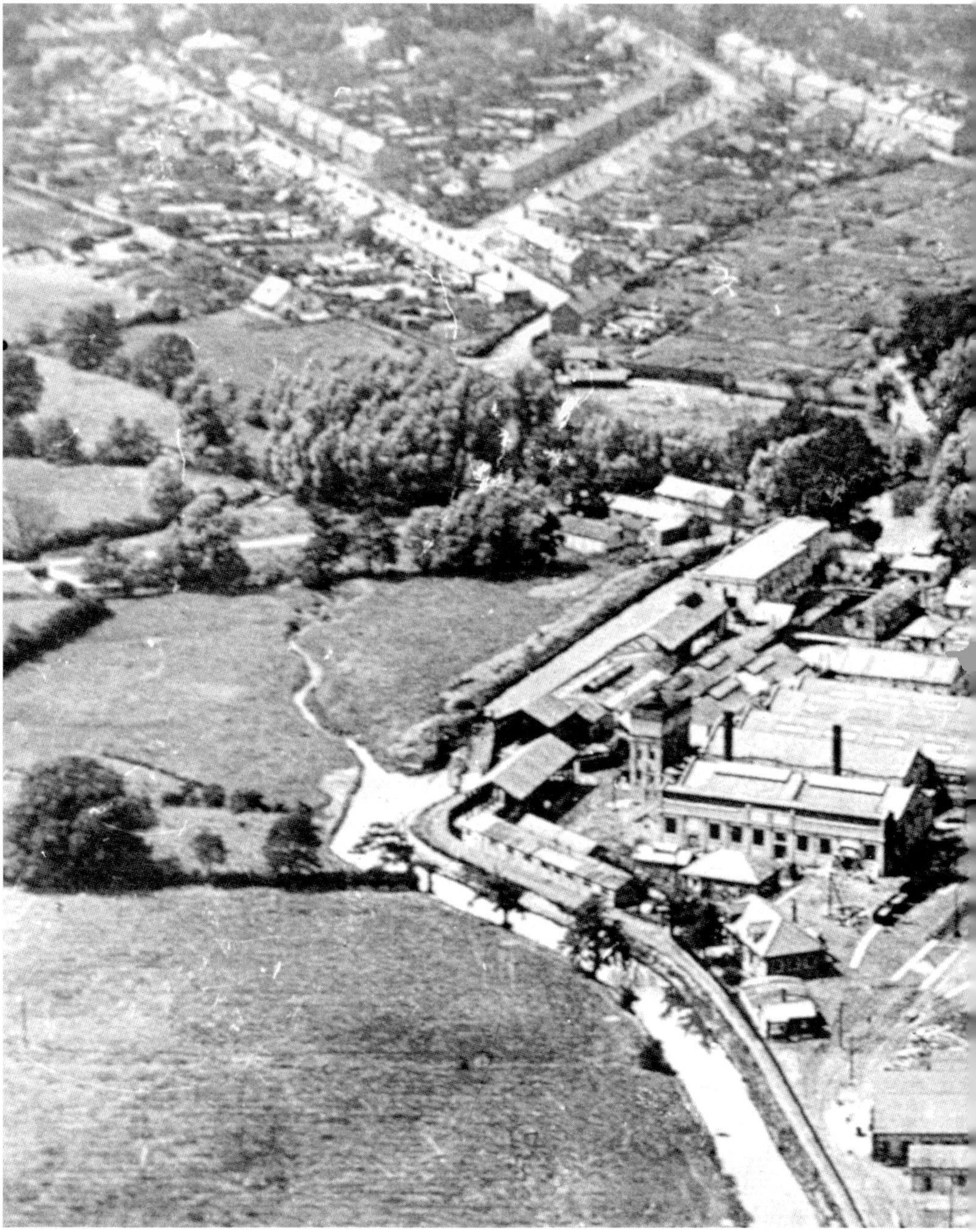

This aerial view taken in the 1920s shows the explosives works in its new guise as a factory for the production of artificial silk. In the lower right-hand corner of the photograph can be seen a small part of the disused cordite works site. There was an

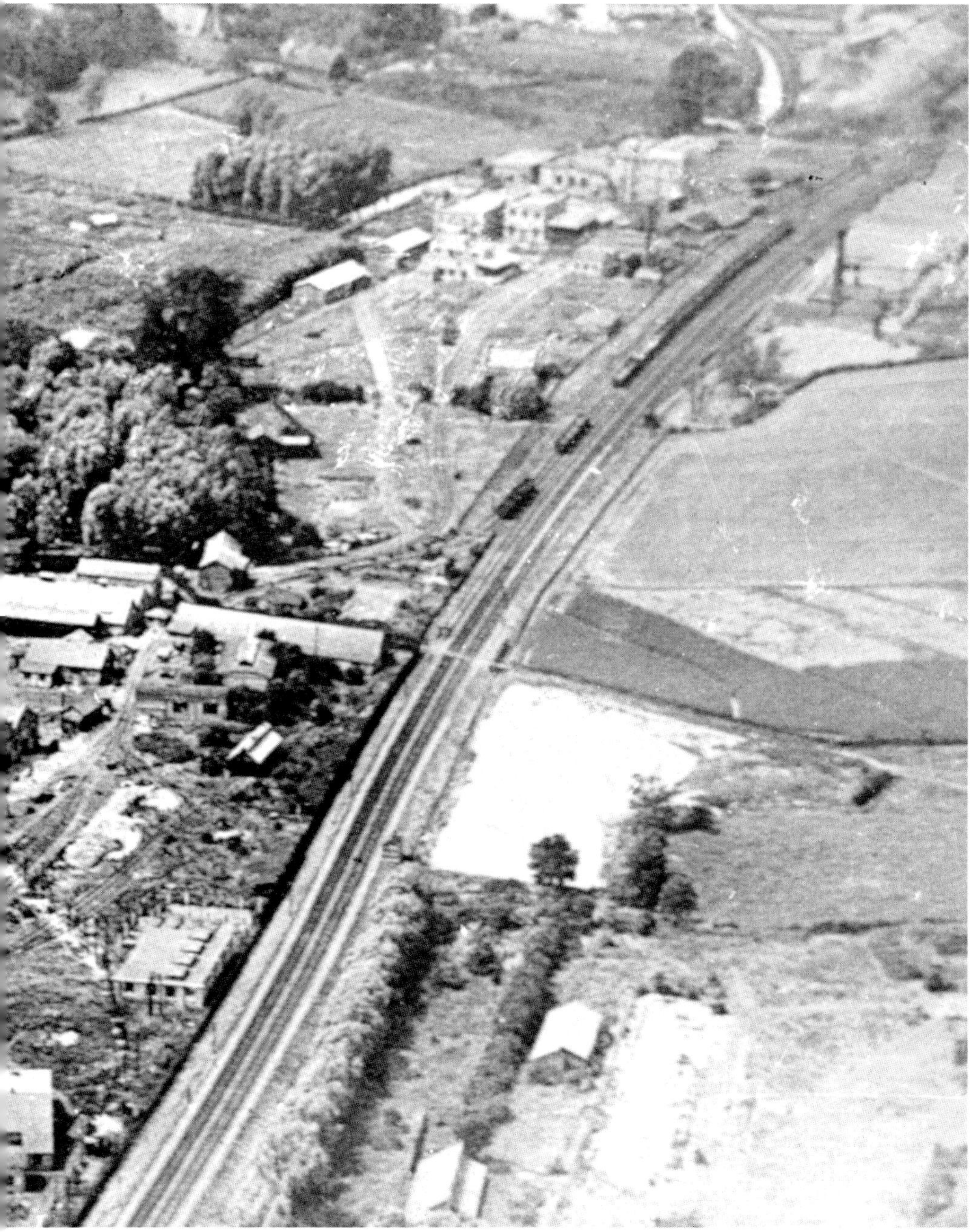

extensive tramway layout within the works which is clear from this view; the tramway passes under the Great Eastern main line to the cordite works site at the extreme bottom of the picture. (Ivan Codd)

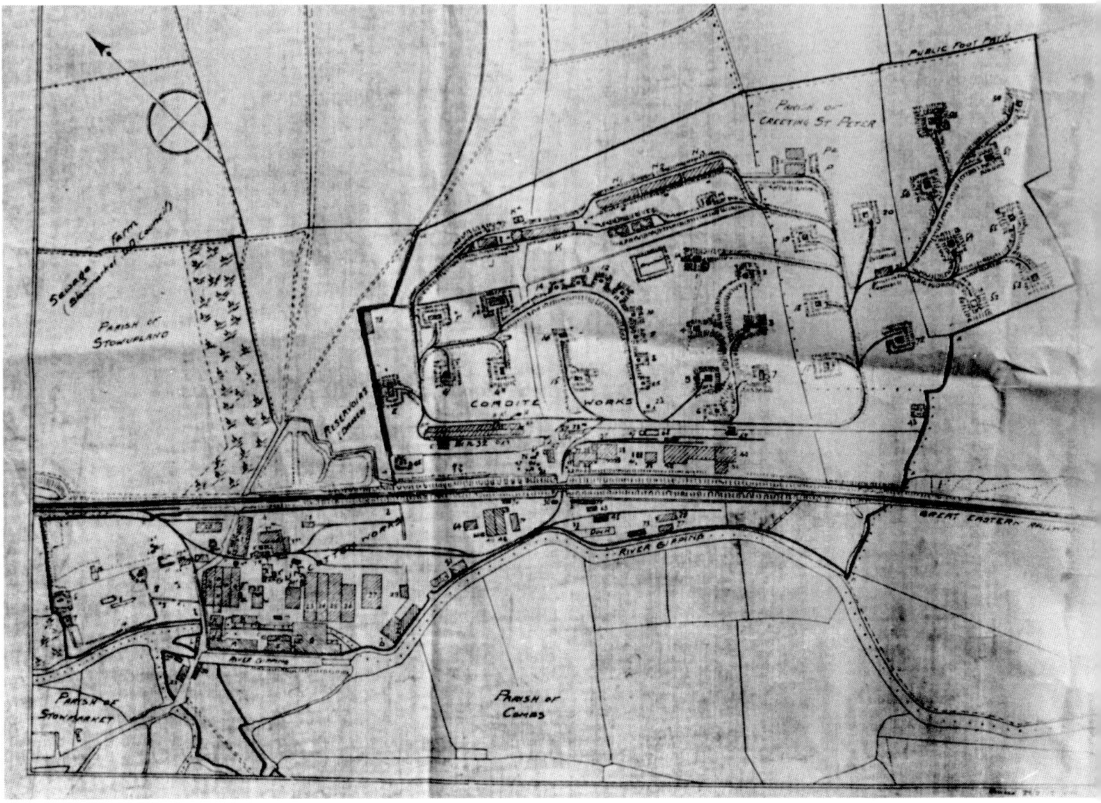


The works produced a range of products including blasting charges and explosives for military use. In 1898 the company embarked on the manufacture of cordite, a smokeless explosive made from nitroglycerin and guncotton, on a new site to the north of the Ipswich–Norwich railway line. This map, dated 1915, shows the guncotton works beside the River Gipping at bottom left and the cordite works on the other side of the railway line. The tramway system linked the dispersed production buildings and magazines. Four workers died when one of the cordite magazines exploded in 1915. (Ivan Codd)

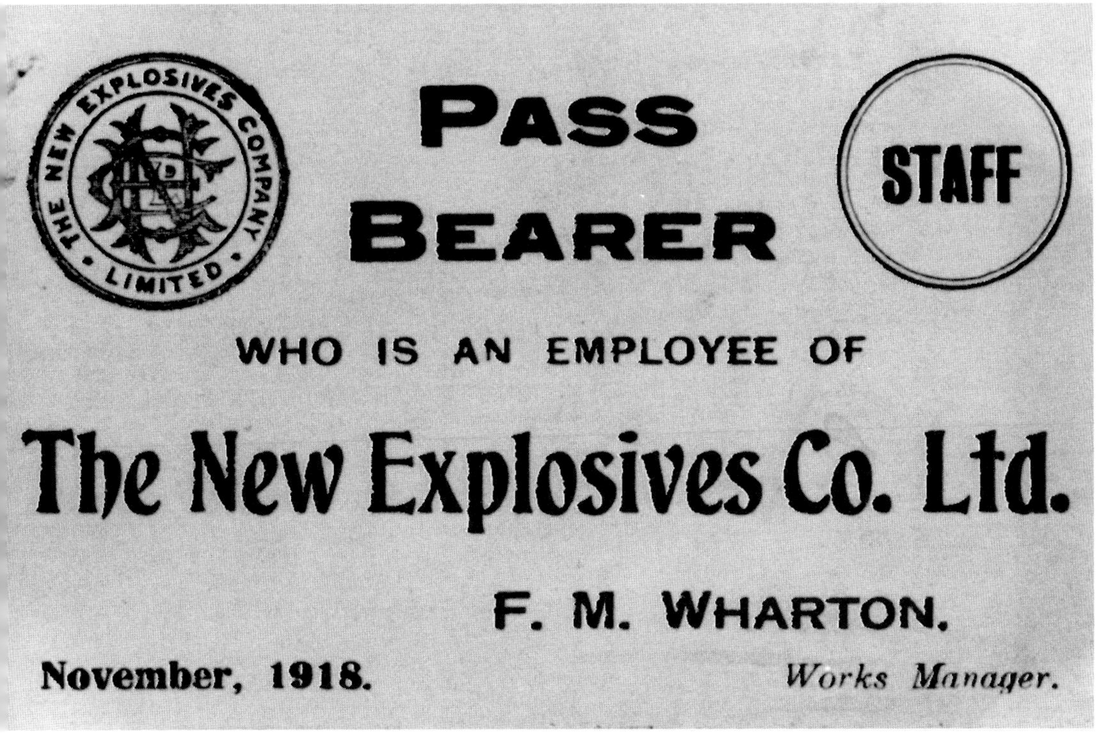


A pass issued by the New Explosives Co. Ltd to an employee in 1918. At this time more than 2,000 people were employed in the works, but almost as soon as the war ended many were laid off and the number of workers shrank markedly. (Nic Portway)

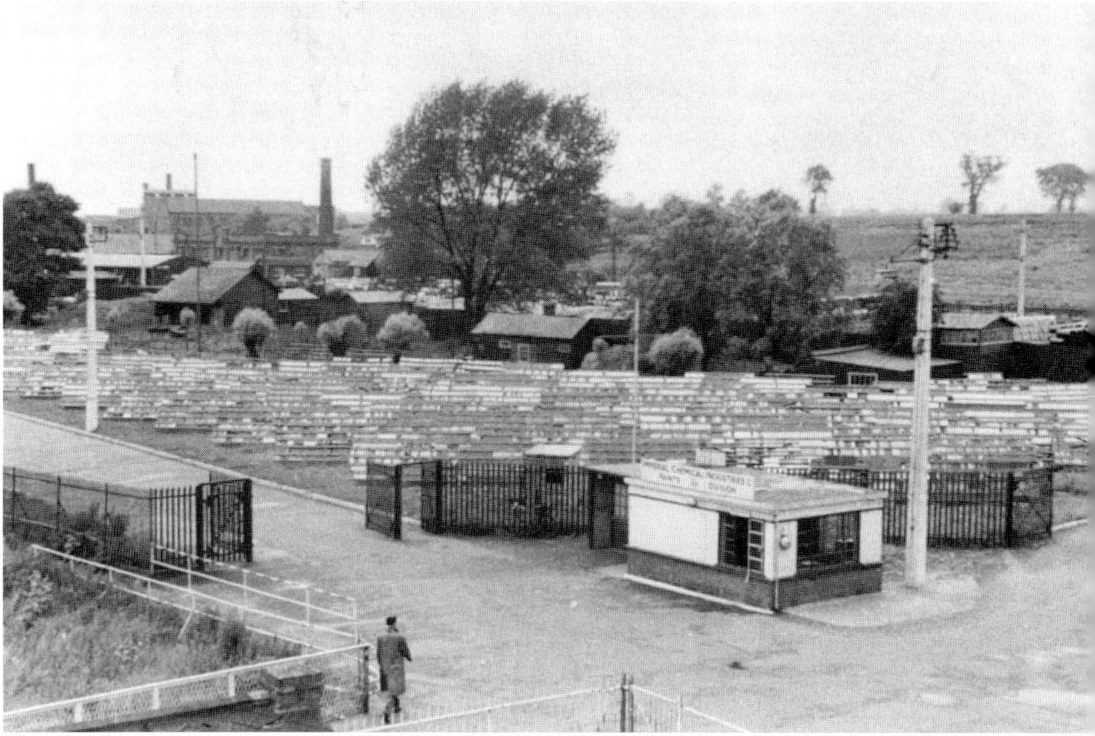

The entrance at the end of Bridge Street to the works of Imperial Chemical Industries Ltd. Laid out on racks are boards bearing samples of the paints produced, being subjected to the weather to discover their relative durability. (Ivan Codd)

*Section Six*

# MILLWRIGHTS AND ENGINEERS

Involved in the maintenance of the old windmills and in the building of their steam-powered replacements were generations of local millwrights. In 1844 Edward Mays, millwright, appears in the directory, located in Bury Street.

Robert Scase Catchpole, engineer and millwright, who had his premises in Regent Street towards the end of the 19th century, was the inventor of 'skyscrapers', as they were popularly termed, longitudinal shutters on the leading

(continued p. 70)

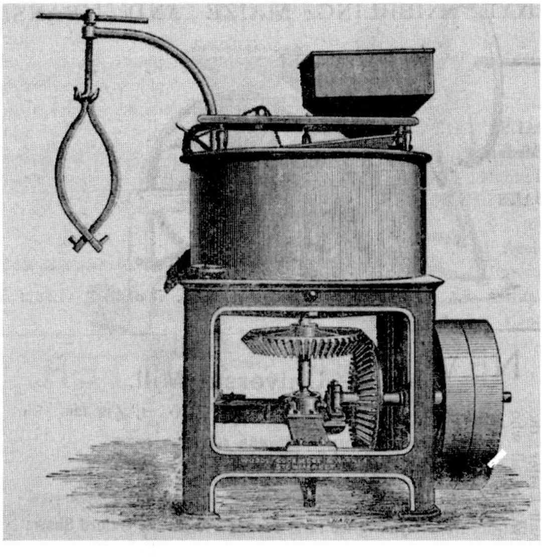

A portable grinding mill for any kind of grain, lump sugar, chicory and other materials, made by Woods at the Suffolk Iron Works.

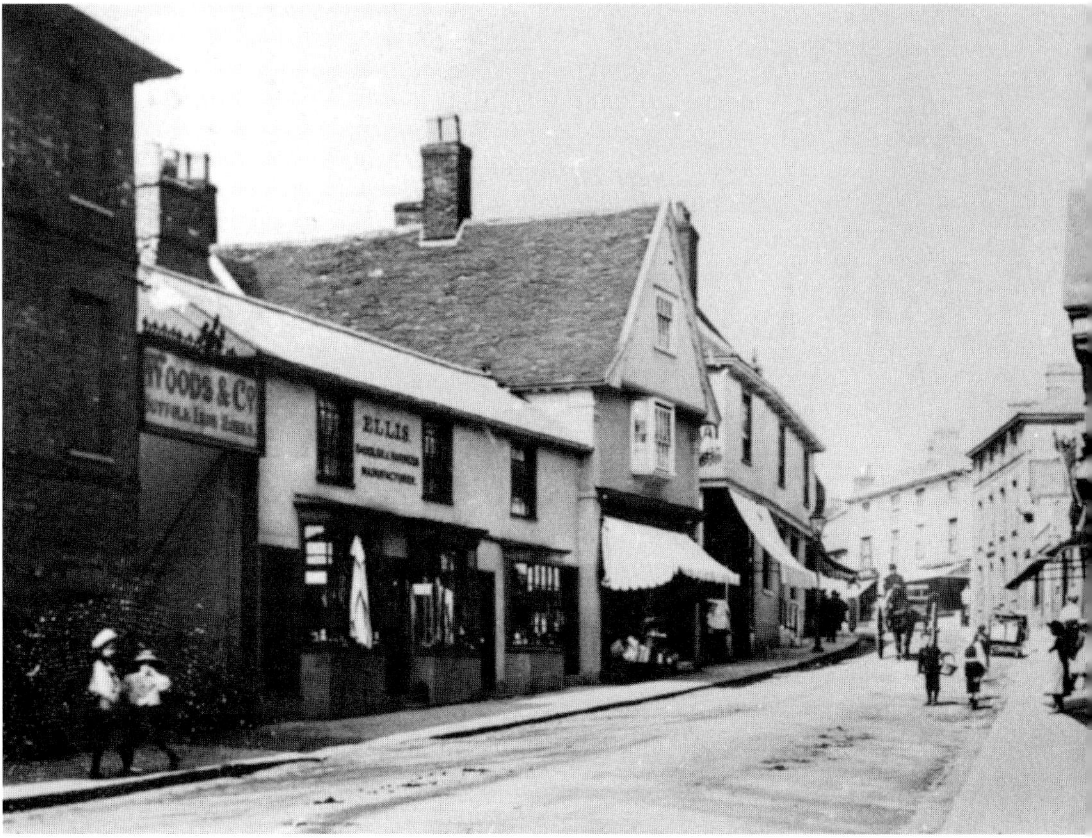


The entrance to the Suffolk Iron Works can be seen on the left of this view of Bury Street in the 1890s. Laid out on what had once been garden ground, the works included a foundry, woodworking shops, fitting shops and other buildings for storage of both raw materials and manufactured equipment. Much of this works was destroyed in 1875 in one of the most disastrous fires Stowmarket has seen, but it was subsequently rebuilt and continued in use for many years. (Ivan Codd)

*Opposite:* A page from a catalogue in French issued by Woods, Cocksedge & Co. and printed by Arthur B. Woolby in Ipswich Street in the 1870s. Illustrated is a very compact 2 h.p. steam engine with vertical boiler on a shared bedplate. (RM)

# MACHINES A VAPEUR,

## Fixes et Transportables,

## À CHAUDIÈRE VERTICALE,

## TRES ECONOMIQUES.

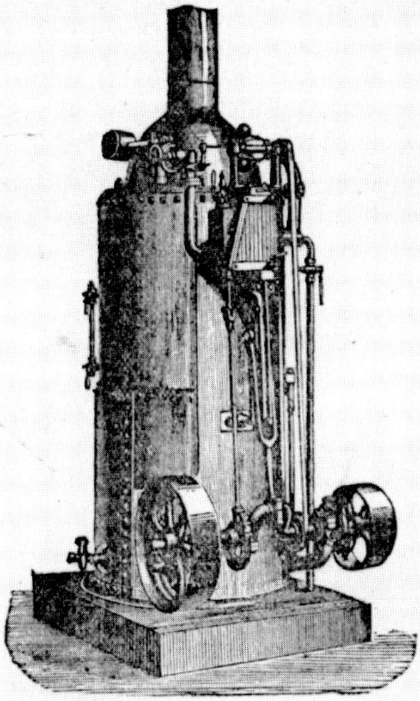

**Force de 2 Chevaux.**

Ces Machines étant très compactes et bien adaptées pour l'exportation, elles sont également utiles dans les ateliers et les Magasins comme dans les Fermes—Le foyer est bien adapté pour Chauffage au bois.

La Chaudière repose sur une forte plaque de fondation en fer de fonte; cette plaque de fondation est en même temps le cendrier et se ferme par un clapet pour éviter et régler le courant d' air. Ces Machines ne demandent pas de maçonerie; les Chaudières sont faites des meilleurs matériaux et soumises à de sévères épreuves avant d' être livrées.

Ci-dessous les Prix des Machines et Chaudières, complètes, avec Gauges, Manomètres, Soupapes de Sûreté et d' arret, Robinet, Modérateur, Pompe d'alimentation, Robinets de Niveau, de vidange, et régulateur modérateur, perfectionné et bréveté.

---

Livrées franco à Londres, Hull ou Liverpool.

---

*Prix de l'Emballage £1 par Chaque force de Chevaux.*

| Force de Chevaux. | Diamètre du Cylindre. | Longueur de Course. | Poids. | Mesurage approximatif. | Prix. |
|---|---|---|---|---|---|
| 2 | $4\frac{1}{2}$ pouces. | 8 pouces. | 20 cwt. Anglais. | 100 Pieds cu- | |
| 3 | $5\frac{1}{4}$ ,, | 11 ,, | 30 ,, ,, | 130 biques An- | |
| 4 | 6 ,, | 13 ,, | 39 ,, ,, | 230 ,, glais. | |
| 6 | $7\frac{1}{4}$ ,, | 14 ,, | 58 ,, ,, | 290 ,, ,, | |
| 8 | $8\frac{1}{2}$ ,, | 14 ,, | 75 ,, ,, | 370 ,, ,, | |

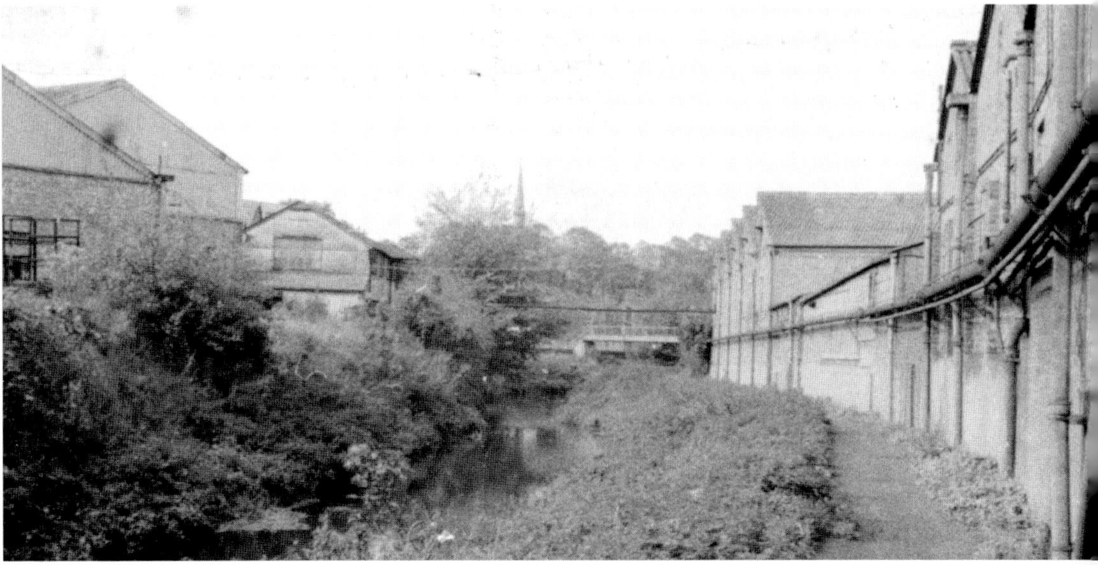

The spire of the parish church peers up above the trees in this photograph of the river which typifies industrial Stowmarket. On the right is Gipping Works, built on the riverside site to replace the old Suffolk Iron Works off Bury Street when the new company of Suffolk Iron Foundry (1920) Ltd was set up by Lewis Tibbenham, who lived at The Limes in Ipswich Road; on the left is the leather factory operated by S.T. Leathers Ltd and earlier by Edwin Stowe. (Ivan Codd)

edge of windmill sails which acted as air-brakes when the sail shutter mechanism was operated to stop the sails. 'Catchpole's skyscrapers' were fitted to a postmill at Combs and to a number of other Suffolk mills. Catchpole, who remained in business into the present century, had worked at Sudbury for William Bear, who moved his millwrighting business to Stowmarket in the 1860s.

The foundry business in Bury Street dated back to 1812, and was carried on for many years by James Woods. In the early part of the 19th century there was also a second iron foundry in Crowe Street operated by Thomas Bewley, who made such machinery as winnowers and chaff cutters. In about 1850 he was succeeded by George Bewley, perhaps a son, but the business did not continue nearly so long as Woods'.

For a time the Bury Street firm was Woods, Cocksedge and Warner, and then in the 1870s Woods, Cocksedge & Co., but after Mr J.S. Cocksedge left the partnership in about 1879 to set up his own engineering firm in Ipswich it became Woods & Co., 'engineers, manufacturers of general agricultural, hydraulic & steam machinery, millwrights, wagon & cart builders, target makers &c. &c'. The firm was based at Suffolk Iron Works on the west side of Bury Street, but also had branches in Bury St Edmunds, Newmarket, Norwich, Ipswich and Sudbury. Steam engines of various kinds were produced between 1862 and 1896.

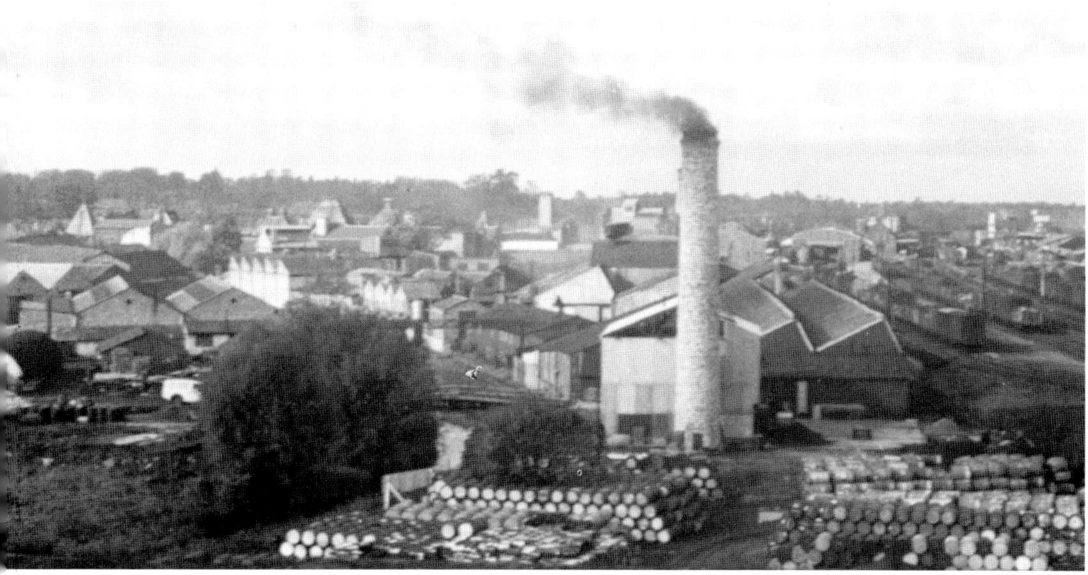

Looking down on Gipping Works. To the right can be seen the railway goods yard, with the curved roof of the goods shed visible just to the right of the foundry chimney; towards the left the kilns of some of the town's many maltings stand out clearly. (Ivan Codd)

At the beginning of this century the firm was facing an uncertain future. An engineer, Lewis John Tibbenham, was brought in as manager in an attempt to restore the company's fortunes, and when the receiver was called in he persuaded him to sell the freehold of the property to a local firm whose principals were friends of his, George Thurlow & Sons, who had been 'oil, belting & machinery merchants & manufacturers, engineers & mill furnishers' in the town since the 1870s.

So it was that in 1914 Tibbenham formed a new company, Suffolk Iron Foundry Ltd, which carried on business on the original Woods site. However, by 1919 the firm had grown so successful that a new works was built on a site between the river and the railway, and with the move the company was also reconstructed, becoming Suffolk Iron Foundry (1920) Ltd.

Thurlows then expanded on to the old Woods site, continuing to operate there until quite recent years.

Suffolk Iron Foundry (1920) Ltd produced a variety of items from mangles to lawnmowers. In 1954 the company bought the old leather factory in Milton Road formerly operated by Edwin Stowe and developed a new works on the town side of the river. Under its later name of Suffolk Lawn Mowers it became well known for its Suffolk Punch motor mower, a machine which was well able to compete with those made by Ransomes Sims & Jefferies in Ipswich. Today it is Atco-Qualcast Ltd.

# MANÈGE ROYAL,
## PERFECTIONNÉ ET BREVETÉ,
## POUR CHEVAUX ET BOEUFS.

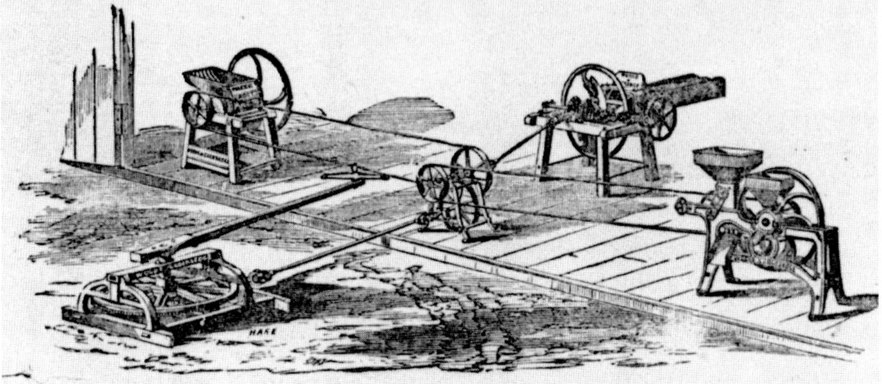

Ces Manèges sont entièrement fabriqués en fer, ils sont très solides, et très simples dans leur construction. La transmission est entièrement en fer et munie d'un Manchon d'embrayage pour mettre en marche et arrêter la Machine sans arrêter le Cheval.

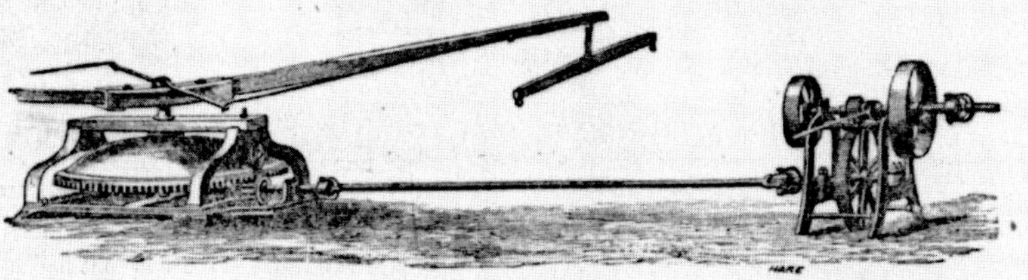

# ROYAL OXFORD MANÈGE, BREVETÉ,
**Pour éviter entièrement les accidents.**

3 MEDAILLES EN OR, 200 PRIMES.

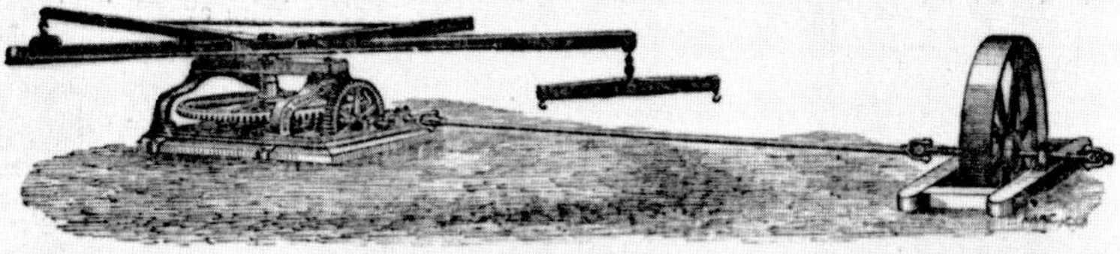

# MANÈGE POUR POMPES & SCIERIES.

**Avec une grande poulie, on peut avoir les 800 à 900 revolutions par minute qui sont nécessaires aux Egreneuses de Coton.**

Ces Machines sont fabriquées en toutes grandeurs, savoir, pour Mules, petits Chevaux, et pour attelages d'un à huit Chevaux.

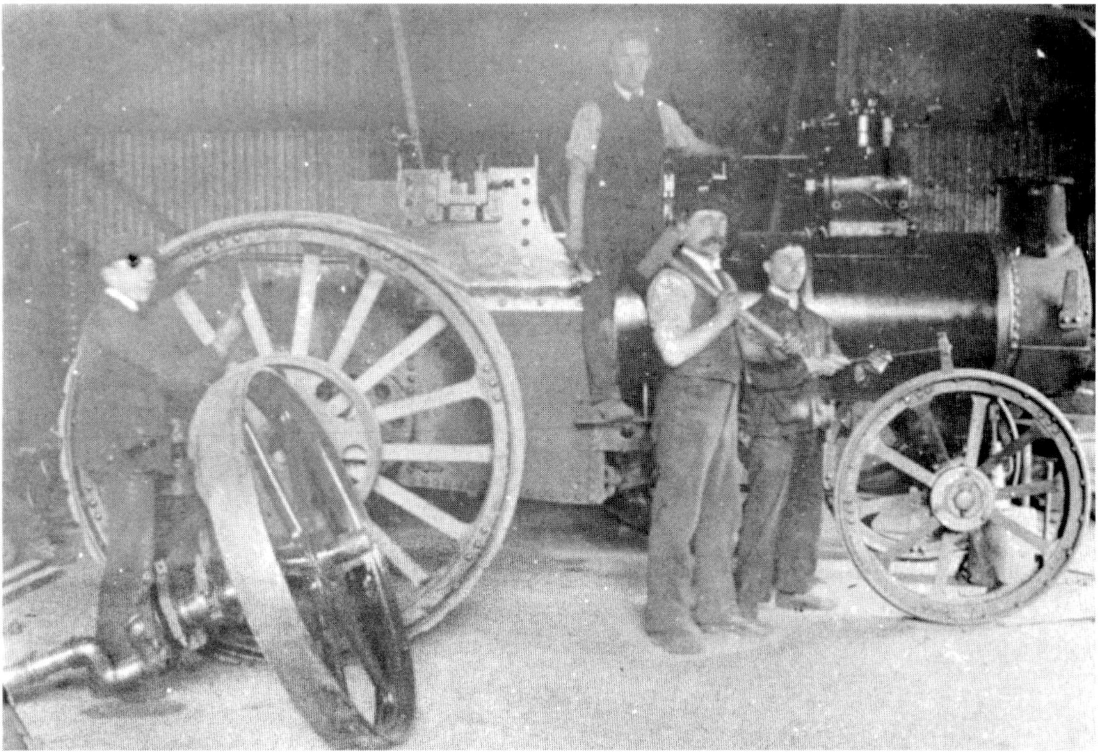

Engineers working on the repair of a steam engine in the Bury Street works of George Thurlow & Sons Ltd, *c.* 1930. Thurlow's had taken over the works of Woods & Co. on the very day that the First World War broke out. The man with a sledgehammer over his shoulder is Mr Scott, who lived in Lime Tree Place, off Ipswich Road. (Ivan Codd)

*Opposite:* A page from the Woods, Cocksedge catalogue with details of horse gears, or groundworks as they were usually known in Suffolk, for operating a variety of machinery. They are, says the description, made in all sizes, for mules, ponies, horses and oxen.

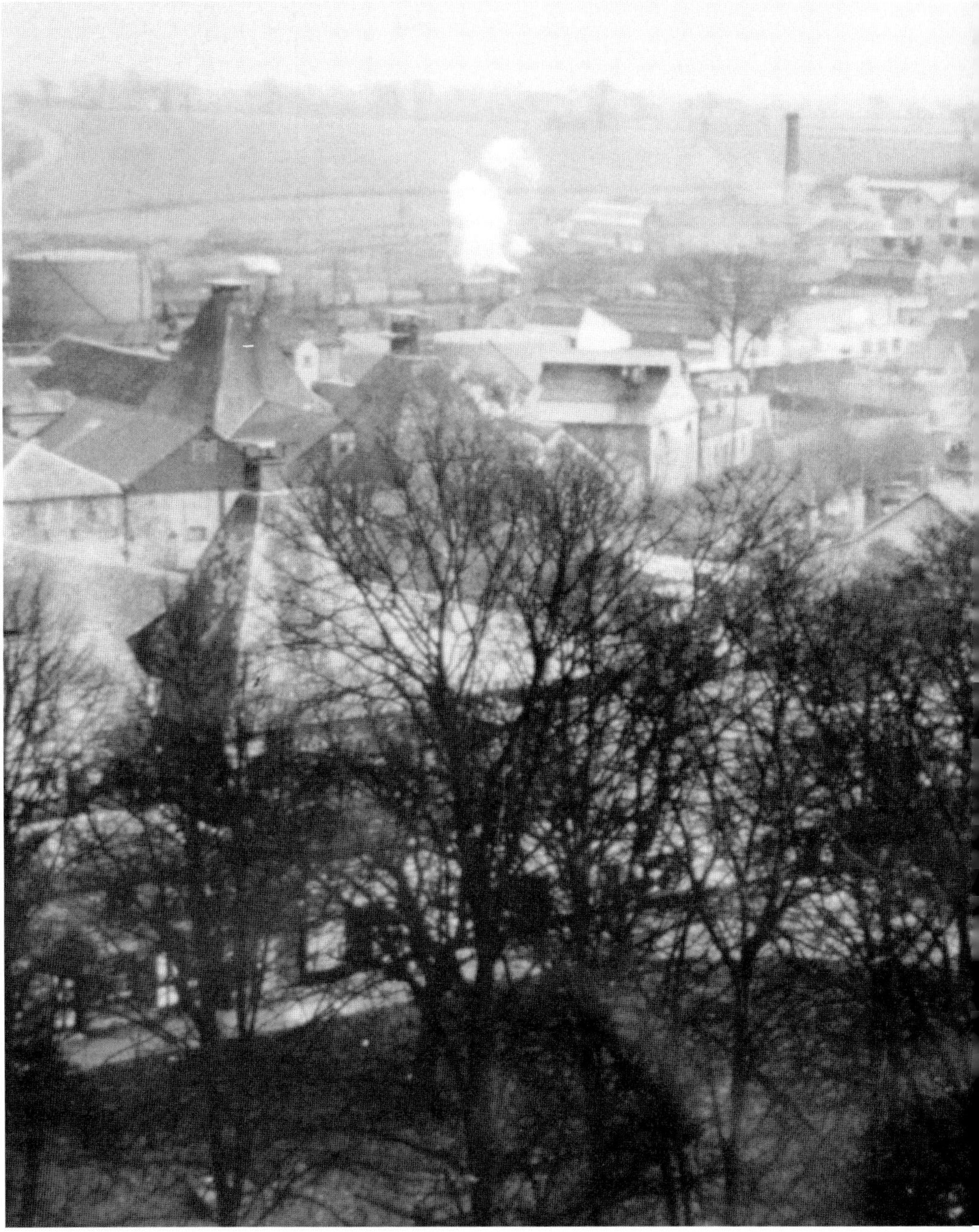

A view of the rooftops of industrial Stowmarket from the tower of the parish church, 1960s. From the left can be seen some of the town's maltings, the gasworks, Suffolk Iron Foundry, and the ICI paint works. (Ivan Codd)

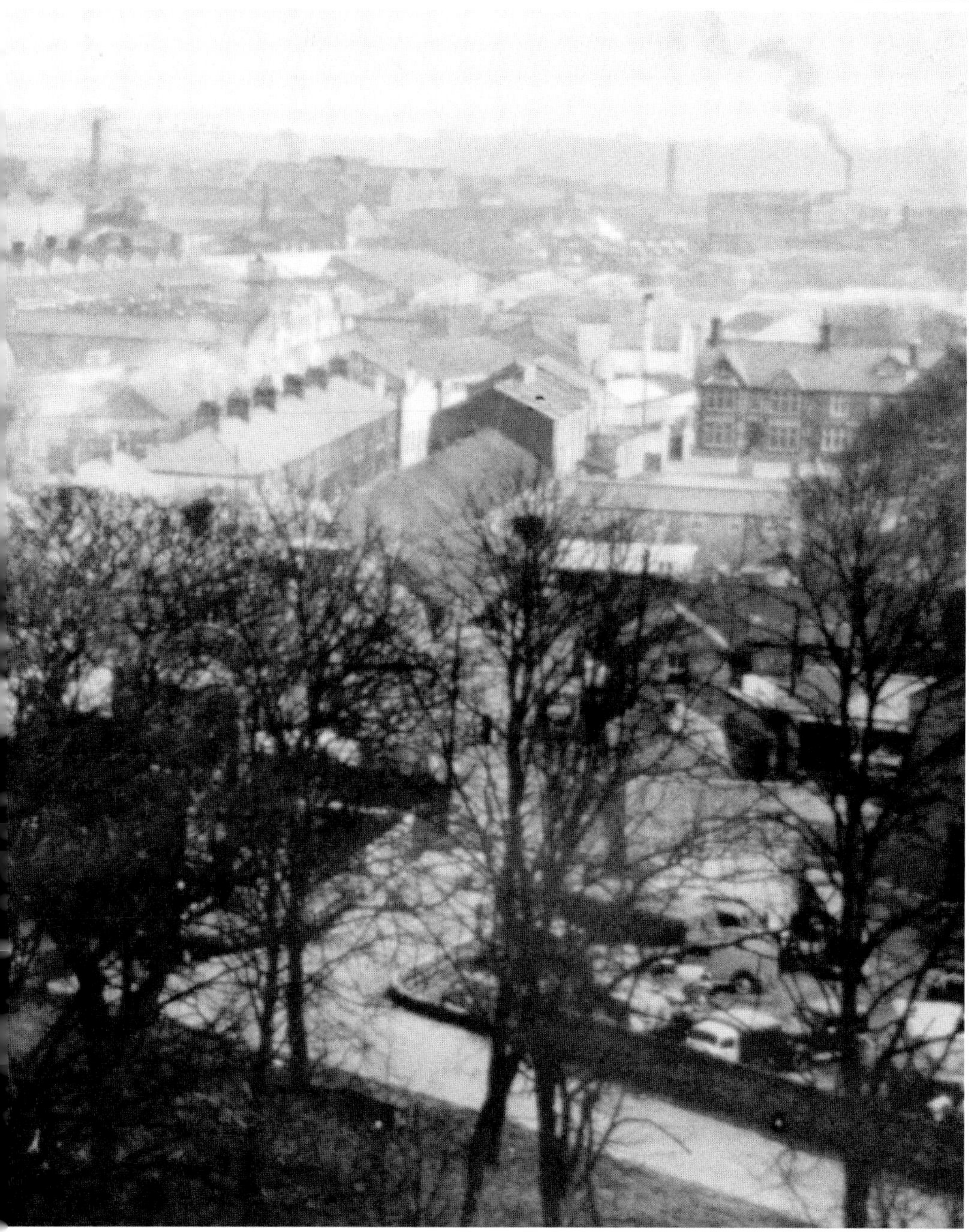

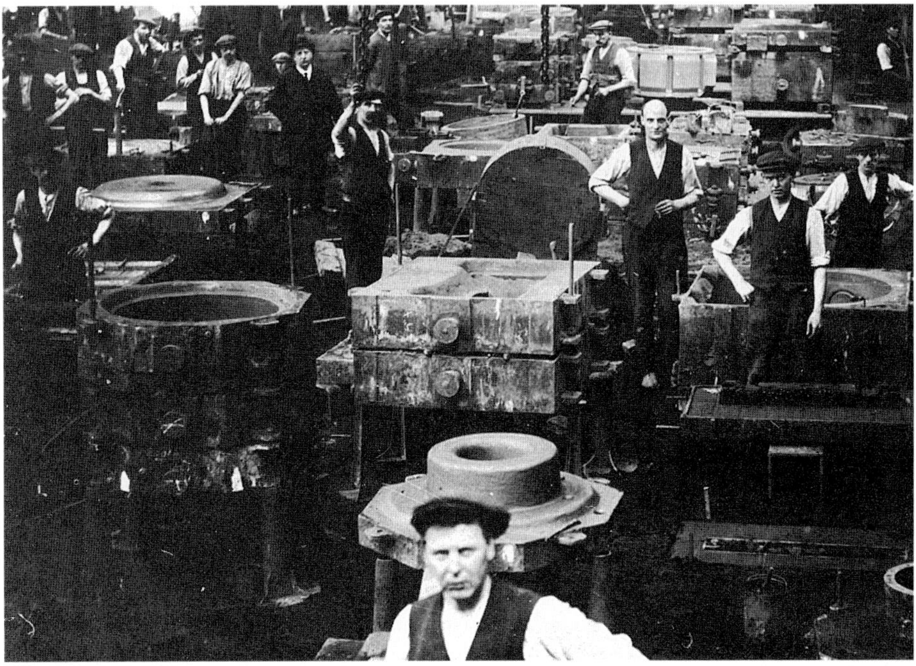

The interior of the foundry at Suffolk Iron Foundry, 1920s. (Harry Double collection, Stowmarket Town Council) Below is a bomb trolley built by Suffolk Iron Foundry in 1952 for use with the RAF's new generation of V-bombers; the firm also built a number of trolleys to carry oxygen cylinders, used to replenish the oxygen system of the aircraft. (Geoff Clarke)

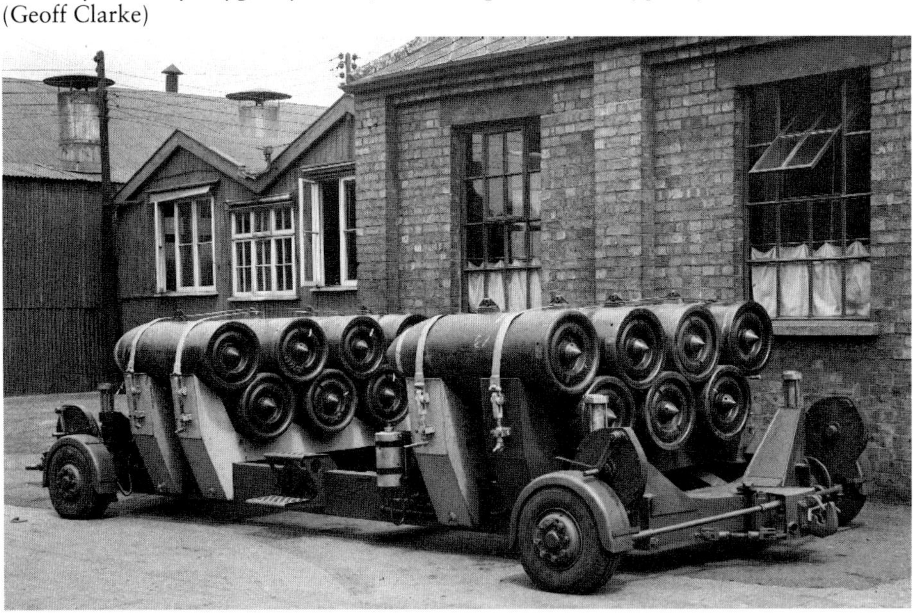

*Section Seven*

# COACHBUILDERS

In the age of horse transport the coach and carriage builder occupied a vital place in the local economy, constructing a variety of vehicles for tradesmen and private owners alike. There seems to have been a coachbuilder's establishment in Tavern Street for much of the 19th century; the premises later became the Salvation Army citadel, and are now occupied by Stannards Stowmarket Ltd. In 1845 William Hewitt was there, and ten years later Samuel Bridges & Son, who also had a similar establishment in Sparhawk Street, Bury St Edmunds. In 1892 Mrs Mary A. Earthy was occupying the premises, but it is not clear what relationship she bore to Reuben Earthy who had a works in Bury Street in 1855, or to Alfred Earthy who was at the Bury Street premises in 1892.

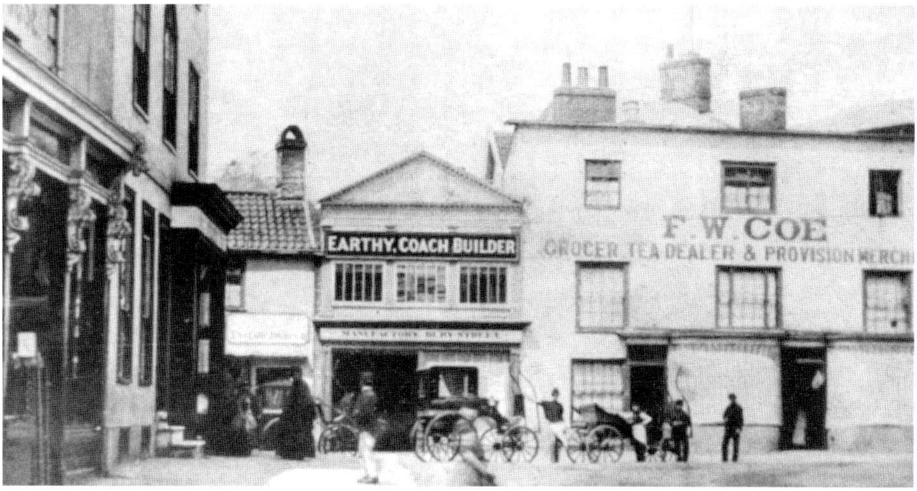


Earthy's premises in the Market Place, *c.* 1880, apparently a showroom as his works was in Bury Street. Frederick Coe's shop on the right gave way to the new post office a few years later. (Ivan Codd)

# J. & R. BAKER,
# COACH BUILDERS
AND
## HARNESS MAKERS,
## STOWMARKET.

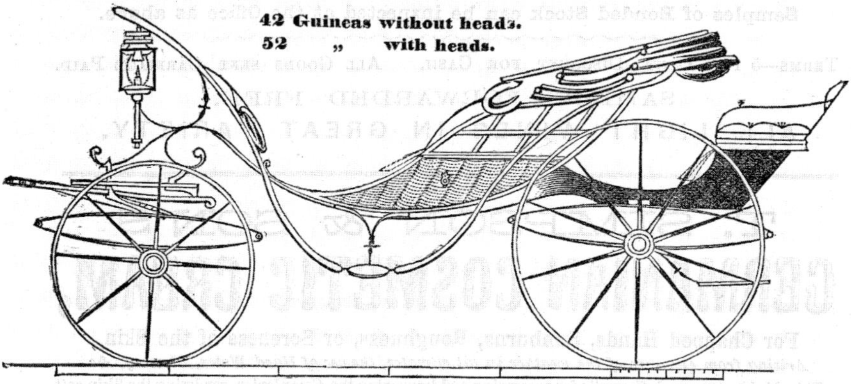


## LANDAUS, BAROUCHES,
## BROUGHAMS,
## SOCIABLES, PARK PHÆTONS, WAGONETTES,
DOG CART PHÆTONS,
## BASKET CARRIAGES,
## GIGS AND CARTS,
OF EVERY DESCRIPTION MADE TO ORDER.

ALL NEW VEHICLES WARRANTED FOR TWELVE MONTHS

REPAIRS NEATLY EXECUTED.

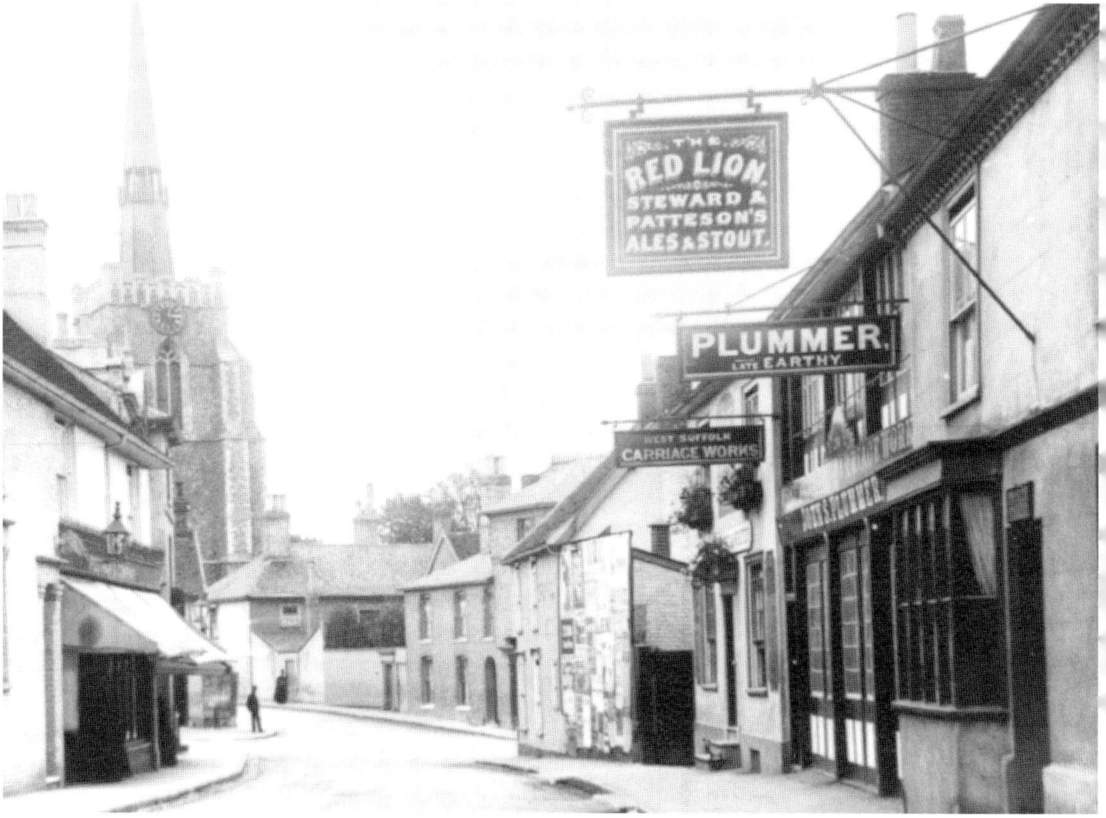


The Tavern Street premises of John S. Plummer, with a sign naming them the West Suffolk Carriage Works. The statement on another sign 'late Earthy' suggests that he might have taken the works over from Mrs Mary A. Earthy, who was there in 1892. (Ivan Codd)

*Opposite:* An advertisement from the 1860s for J. & R. Baker, who seem to have made a wide variety of vehicles. The one illustrated is a phaeton, apparently with a basketwork body for lightness.

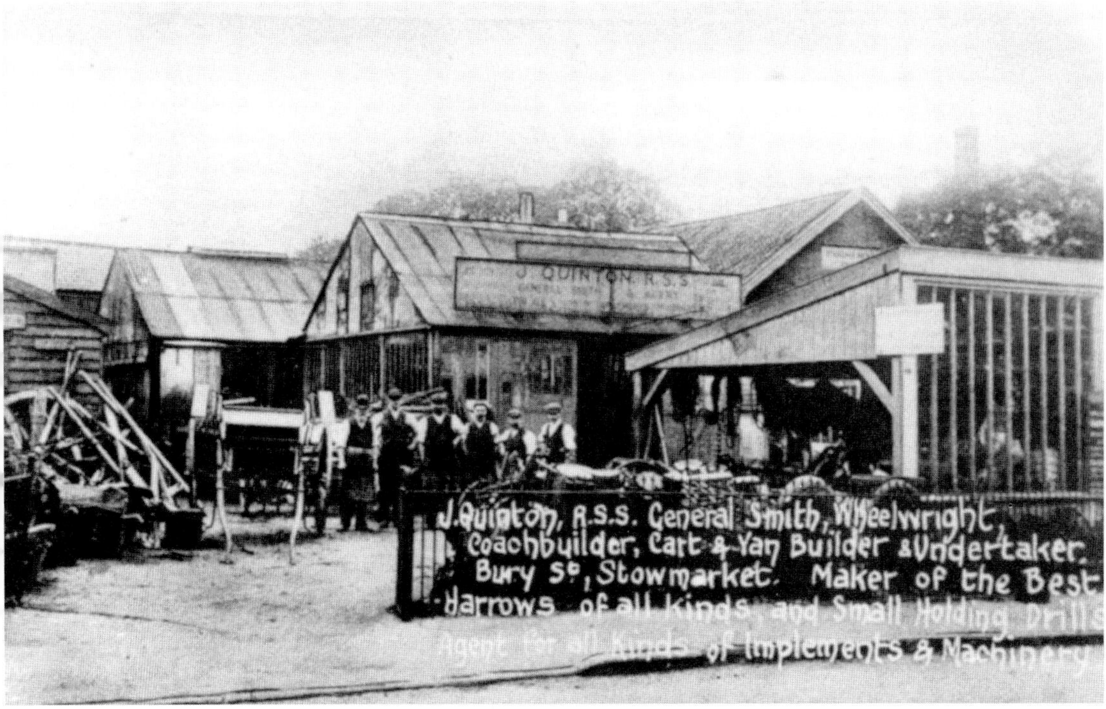


In Bury Street was the works of Jesse Quinton, who had his home in Regent Street. He was never listed in directories as a coachbuilder, but on the advertising card illustrated here he describes himself as such, and also cart and van builder. (Ivan Codd)

*Section Eight*

# COMBS TANNERY

The smelly but economically important work of preparing leather was carried on at Combs for the best part of three centuries up to 1988, when the tannery became a victim of changing times and economic circumstances, and ceased production. It had been a considerable employer of labour, though situated in a rural village with a population in the late 19th century of little more than 1,000.

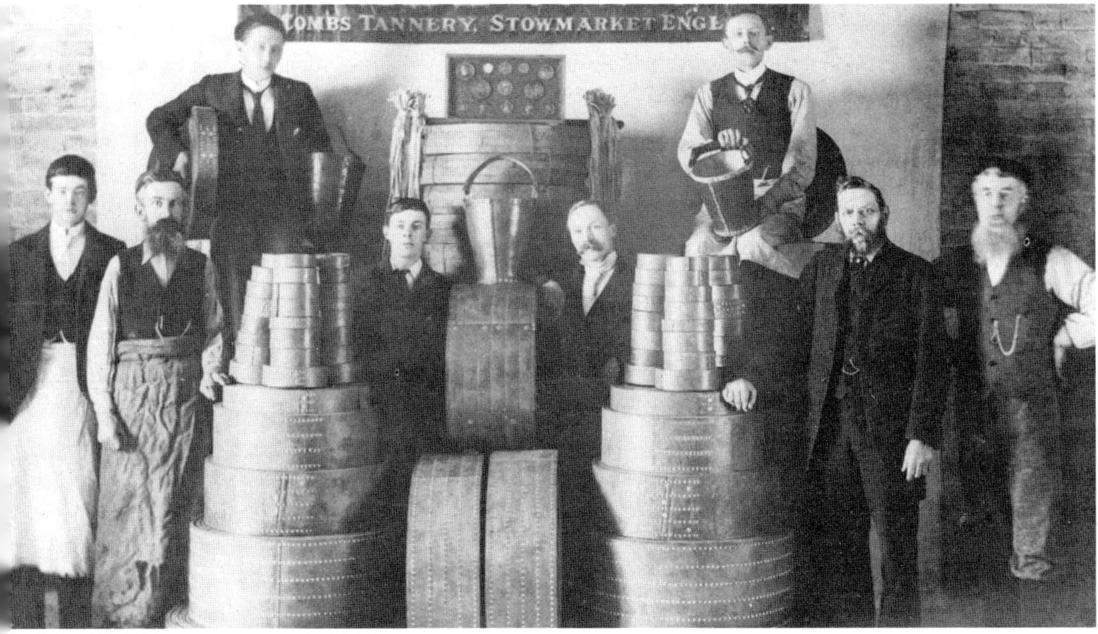


Machine belts large and small and leather fire buckets are among the products of the tannery being displayed here, *c.* 1905. On the wall hangs a frame containing medals awarded at various important shows. (Nic Portway)

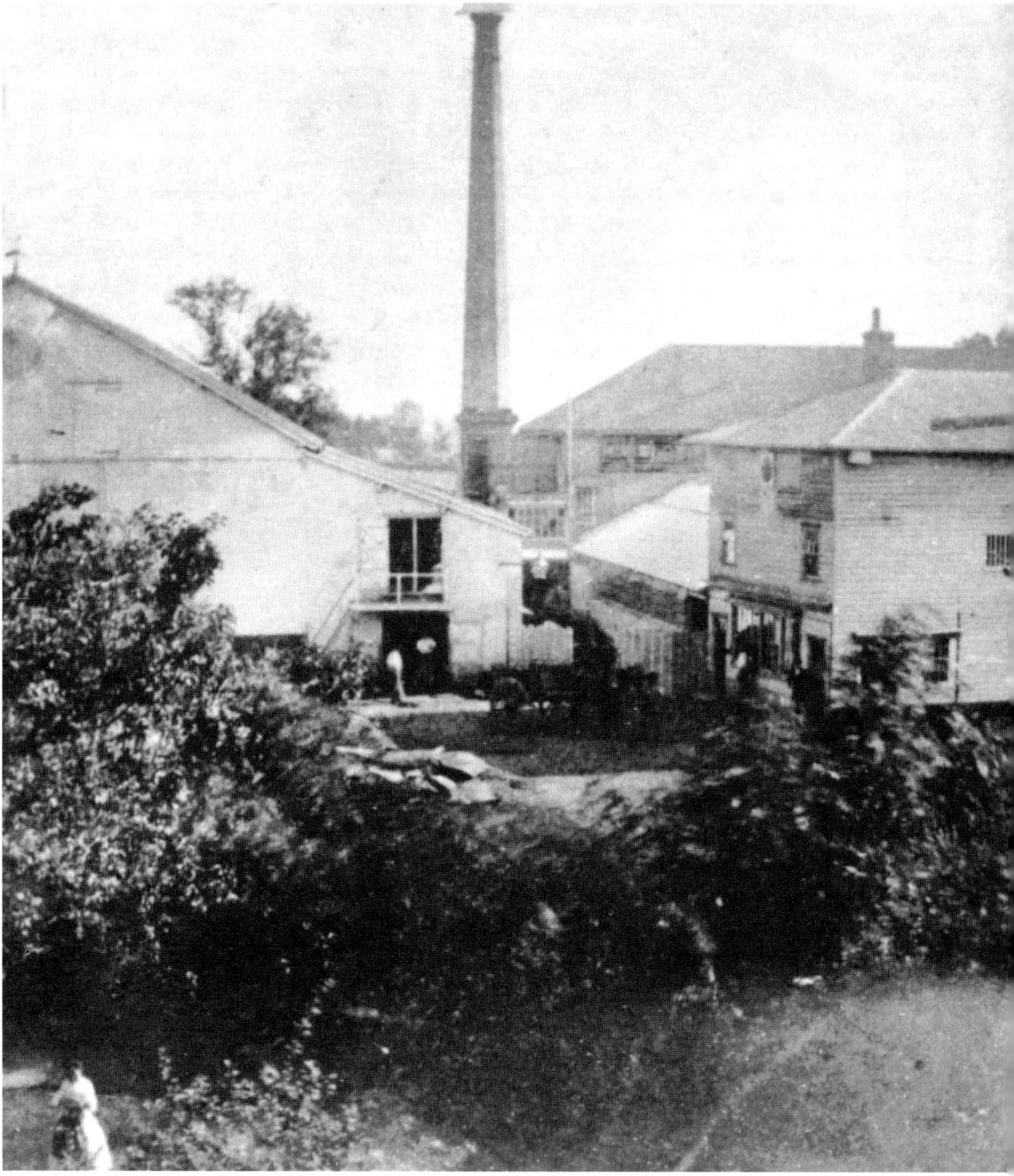

The tannery, *c.* 1860. The building just to the right of the chimney was later heightened by the addition of another floor. (Nic Portway)

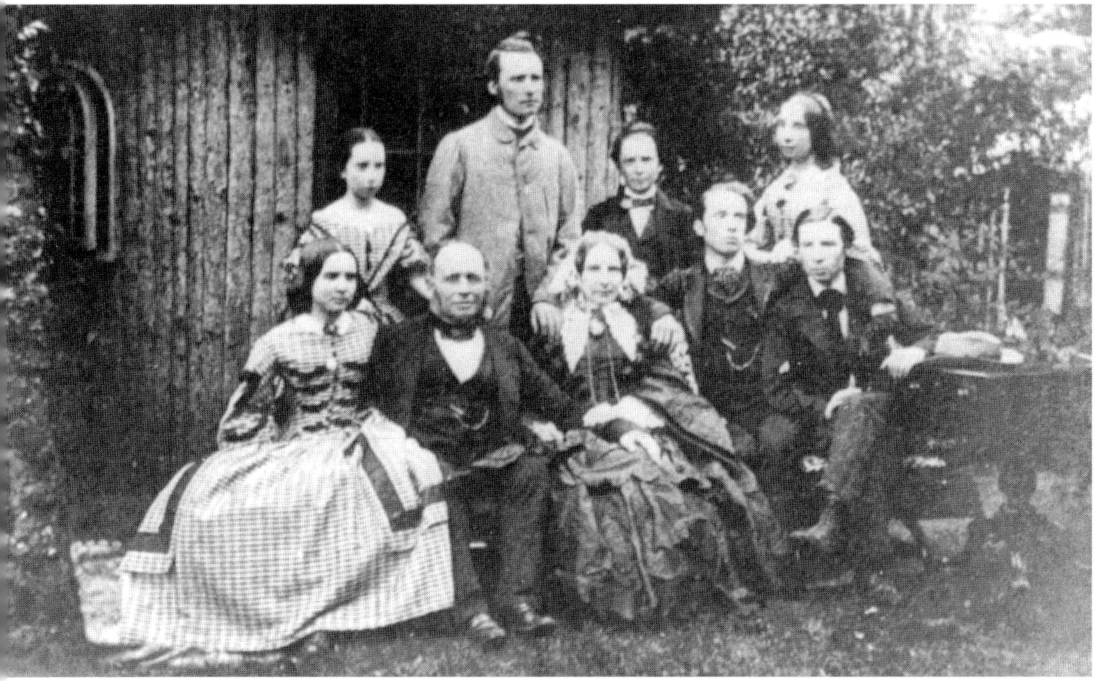

Lankester Webb with his wife and children sitting outside the summer house at Tannery House. Only the youngest son, Joseph, survived the age of 25, and he died unmarried in 1908. One of the daughters, Annie, married George Portway. (Nic Portway)

The tannery was established in 1711, after Thomas Denny had advanced 'the sum of £100 to his son Thomas Denny to sink a tanyard . . .'. The younger Thomas Denny (1690–1772) retired in 1748, leaving the tanyard to his son, another Thomas (1720–1803), who in 1776 let the premises to Joseph Antrim Webb (1745–1809).

Rather confusingly, Joseph Antrim Webb entered into partnership with his son Joseph Antrim Webb (1777–1864), and the son in turn entered into partnership in 1832 with his son Joseph Antrim Webb. The latter, however, died the following year at the age of 23, and a partnership was then formed with his second son, Lankester Webb (1812–87).

Lankester Webb, a man of wide interests and a stalwart of the Stowmarket Congregational Church, built up the tannery business after his father retired in 1848, and by the time of his own death in 1887 it was a very prosperous concern indeed. At that period the business was described as being curriers, tanners, manufacturers of leather machine bands, buckets and hose, fellmongers, glove leather dressers and wool merchants, and it was trading all over Britain and even overseas.

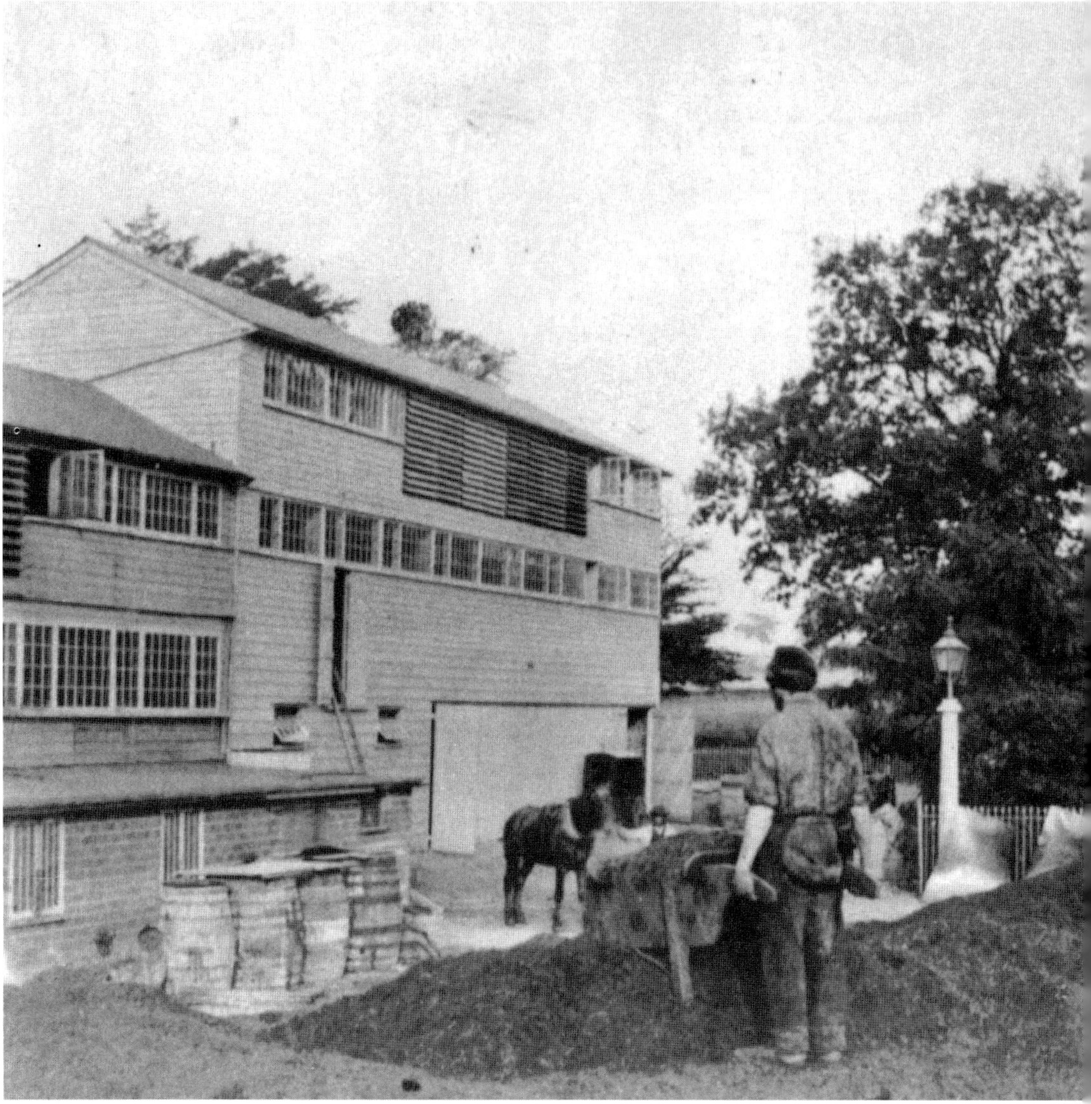

A tannery worker brings out a barrow-load of spent tan, ground oak bark which has been used in the tanning process. Spent tan had a number of uses, including use as a material for making up garden paths in the village. (Nic Portway)

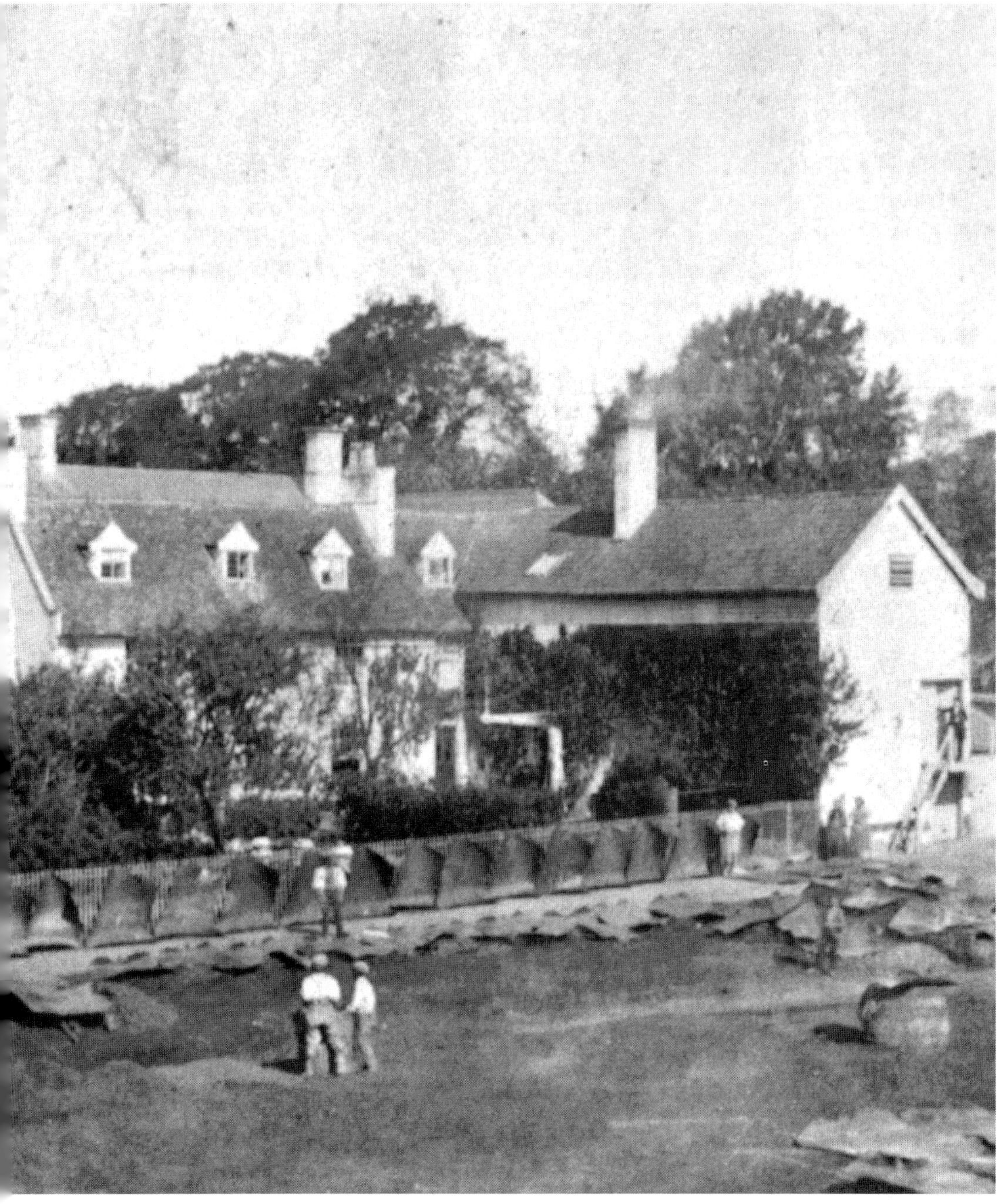

Another photograph in the same series, thought to have been taken in the 1860s, shows workmen hanging calf hides out to dry on the fence of the Tannery House. (Nic Portway)

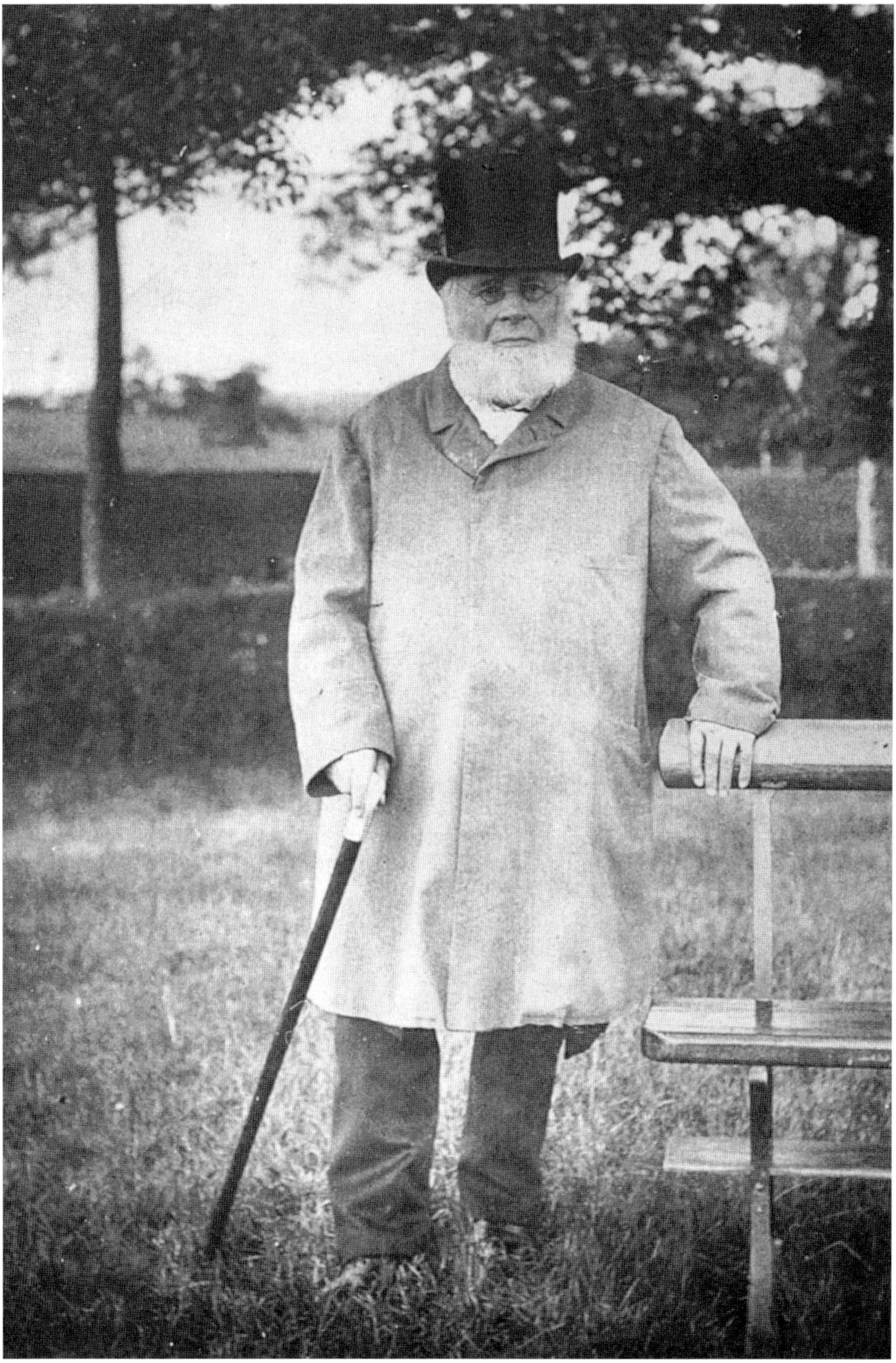

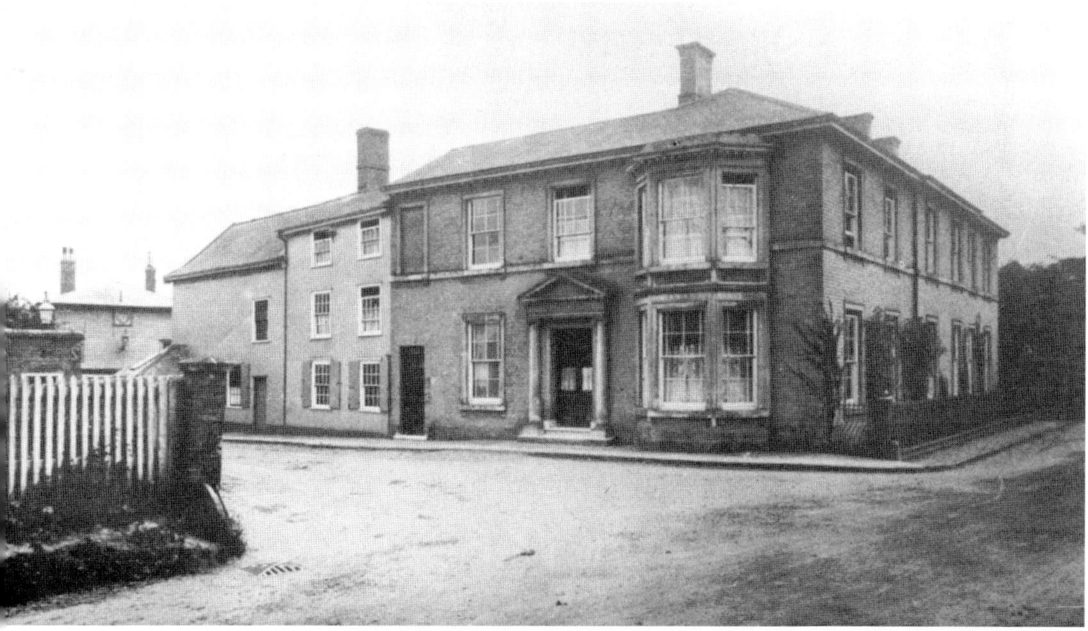

Combs Tannery House in the early years of this century, when it was the family home of the Webbs. The bay window reaches both floors, but earlier photographs show that it had been an addition on the ground floor only, subsequently being extended upwards. (Nic Portway)

*Opposite*: Lankester Webb (1812–87); this photograph was taken by Stowmarket photographer Arthur Bugg towards the end of Webb's life. Lankester Webb, the son of Joseph Antrim Webb who had purchased the tannery in 1843, not only built up the tannery business but also farmed at Model Farm, which he built in 1865. He was one of the leading members of Stowmarket Congregational Church. (Nic Portway)

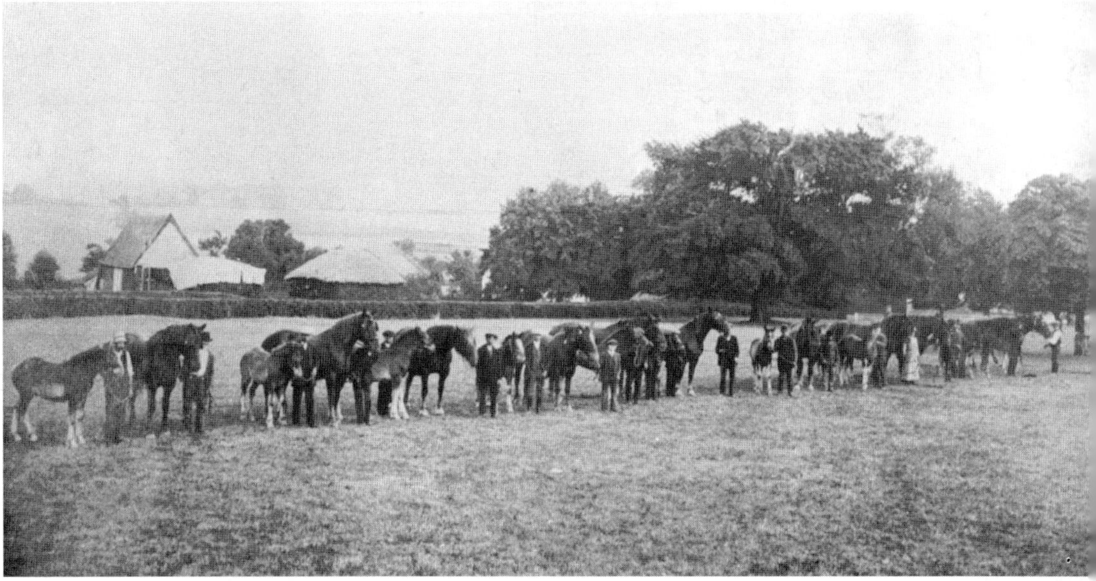

Suffolk mares and their foals photographed in the park at Combs, possibly before the 1919 horse sale. It was said that Model Farm could field 14 teams (two horses to a team) of plough horses fully brassed; no fewer than 45 men were employed on the farm. In the background can be seen stacks of bark, covered with thatch, for use in the tannery. Below we see the building of a stack in the stackyard at Model Farm; it is raised on staddle stones both to keep it dry and to keep out vermin. In the background the farm's portable steam engine can be seen at work. (Nic Portway)

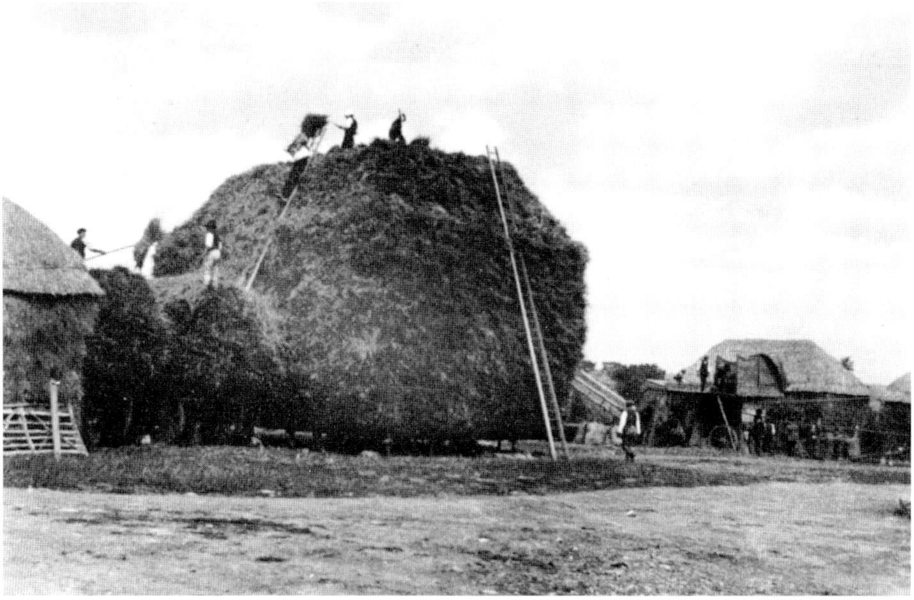

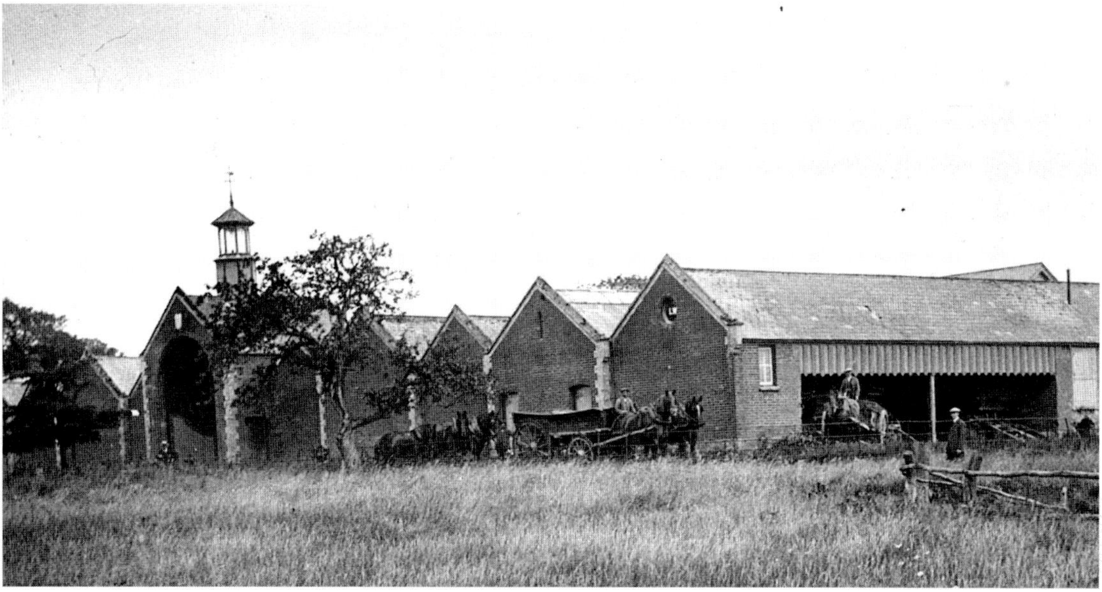

The buildings of Model Farm, Combs, built by Lankester Webb in 1865 at a time when many landowners were rebuilding their farms to take advantage of new sources of power and new methods. The farm had its own small gas-producing plant for lighting, and made use of a steam portable engine for operating a variety of machinery. (Nic Portway)

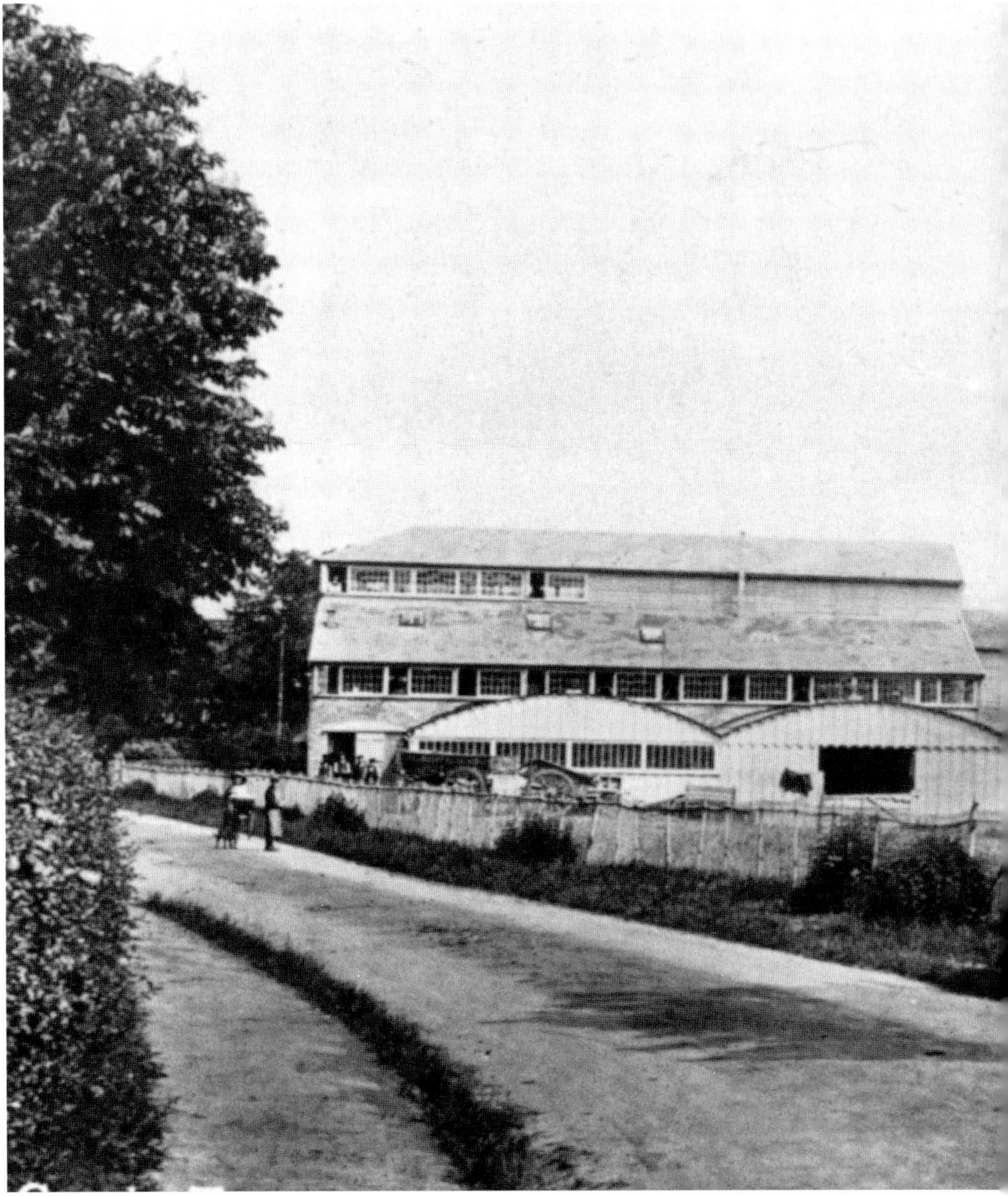

A view of the tannery dating from about 1910, showing the extensive range of buildings which had grown up over the years. The large chimney marks the position of the grasshopper steam engine built and installed in 1851 by William Pickford Wilkins, an Ipswich engineer and millwright. When the tannery ceased to operate in 1988 it was dismantled and taken to the Museum of East Anglian Life, where it is to be re-erected as an exhibit. (Nic Portway)

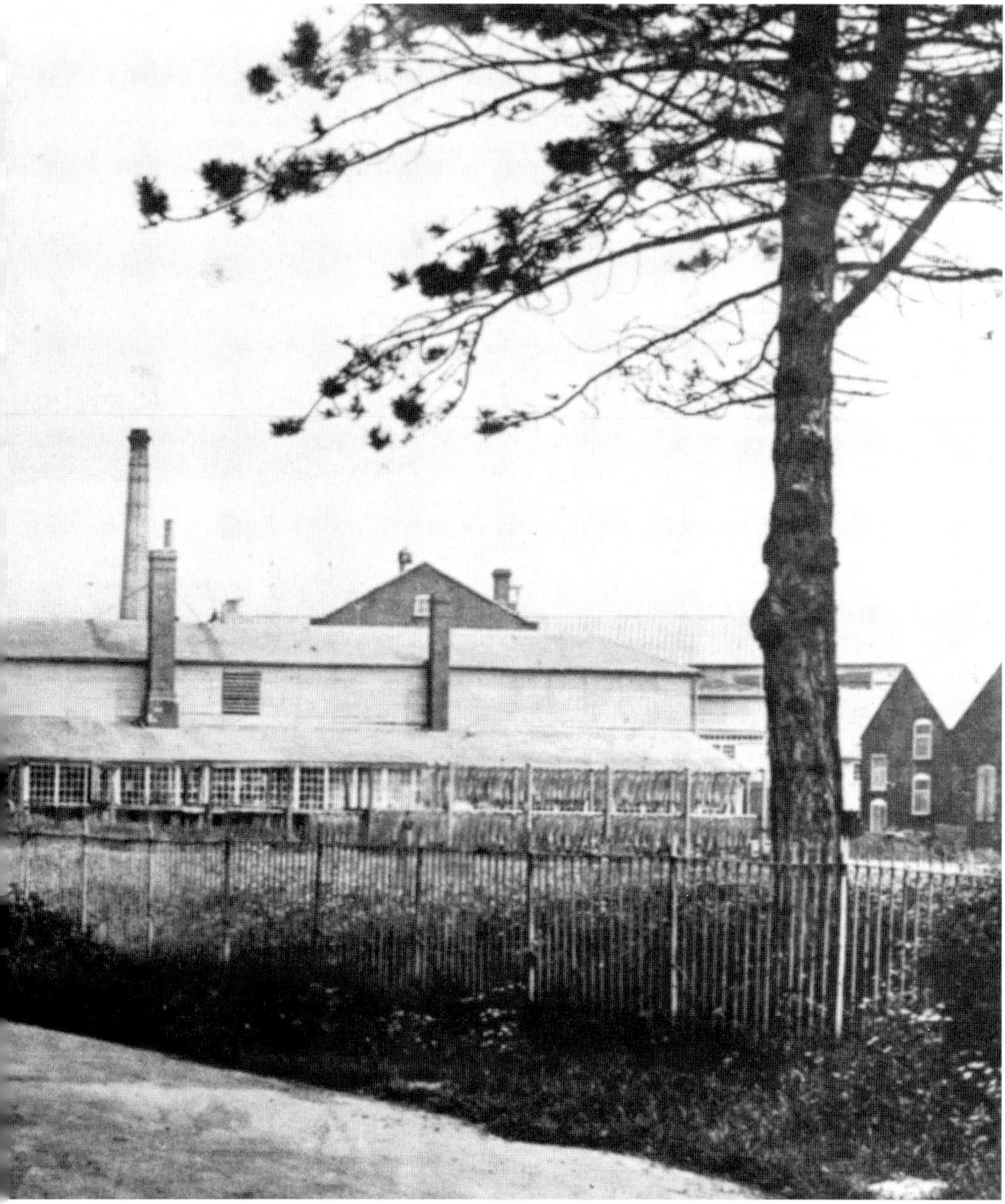

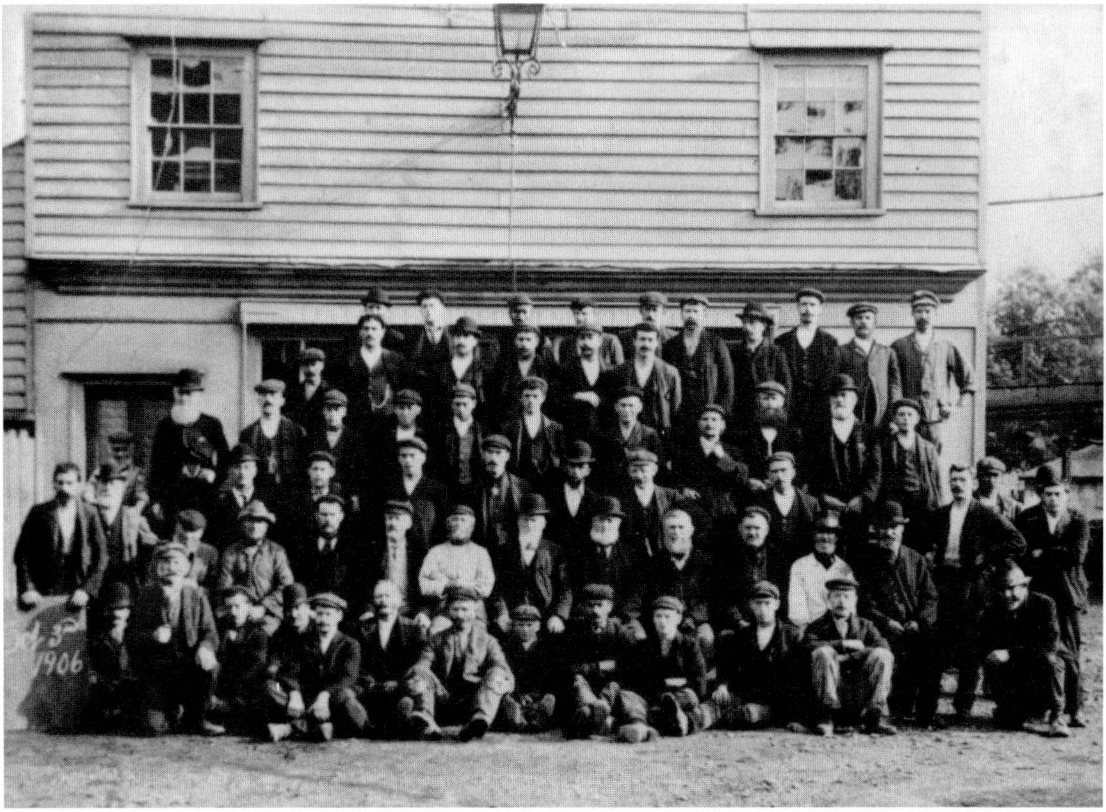

The men of Combs Tannery, 3 February 1906. There are more than 60 men and boys in the picture. (Nic Portway)

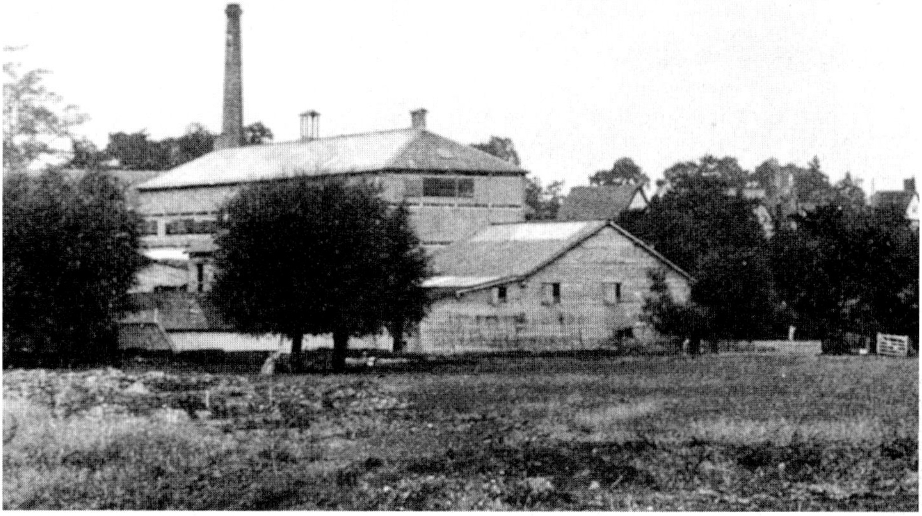

The tannery from the south-east, probably *c.* 1910. The tall building seen to the right of the chimney is the same one seen in the picture on page 82, but with an extra floor added. Below, oak bark brought in from local woodlands is made into a giant stack, using a special lifting device probably operated by horses to raise baskets of bark to the top of the stack. Bark was needed in great quantities for the tanning process. (Nic Portway)

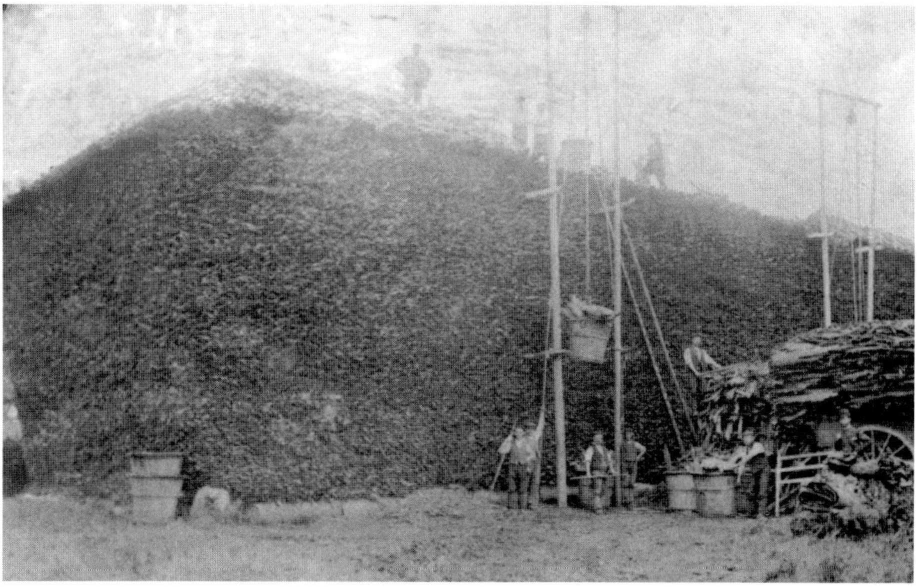

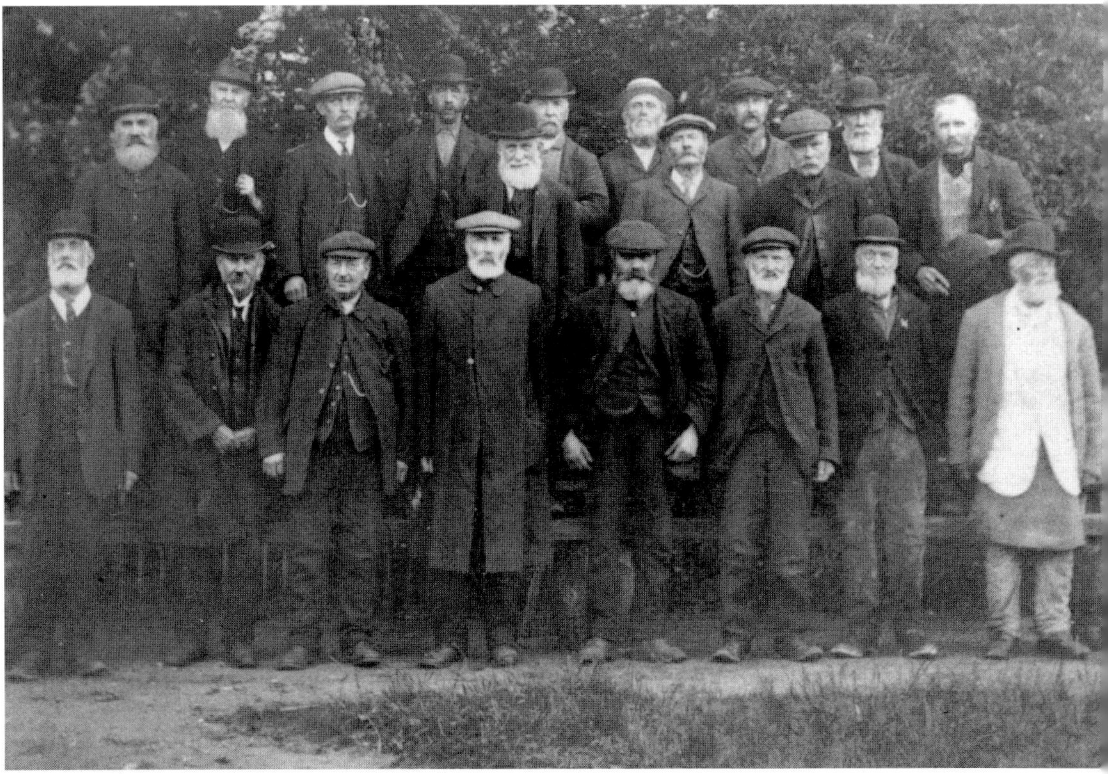

Some of the older workers at the tannery, 27 May 1914. The service at the tannery of these 20 men is said to have added up to 979 years. (Nic Portway)

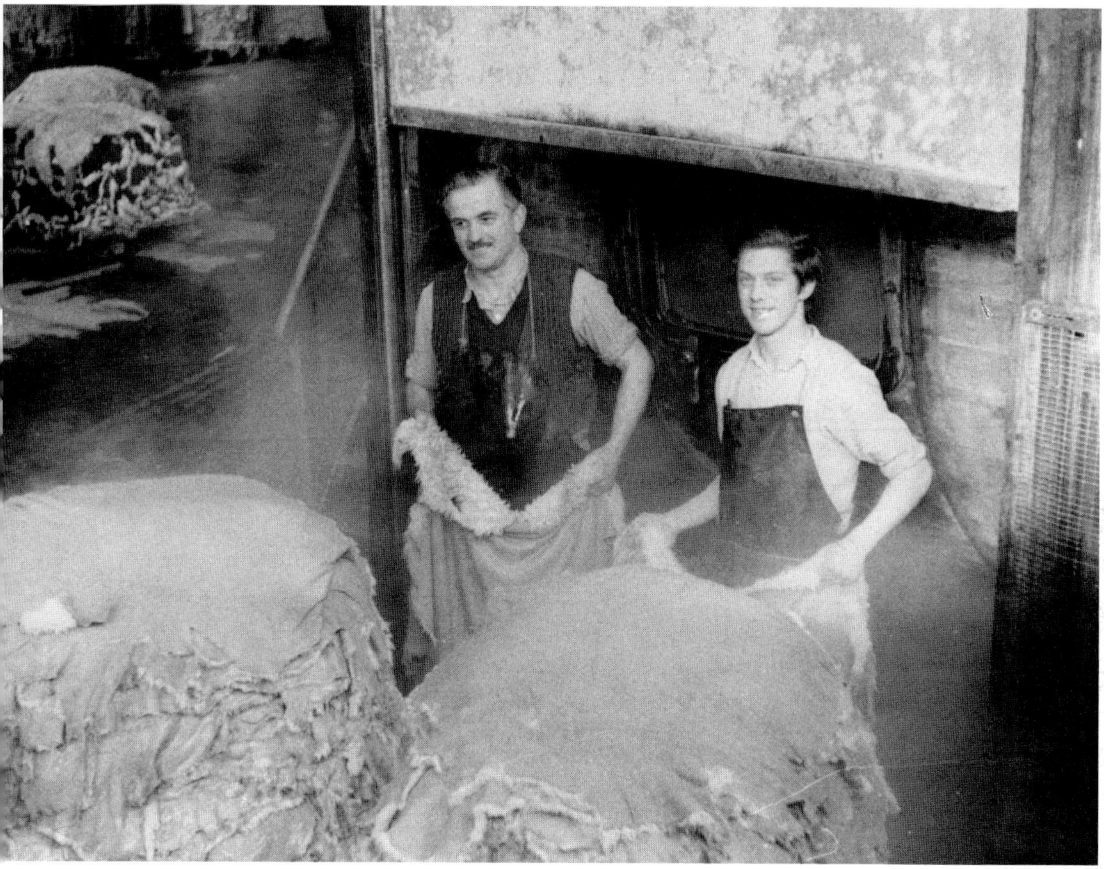

Employees of a later era: Eric Potter and Kevin Meade removing shearlings from a drum. (Nic Portway)

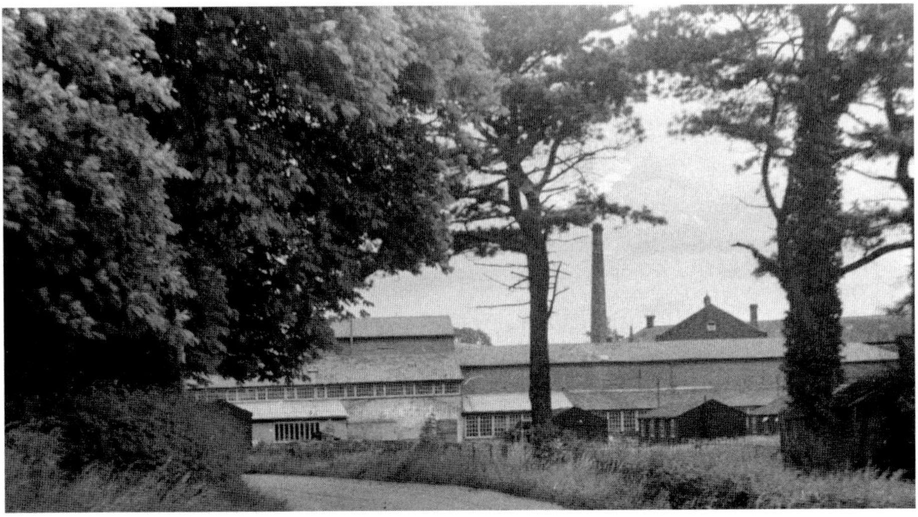

This view of the tannery was taken just after the Second World War. The huts alongside the tannery buildings were Army huts, which came from a searchlight battery placed in the Slough, between Combs and Stowmarket, to illuminate raiding Zeppelins during the First World War. In the picture below Jack Robinson is operating some of the machinery at the tannery. During the Second World War Jack escaped by parachute from the rear gun turret of a burning bomber and spent some years as a prisoner-of-war. (Nic Portway)

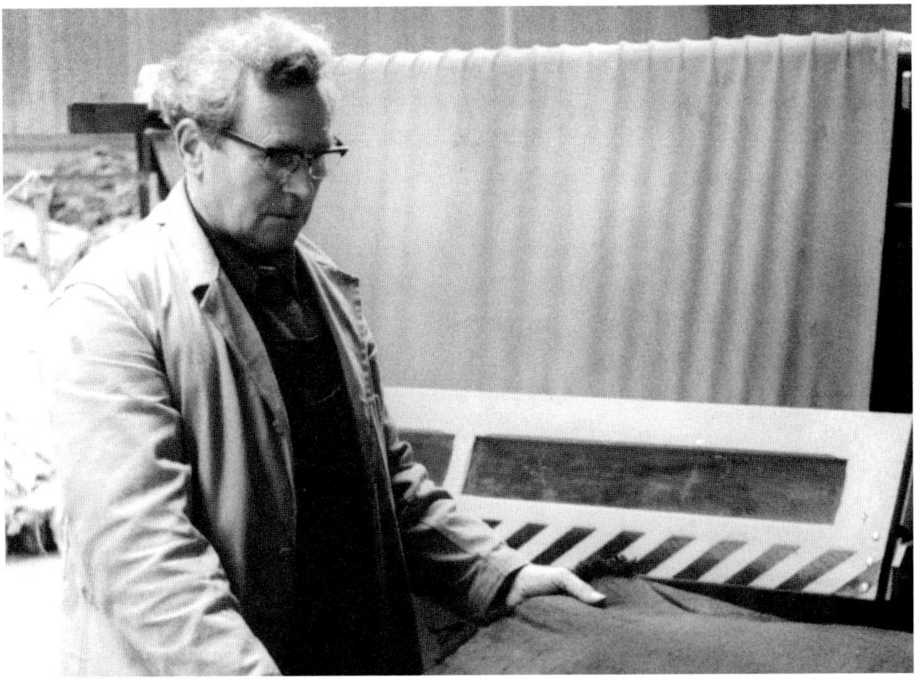

*Section Nine*

# THE TOWN AT WAR

With the New Explosives Company's works on the outskirts of the town, Stowmarket attracted the attention of Zeppelin raiders during the First World War, though such were the deficiencies of the attackers' navigation that the bombs intended for the guncotton works often fell on other towns. Those airships that did find Stowmarket came under fire from guns at Badley and on Thorney Green, Stowupland, and in Stowmarket itself.

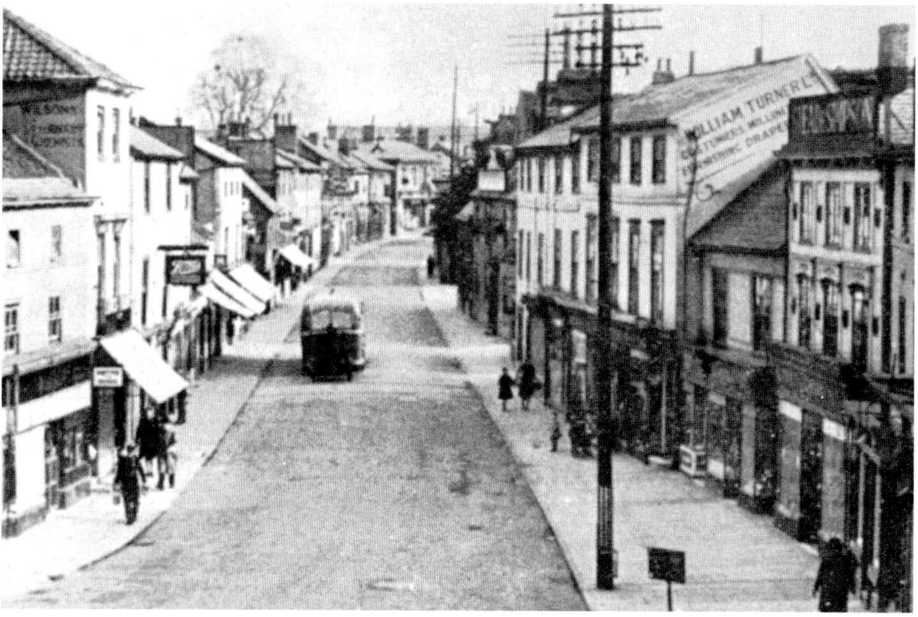

Ipswich Street during the Second World War. Petrol rationing has cleared traffic from the street, and the Eastern Counties bus departing for Ipswich tows a trailer bearing a producer gas plant; this provided sufficient power on the flat, but it was not unknown for passengers to have to leave the bus and walk up hills. (Ivan Codd)

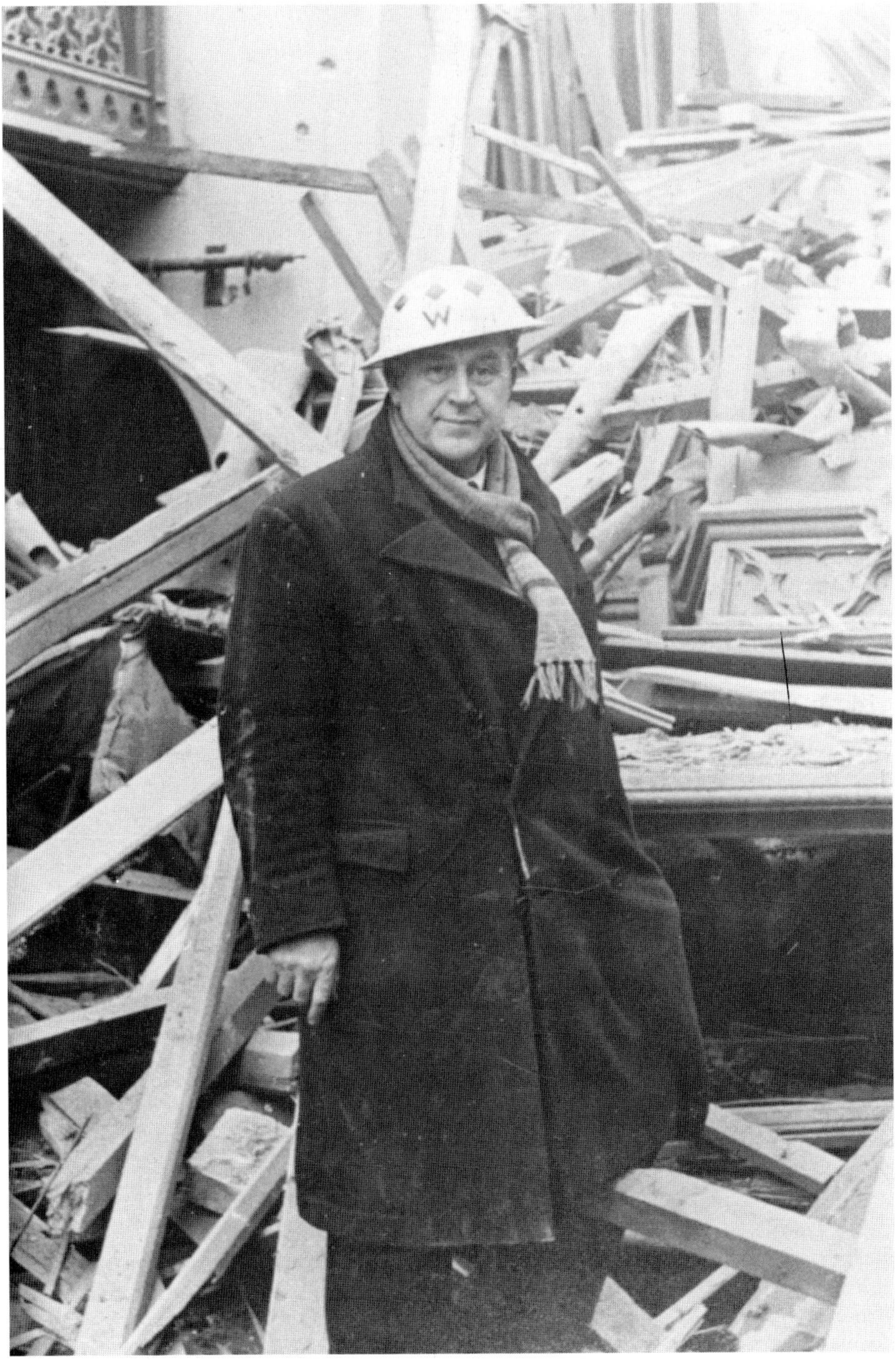
W

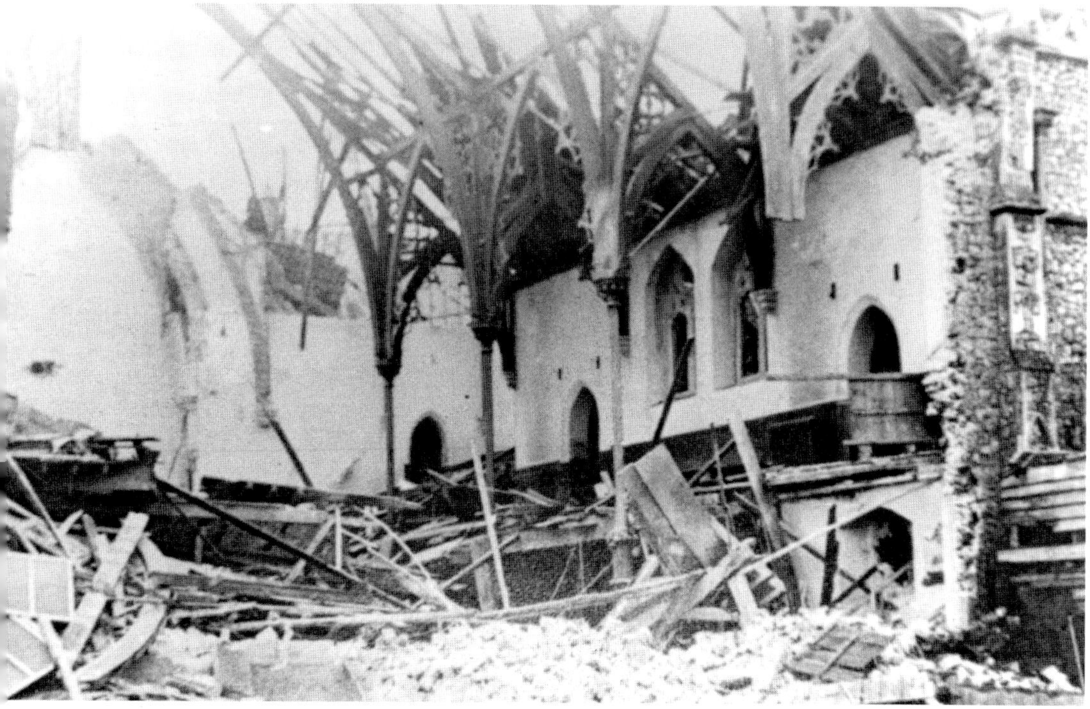

The ruins of the Congregational church after the air raid of 31 January 1941. Designed by Frederick Barnes, who was also responsible for the design of Stowmarket and other stations on the Ipswich and Bury Railway, the church was built in 1861. In the photograph on the opposite page the Rev. Eric Weir, who had been appointed Chief ARP Warden for the town in 1939, stands amid the ruins of the church of which he was pastor. Following the destruction of the church the congregation held their services in the Regal cinema, funerals and similar services being conducted in the parish church until a new Congregational church was opened in 1955. (Both Ivan Codd)

In the Second World War the town came under more severe aerial attack, and on the last day of January 1941 a raiding aircraft scored direct hits on the Congregational church in Ipswich Street and on a nearby house; perhaps the Suffolk Iron Foundry on the other side of the Gipping had been the real target, for in common with other similar factories elsewhere it was engaged in war work.

It was a war in which the people of Suffolk found themselves playing a more significant role than ever before. Unfamiliar accents were heard in the streets of Stowmarket as American airmen from nearby bases sought refuge from the stresses of war in the town's hostelries, and even more strange to local people was the presence of black servicemen at nearby Haughley Park, though it appears that their swing bands proved popular.

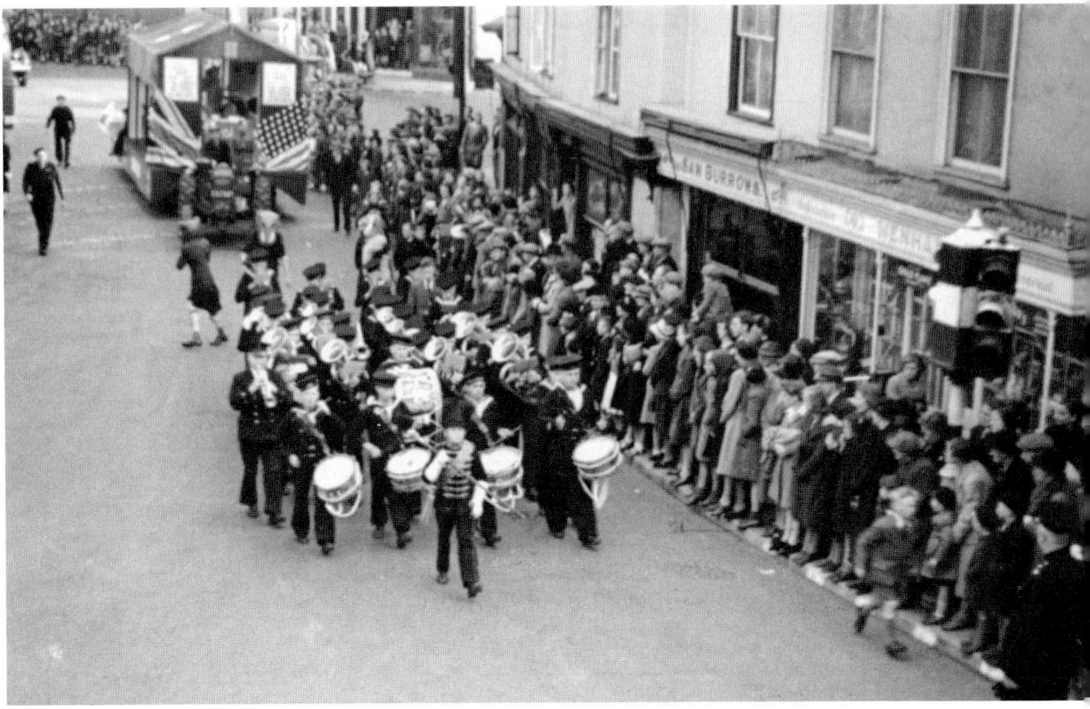

The band of the Royal Hospital School at Holbrook leads the 'Salute the Soldier' Week carnival parade through the town on 17 June 1944. At the time of the parade Stowmarket was £7,000 short of its target of £75,000 savings, but by the following Monday it was possible to announce a total of almost £77,500. On the opposite page the procession negotiates the Market Place. (Geoff Clarke)

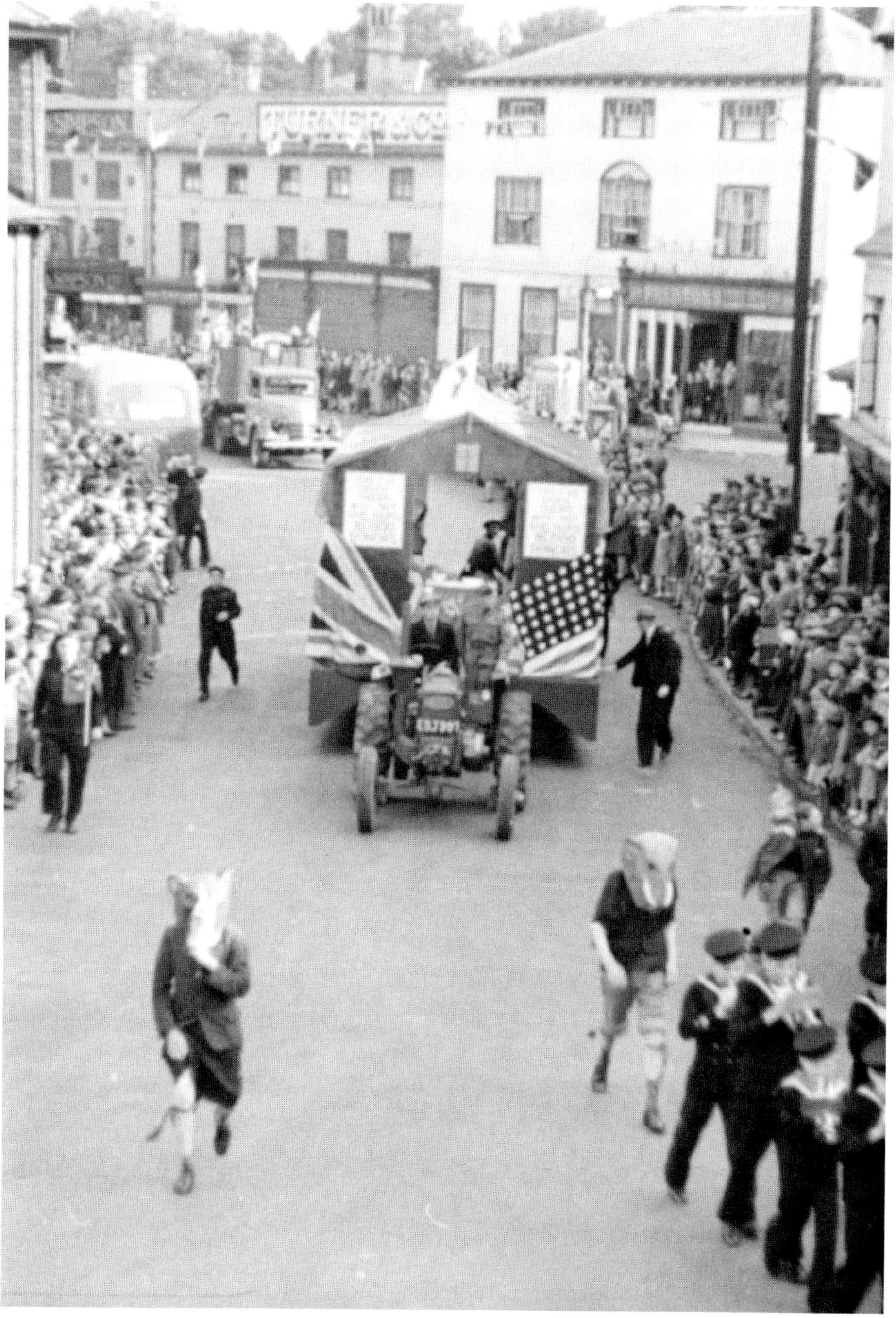

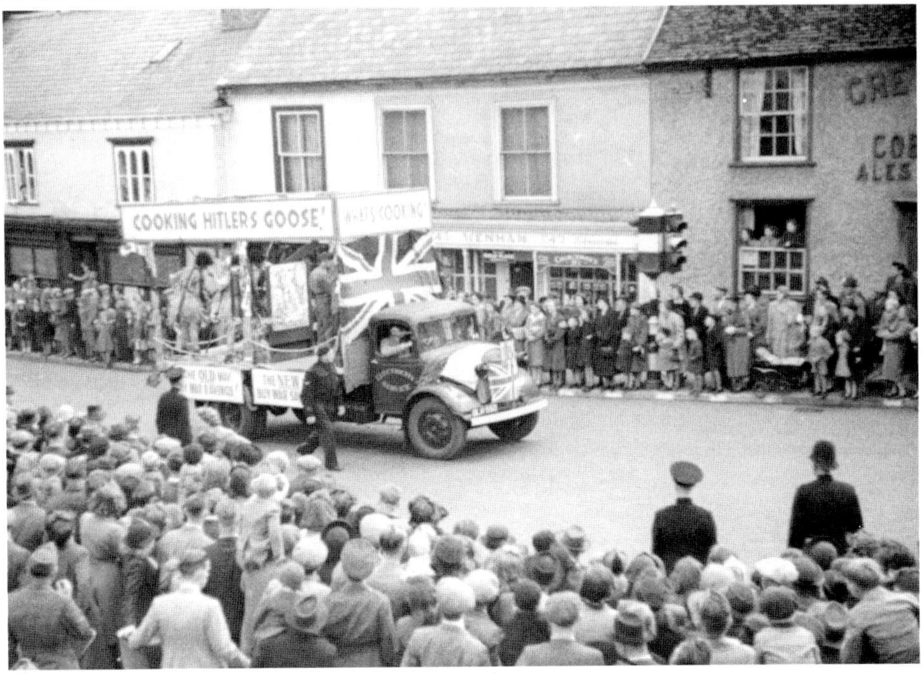


'Cooking Hitler's Goose!' announces one of the entries in the 'Salute the Soldier' Week procession. American and British airmen are among the spectators outside the Greyhound Inn watching the procession, below. (Geoff Clarke)

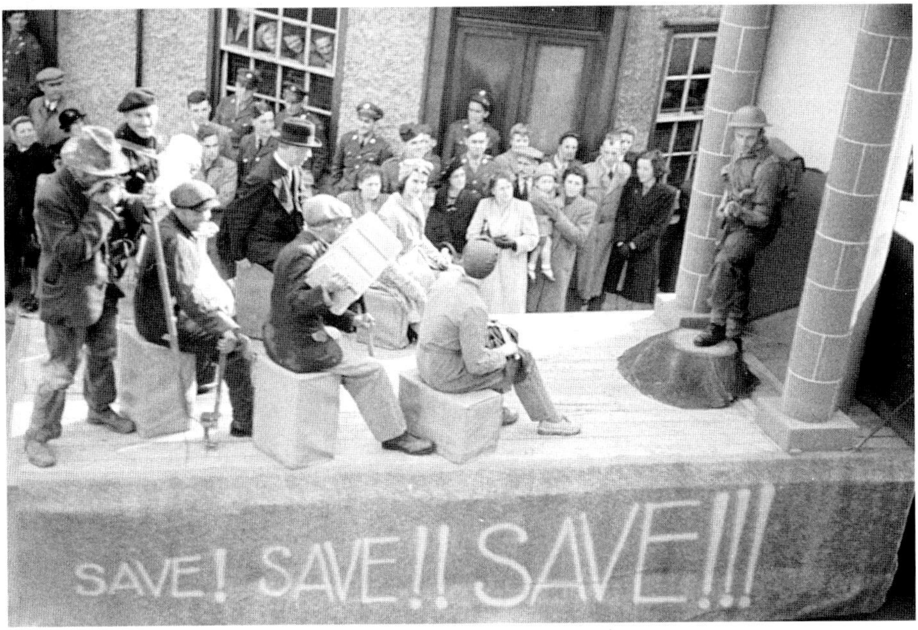

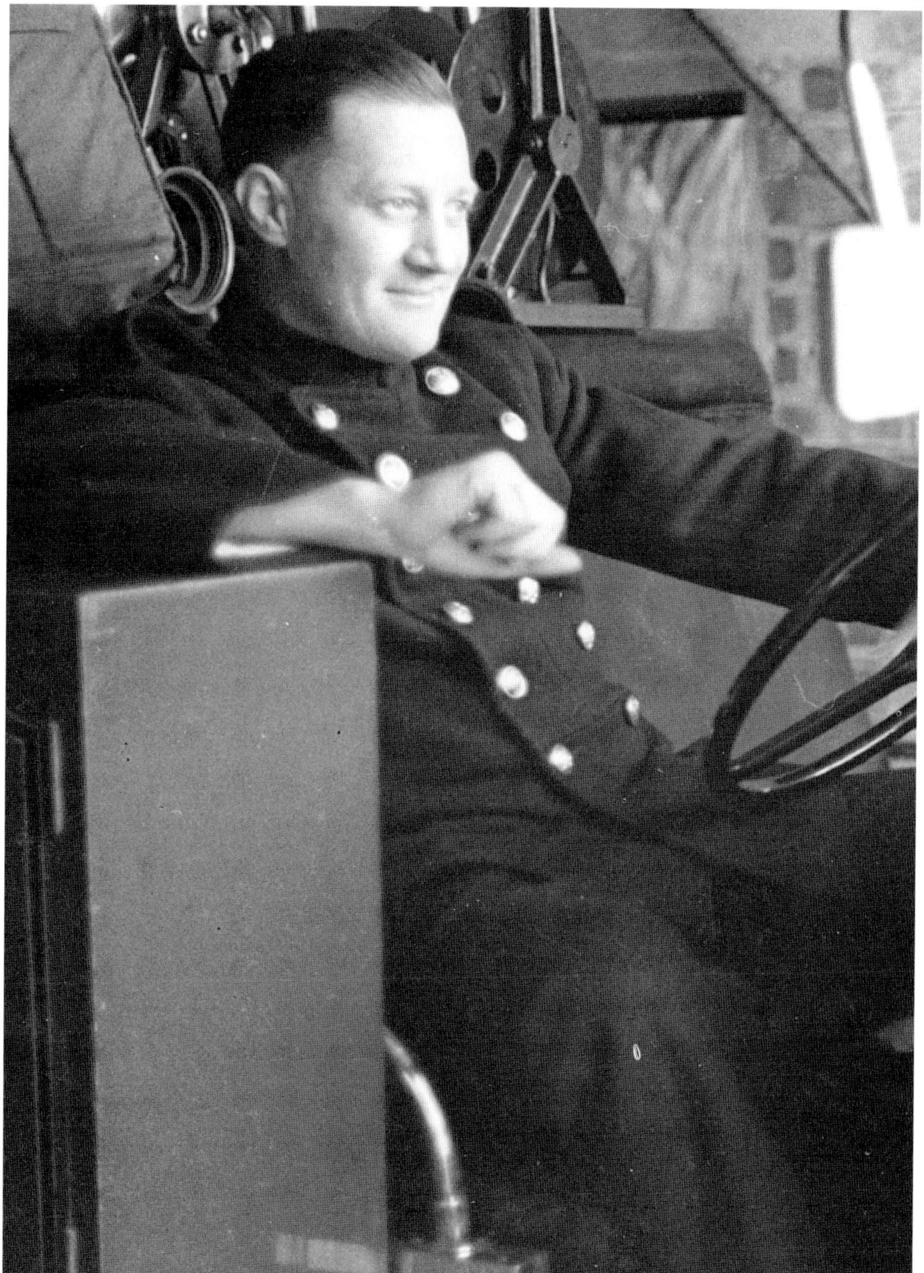

George 'Tich' Wilden, photographer and part-time fireman, at the wheel of Stowmarket Urban District Council's fire engine. Many of the pictures in the wartime and post-war sections of this book were taken by him. (Geoff Clarke)

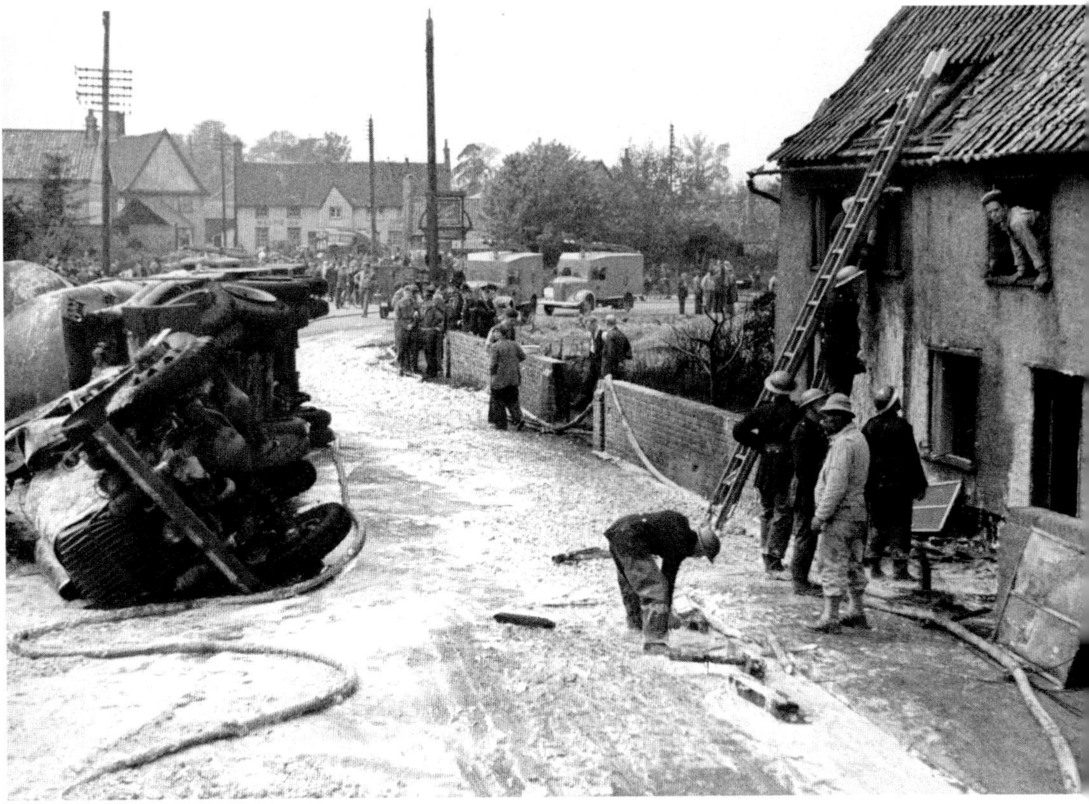

Foam covers the road and a US Army Air Force petrol tanker lies on its side following a serious accident at Combs Ford, 24 May 1944. Coming round the bend from Stowmarket rather too fast, the tanker overturned in the path of a CWS milk tanker coming the other way and burst into flames. The driver of the milk tanker, Albert Goodchild, a Stowmarket man and a special constable, died in the flames as he ran from his wrecked lorry, and one of the three American servicemen in the petrol tanker died later. In George Wilden's picture on the opposite page local people watch as flames and smoke billow up from the burning petrol, which ran down the road and set light to nearby cottages. (Geoff Clarke)

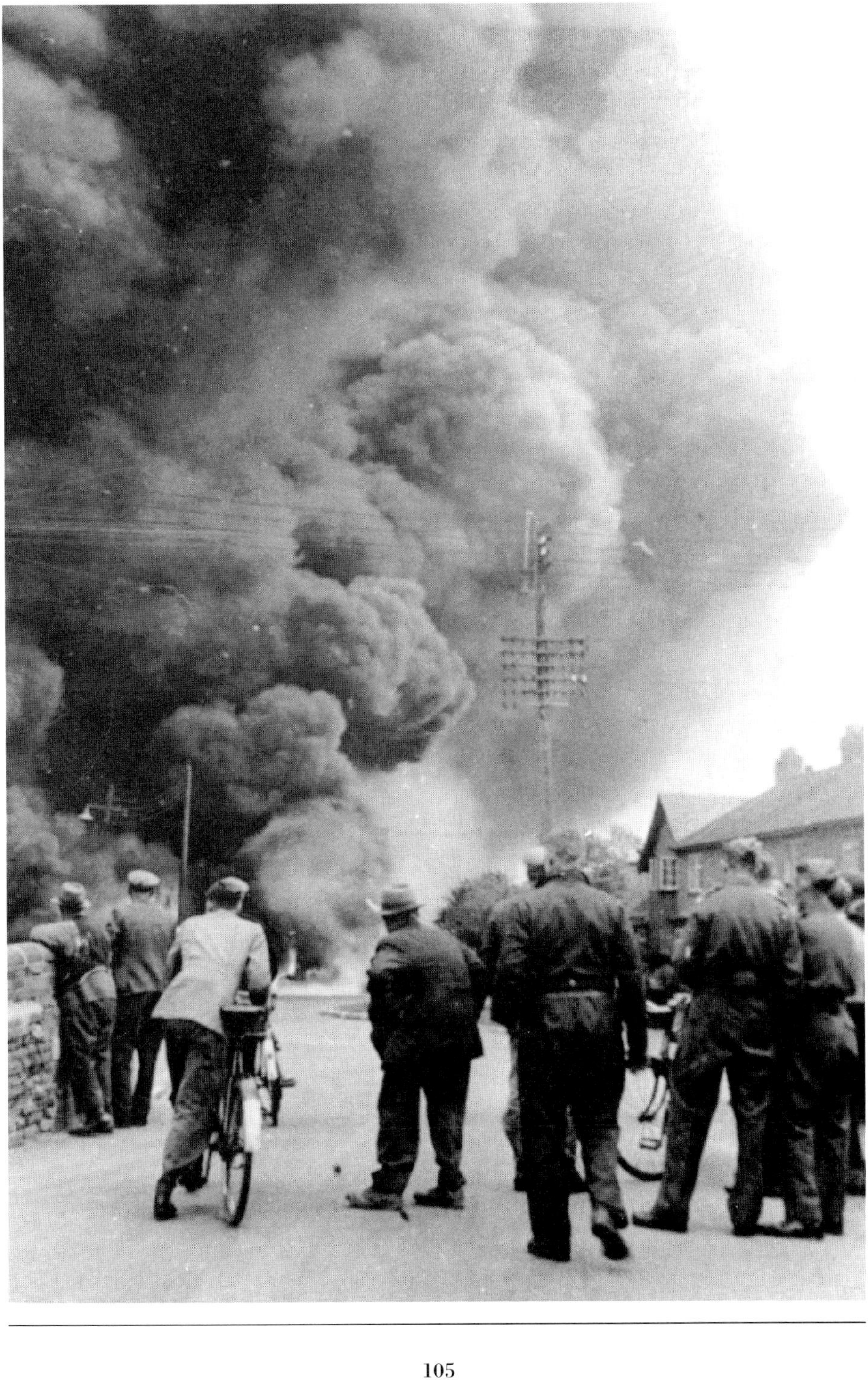

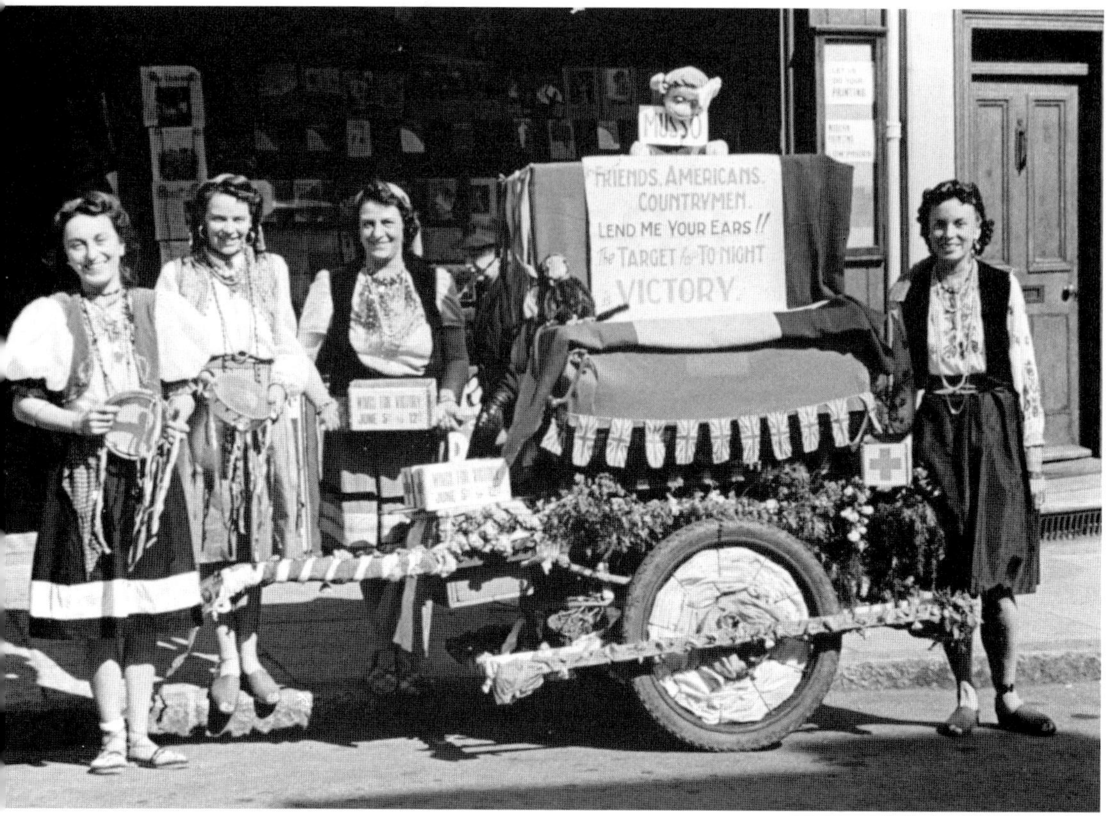


During 'Wings for Victory' Week in June 1943, Brenda Wilden, Vera Cole and Lilian Thurlow, aided by an unnamed friend, set out with their street piano to raise money towards the town's target. (Geoff Clarke)

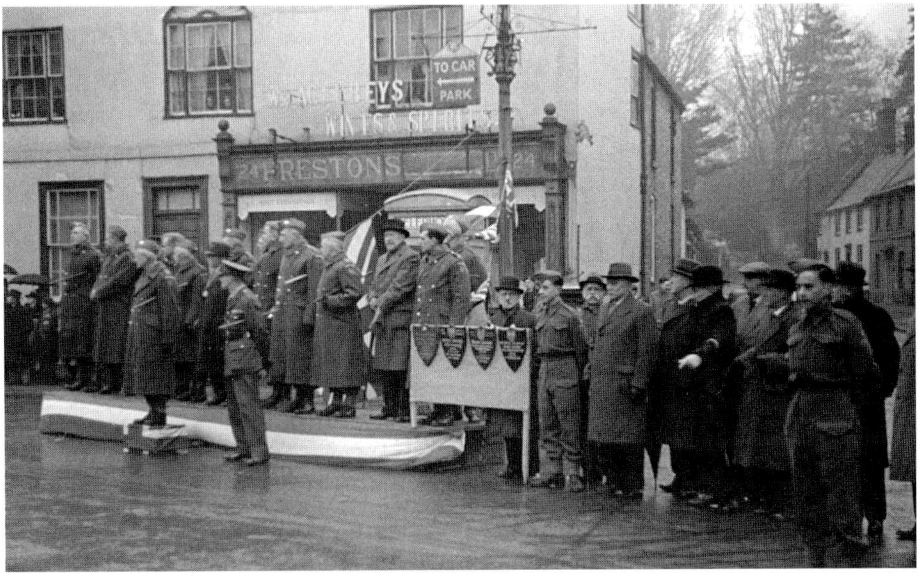


On a wet Sunday afternoon in December 1944, Lt.-Col. D. Ovey takes the salute at the stand-down parade of the 7th Suffolk Battalion, Home Guard. More than 1,000 men marched past to the music of the Gislingham Town Band. Behind the saluting base in the Market Place the fascia of Prestons (Stowmarket) Ltd has been suitably masked to avoid an invading German army discovering its whereabouts. In the picture below the battalion marches into the Market Place. (Geoff Clarke)

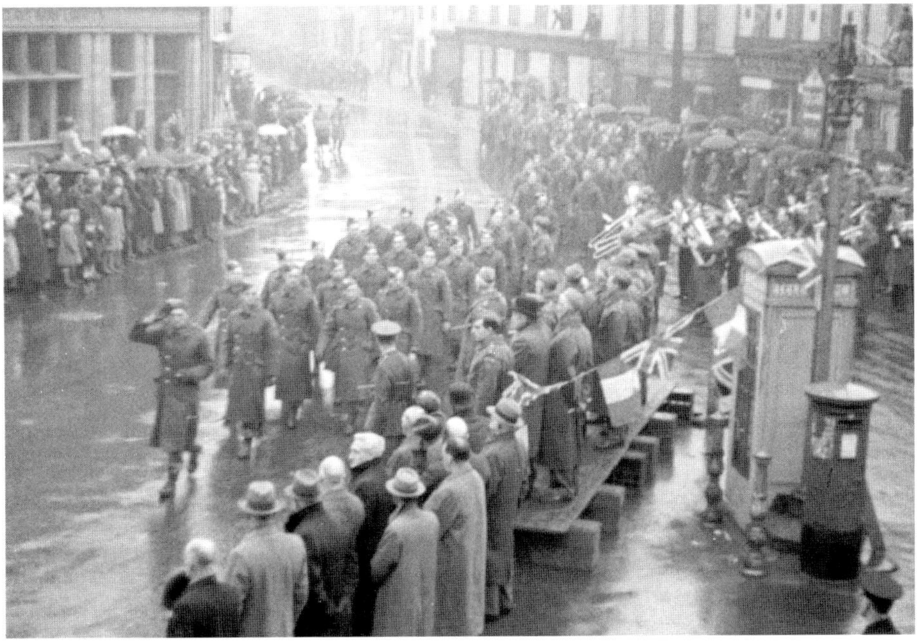

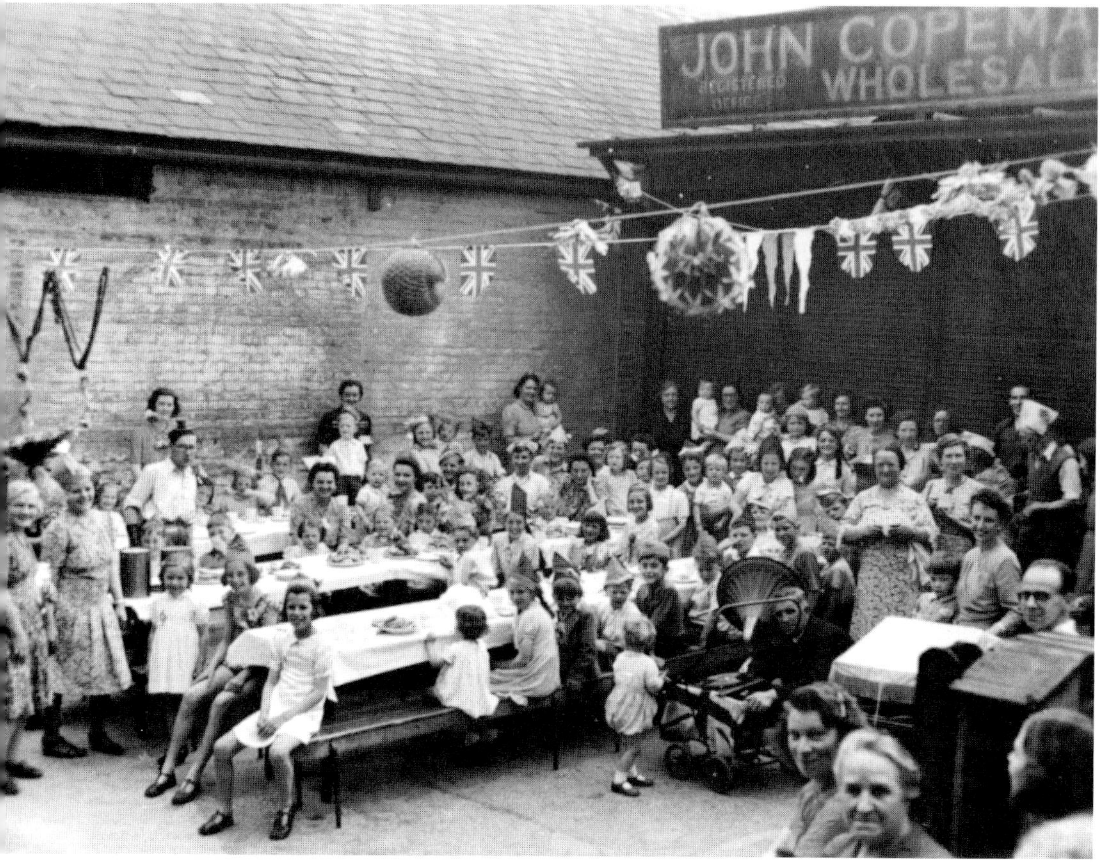


With the ending of the war in 1945, the people of Stowmarket celebrated along with the rest of Britain. This party for the children of Violet Hill was held in the yard of John Copeman & Sons Ltd in Violet Hill Road. (Ivan Codd)

*Section Ten*

# REDEVELOPMENT

The immediate post-war period was a time of austerity, but as the country recovered from the effects of war plans were made for what was euphemistically called redevelopment. Long-established shops disappeared as the developers moved in and cleared away buildings like the King's Head in Ipswich Street, which had stood firm for perhaps three centuries.

With the benefit of hindsight some people are now asking whether the buildings which have replaced them have in any way enhanced the appearance and character of the town. Yet the fact remains that the changes of the sixties and seventies will be with us for many years to come, and that the construction of the Gipping Valley bypass and other new roads will influence life in the town for good or bad in the century soon to come.

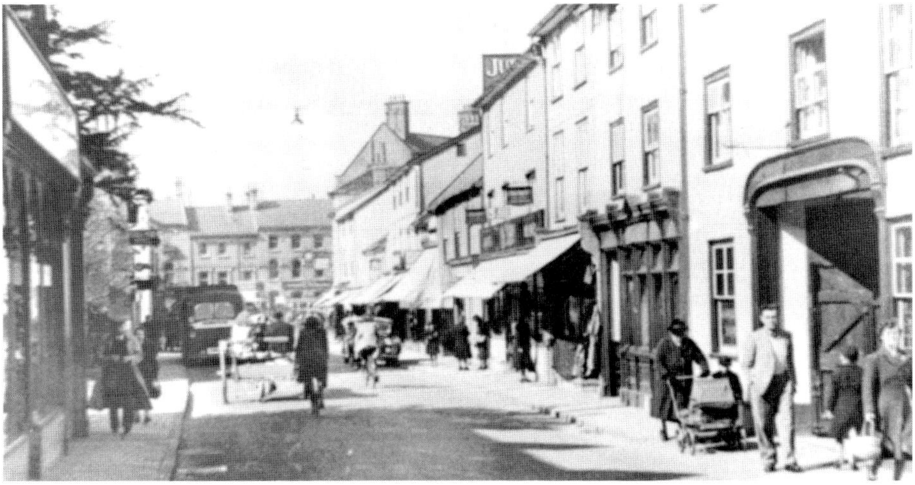

Ipswich Street just after the end of the Second World War. On the right, walking past the entrance to the Fox Hotel yard, is Ivan Codd, home on demob leave from the RAF. (Ivan Codd)

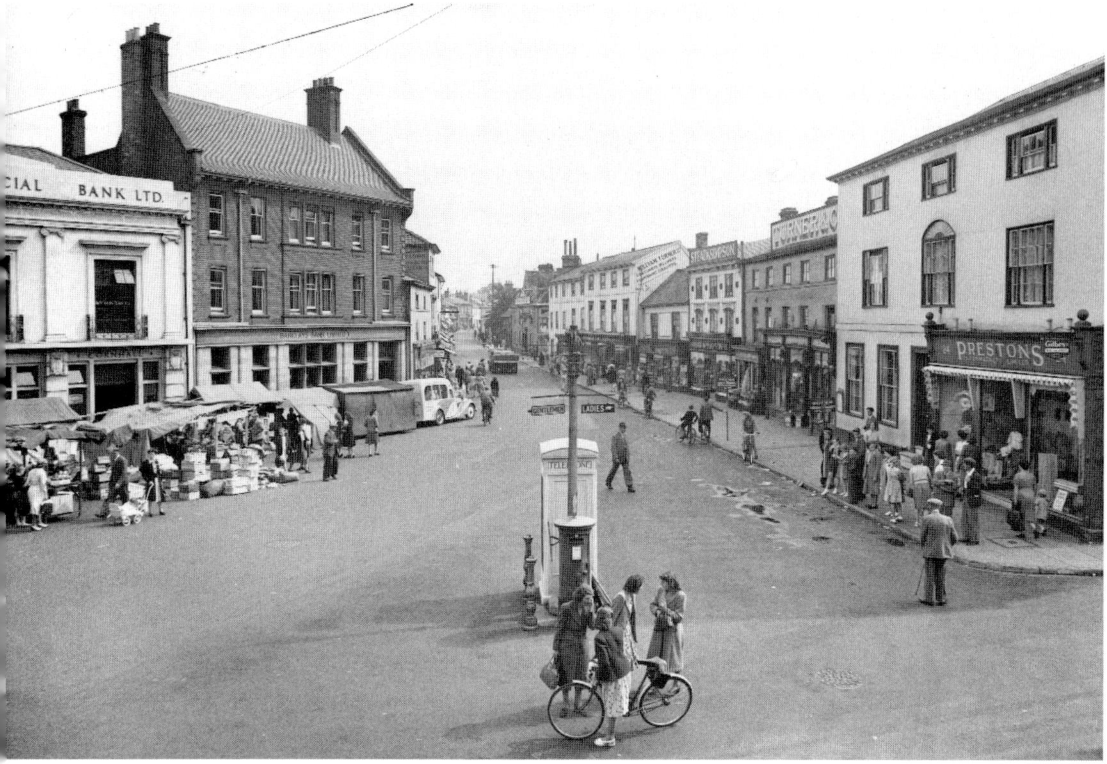


Looking along Ipswich Street from the Market Place on a market day, not long after the end of the Second World War. The market is now confined to one side, and the Crowe Street side is clear. Two shops can be seen with the name Turner; the nearer is that of Turner & Co., grocers, and further along in Ipswich Street is that of William Turner (Stowmarket) Ltd, furnishing drapers and dressmakers. (Geoff Clarke)

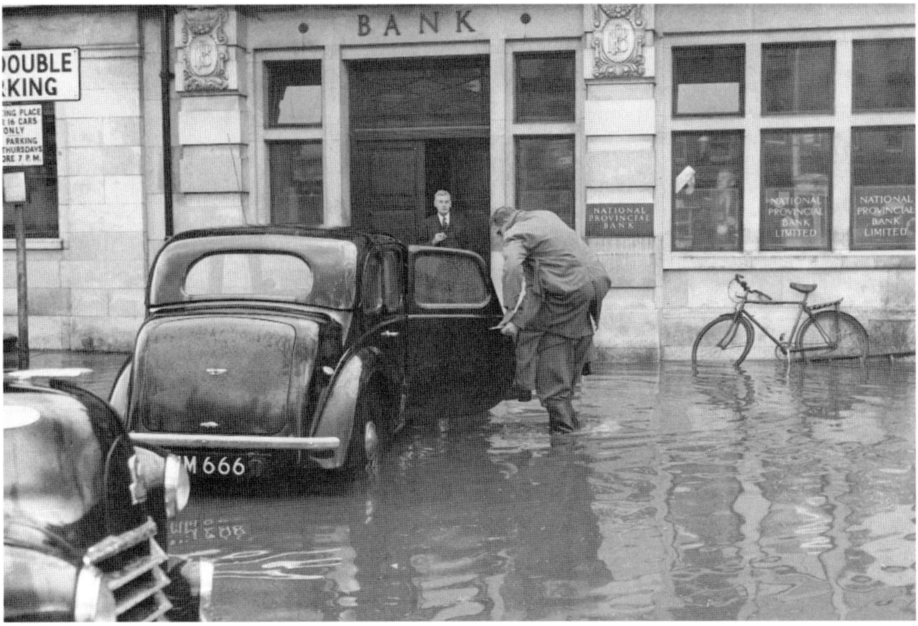


A motorist is given a helping hand to reach his Morris dry-footed during flooding in the Market Place. The National Provincial Bank (now National Westminster) had a stylish building erected for it in the 1920s. (Geoff Clarke)

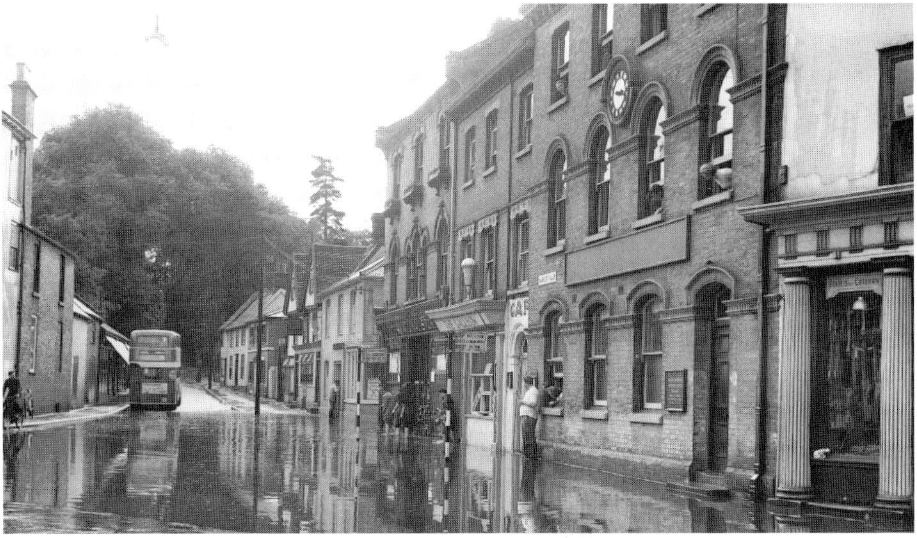

Flooding in the Market Place and Crowe Street, late 1940s. The building with the clock was the post office until the opening in 1937 of a new one in Ipswich Street; further along is the International Stores, which occupied the same premises for more than 50 years. (Geoff Clarke)

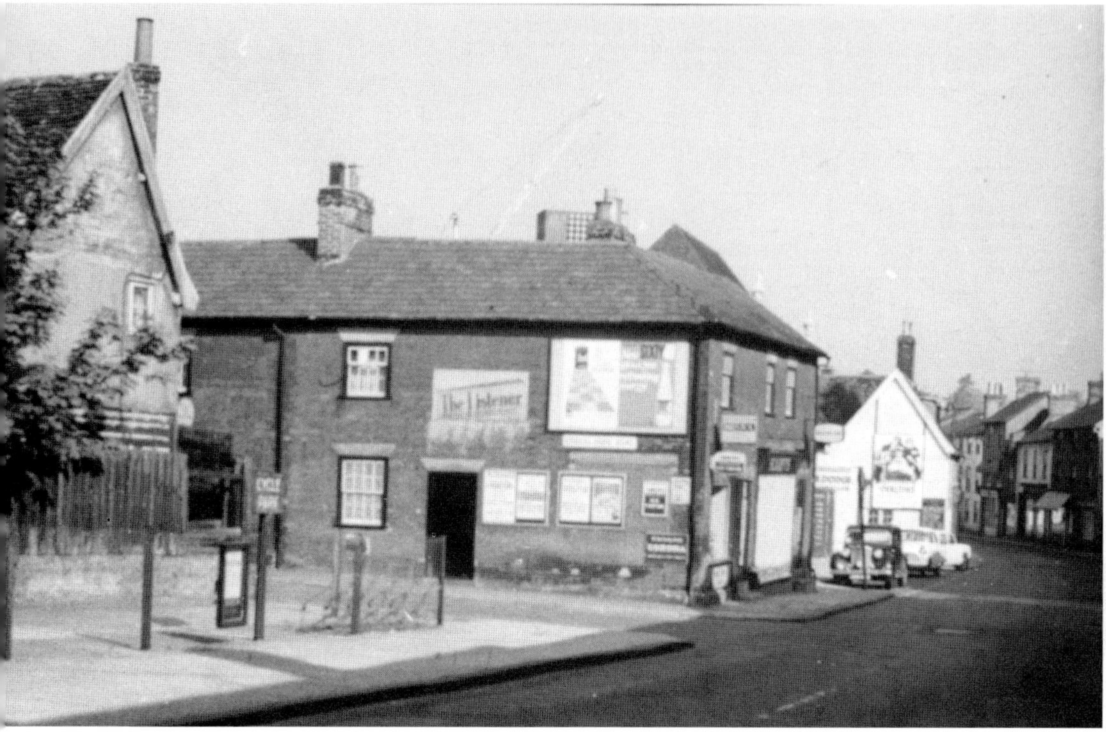


The corner of Ipswich Street and Stricklands Road (formerly Stricklands Lane), *c.* 1950. A pair of K6 telephone kiosks have been placed outside the post office, which is largely hidden; demolition of Charles Scarff's shop and the other buildings will soon open it up to view. (Ivan Codd)

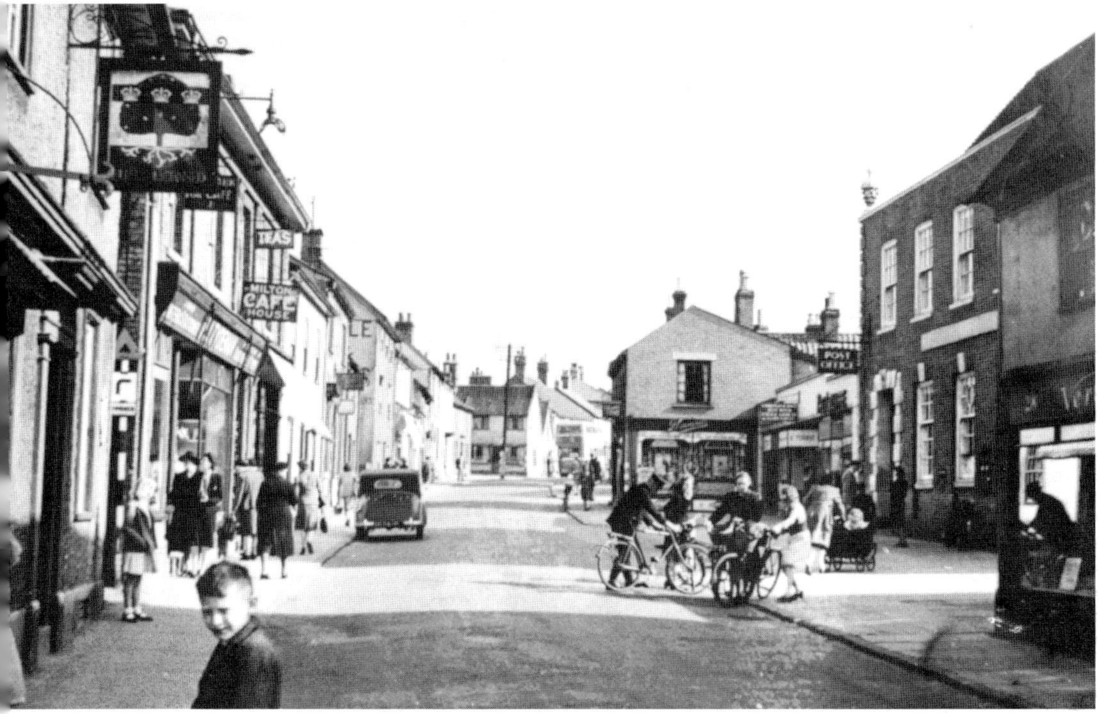

Ipswich Street during the Second World War, with the Royal Oak on the left. The new post office had been opened on a new building line on the west side of the street in 1937. The words 'Stowmarket Post Office' on the wall of the building are blanked out to avoid giving invading Germans any clue to their whereabouts. (Ivan Codd)

*Following pages*: Ipswich Street, 1950s. William Turner (Stowmarket) Ltd is still there, but Turner & Co. has given way to F.W. Woolworth's, opened in 1953; cats'-eyes have been laid down in the road and new bus stop signs have appeared. (Geoff Clarke)

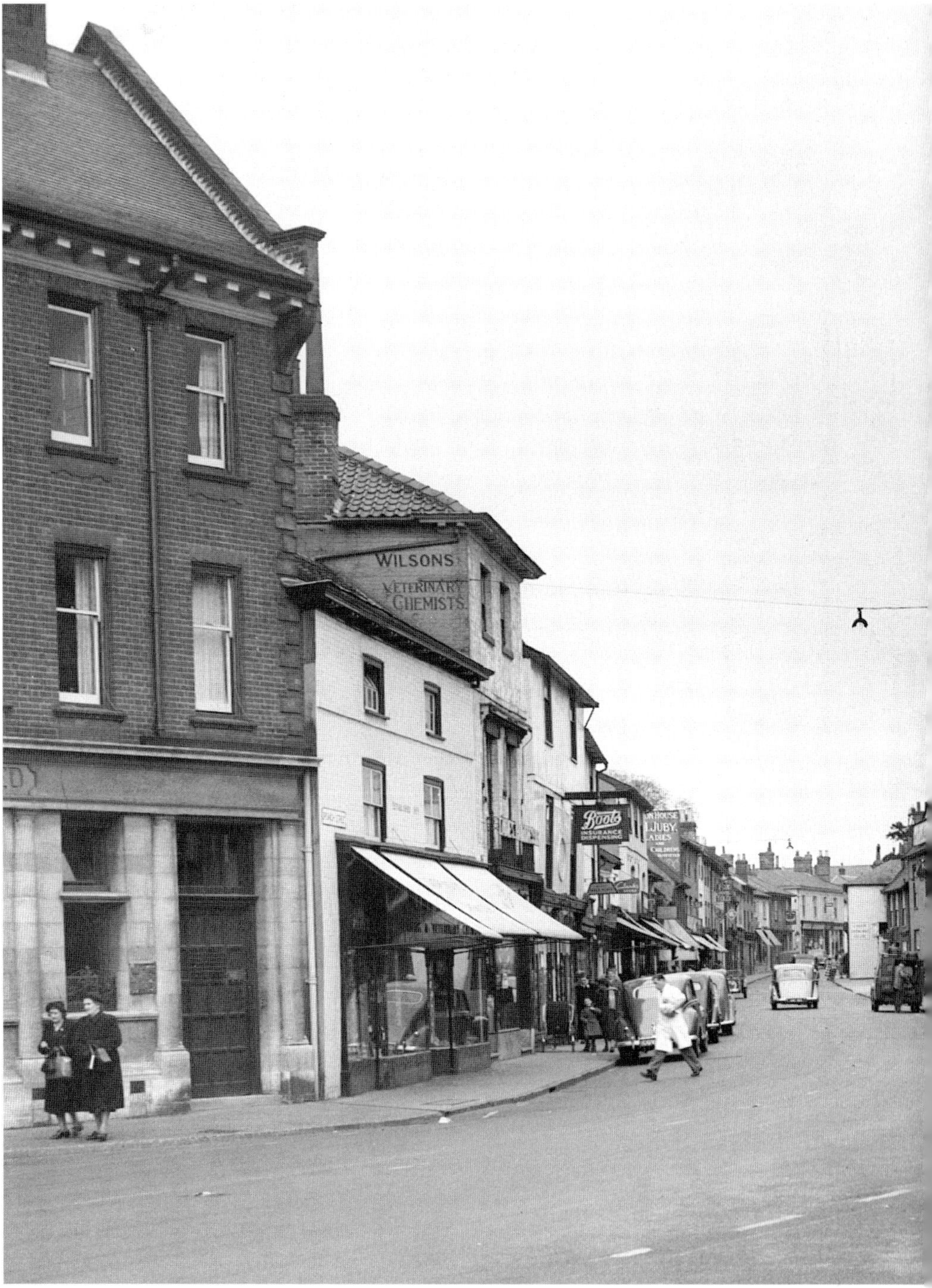
WILSONS
VETERINARY CHEMISTS
Boots
INSURANCE
J. JUBY
LADIES

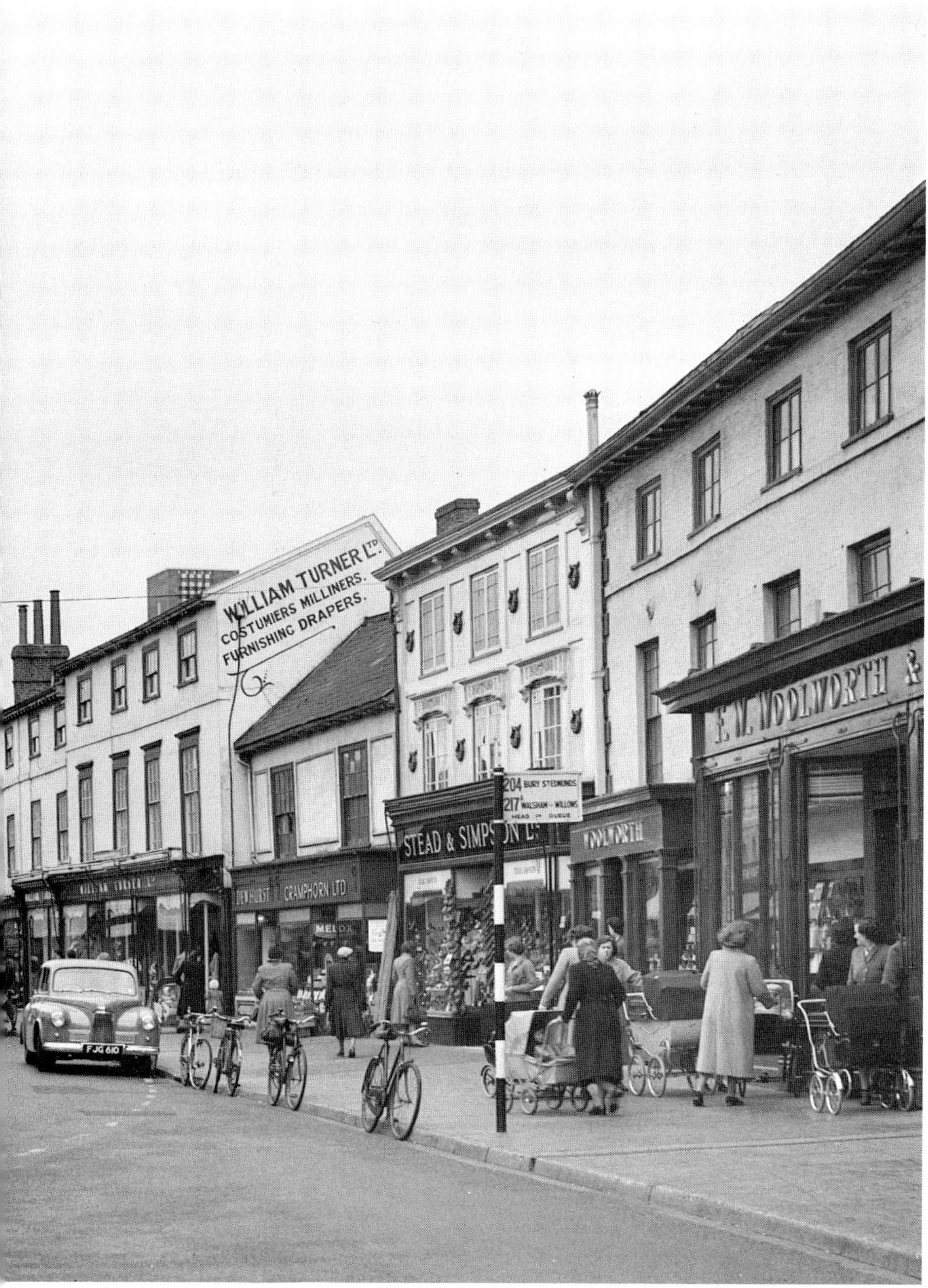
WILLIAM TURNER LTD.
COSTUMIERS MILLINERS.
FURNISHING DRAPERS.
STEAD & SIMPSON LTD
DEWHURST
CRAMPHORN LTD
204 BURY ST EDMUNDS
217A WALSHAM-LE-WILLOWS
HEAD OF QUEUE
WOOLWORTH
F. W. WOOLWORTH &
FJG 610

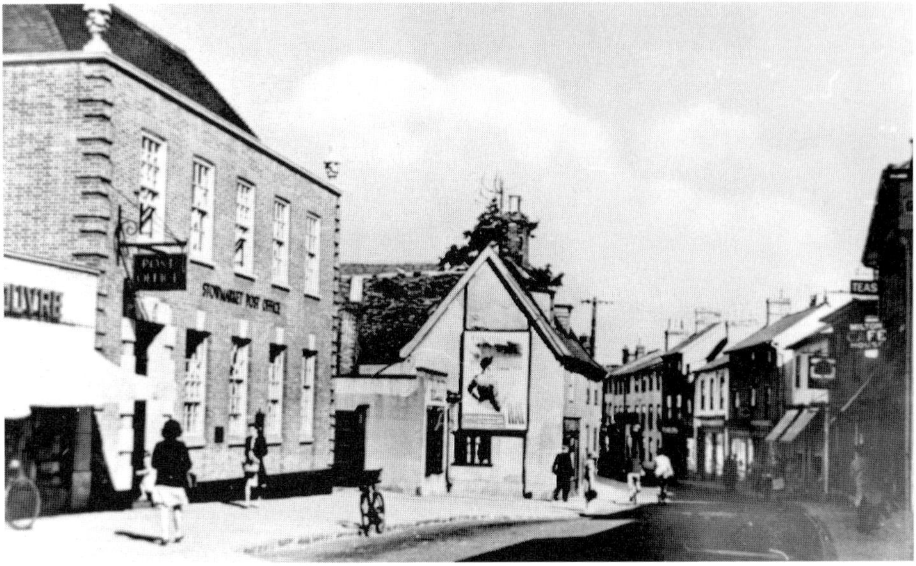


A later picture of the post office, with the town's name revealed; the building bearing an RAF recruiting poster was soon to come down to make way for redevelopment. In the picture below new shops have taken the place of the old, and the tower of the new Congregational church rises above the roof, but one's view of the lower part of the new buildings is blocked by heavy traffic on the A45, a feature of Stowmarket in the 1960s. (Both Ivan Codd)

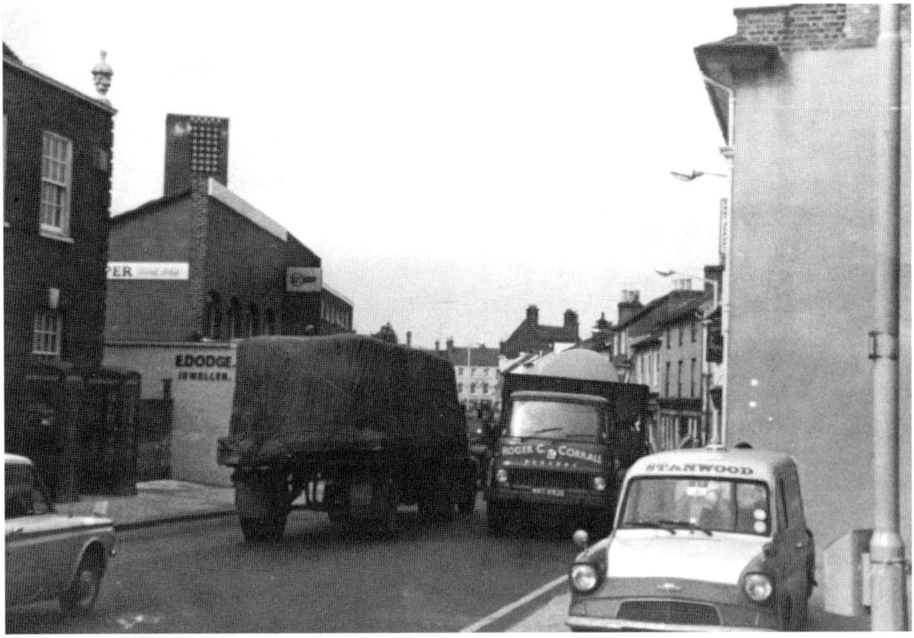

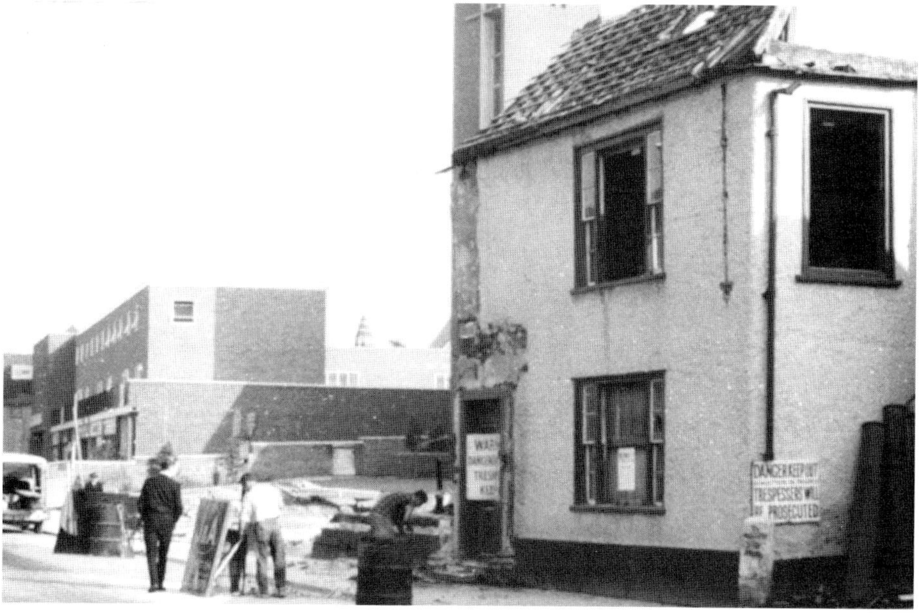

The demolition of the King's Head in the later 1960s to make way for new shops; it had closed in 1964. The new shops already built further along Ipswich Street clearly lack the character of the buildings that are being lost. Below, Frank Ward's outfitters, which had been a feature of Ipswich Street since some time last century, is demolished to make way for more new shops. (Both Ivan Codd)

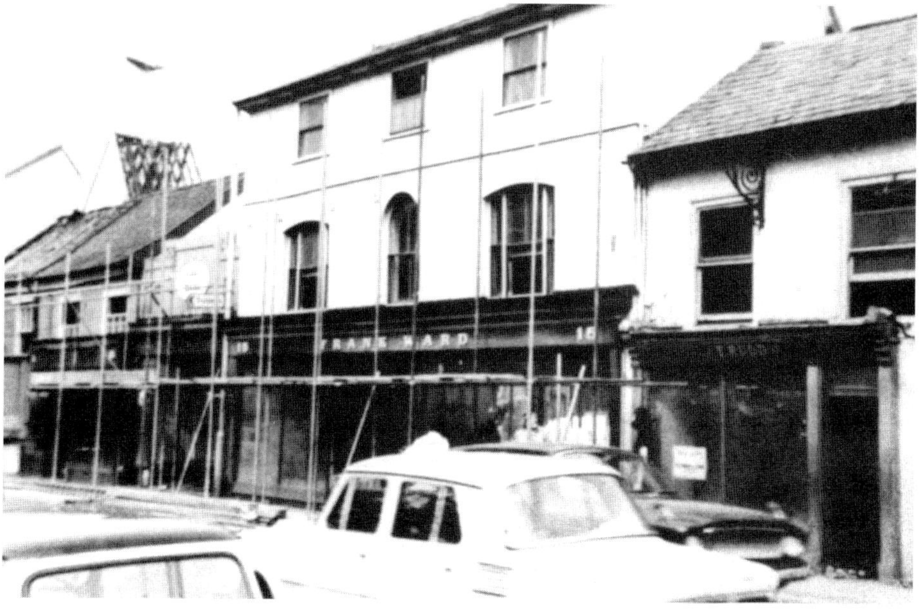

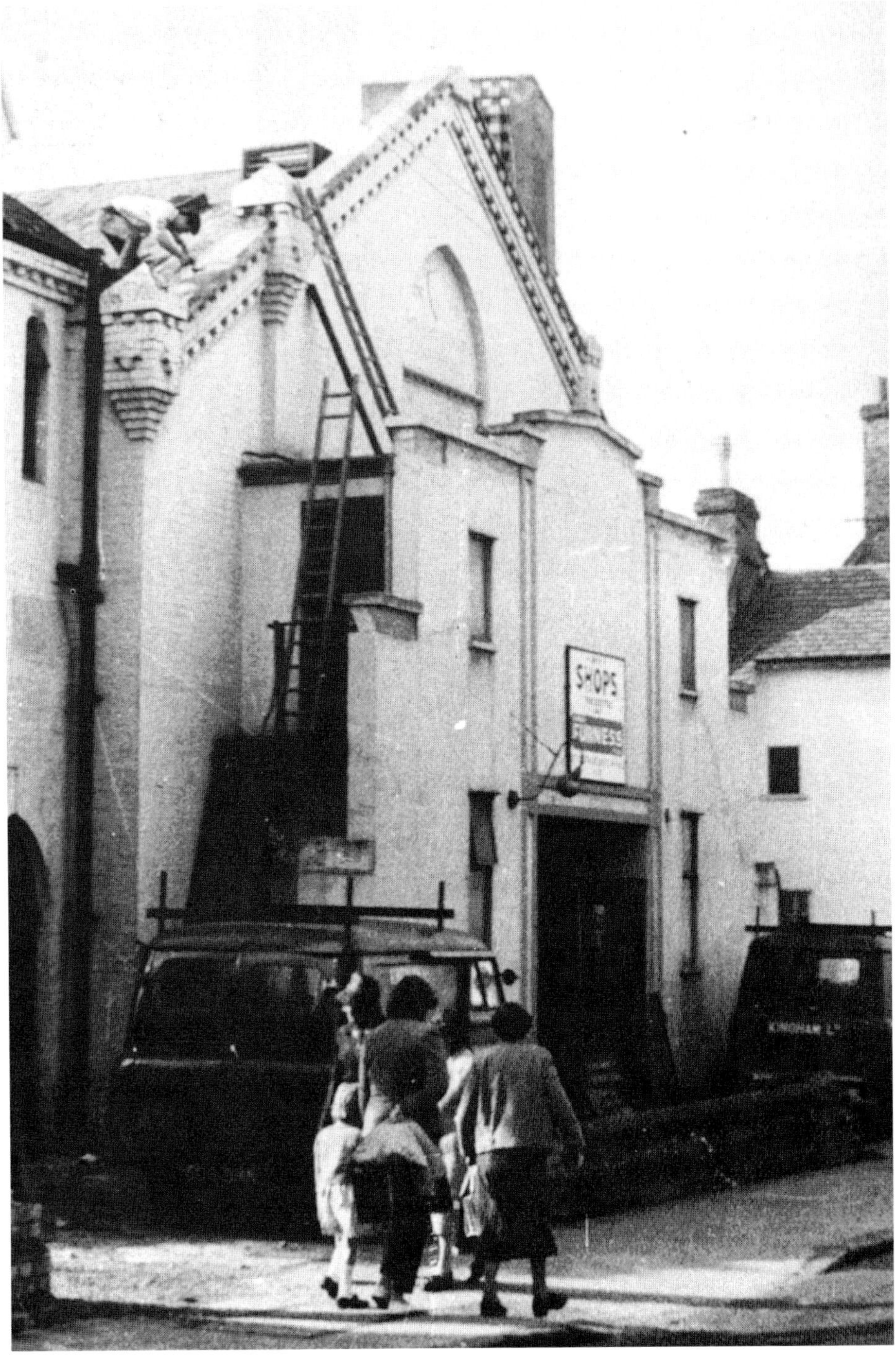
SHOPS

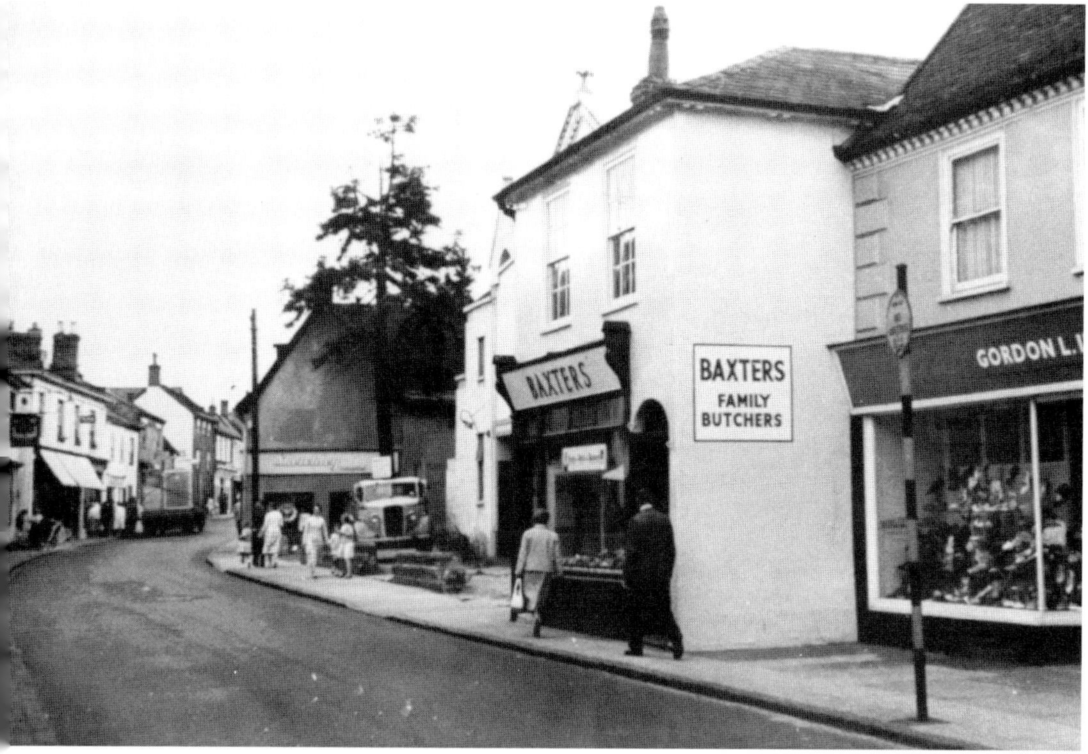


*Opposite*: The end of the Palladium cinema in Ipswich Street, which had closed in 1959 after almost half a century of 'the flicks'; it had opened as a cinema in 1911, but the building had had a previous existence as the Stowmarket Institute. The Institute, which began life in 1874 following an amalgamation of the Literary Institute and the Young Men's Society, contained a library and a reading room, and a hall said to be capable of seating 400 people; it was this hall that became the cinema. Baxters family butchers, which almost hides the Palladium in the photograph above, had in pre-war days been the London Central Meat Company. (Both Ivan Codd)

*Following pages:* A view looking south-west from the church tower in the late 1940s, with the former post office in the Market Place in the left foreground and the Greyhound Inn on the corner of Tavern Street in the right foreground. In the middle is the saleyard of R.C. Knight & Sons, tennis courts and the Stowmarket Football Club ground, while in the distance can be seen the claypit of Fison & Company's brickworks, closed in 1940. (Ivan Codd)

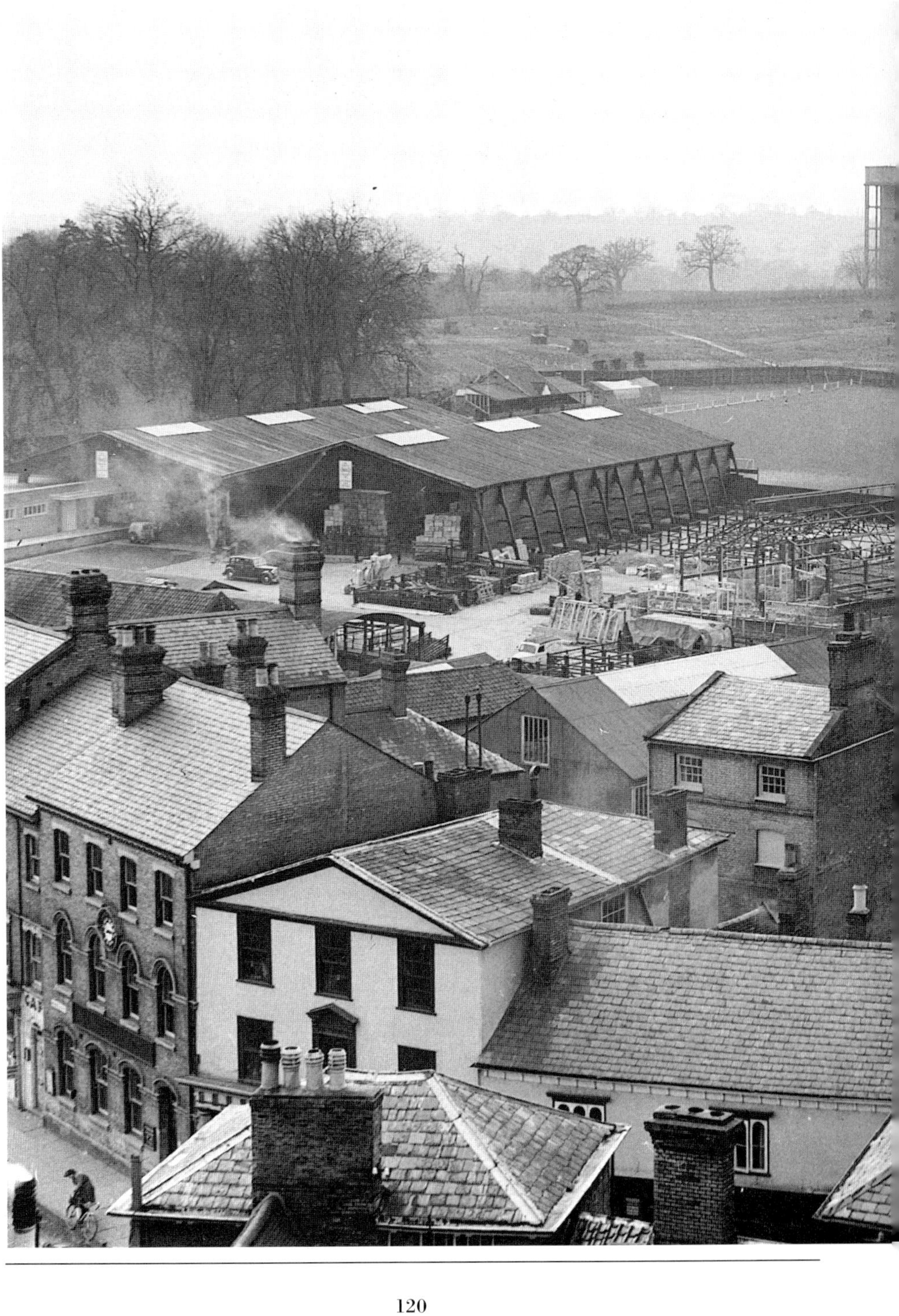

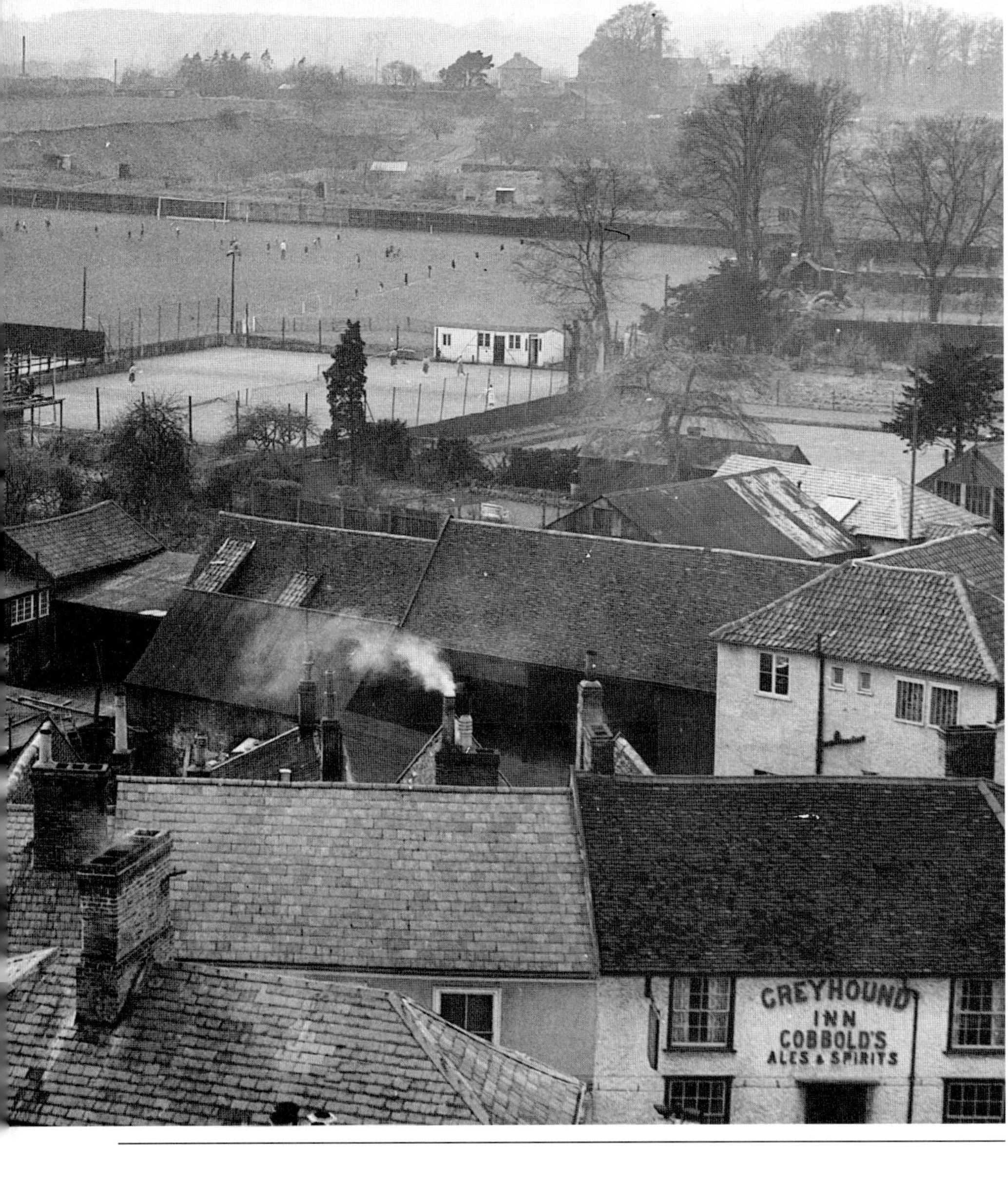
GREYHOUND
INN
COBBOLD'S
ALES & SPIRITS

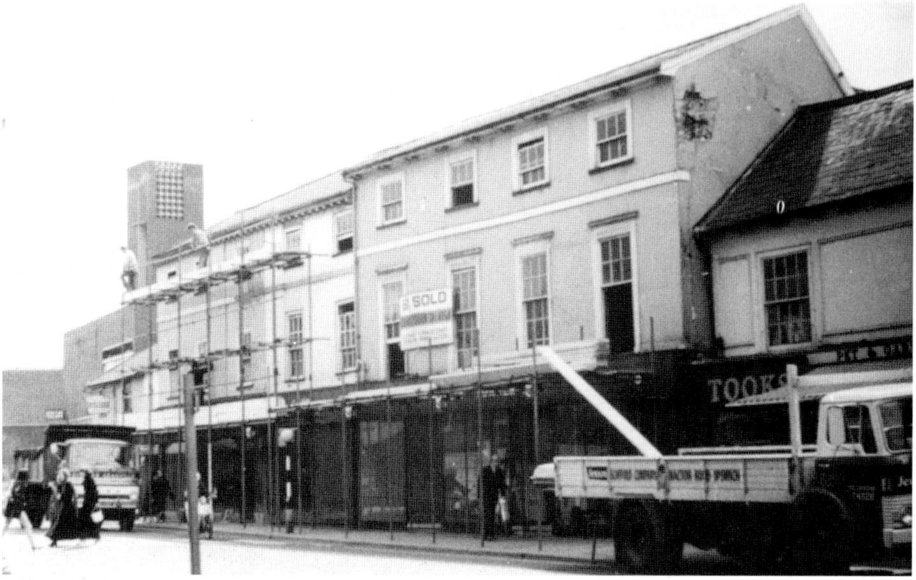


Redevelopment gains pace: the premises of Turner & Co. (Stowmarket) Ltd and neighbouring shops are torn down in June 1970. In the left background is the tower of the new Congregational church. Below is the scene looking in the opposite direction from Marriott's Walk, with the spire of the parish church showing clearly above the roofs. (Both Ivan Codd)

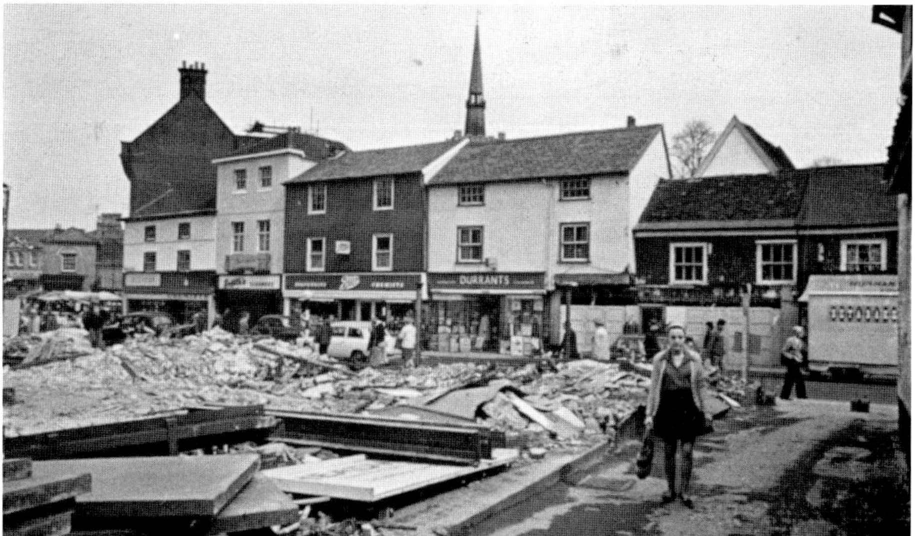

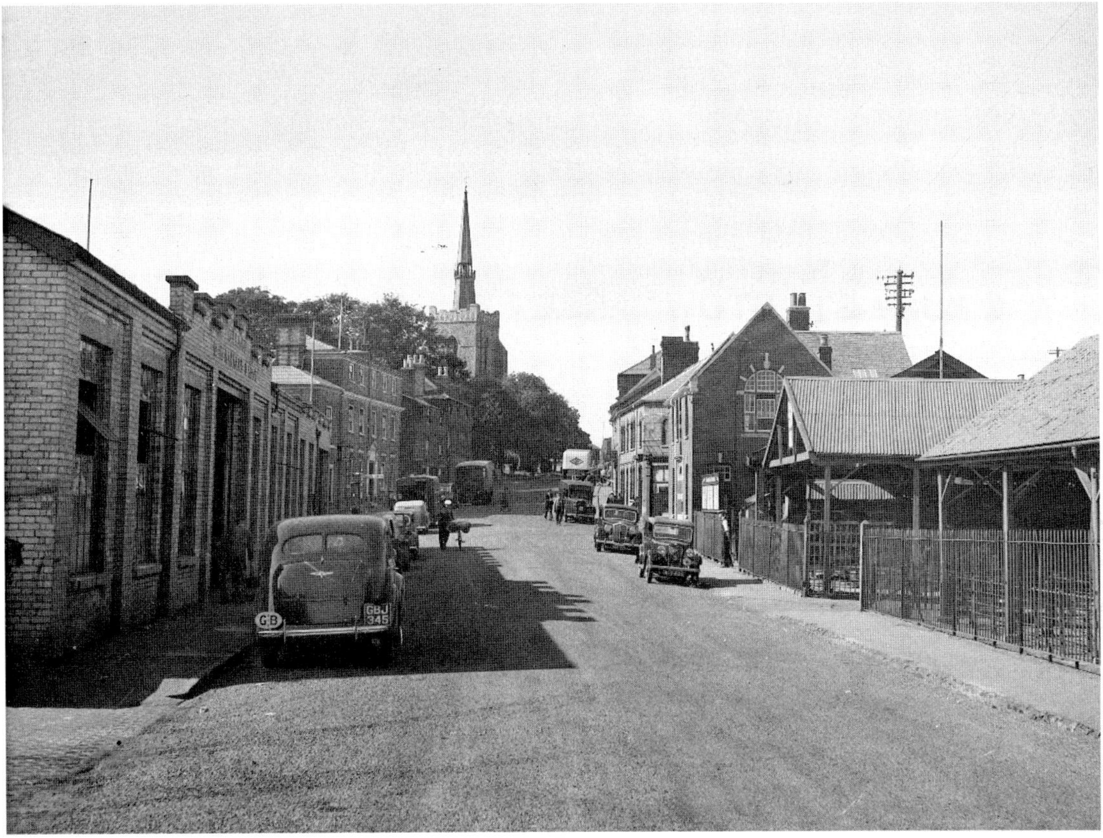


Looking up Station Road soon after the Second World War, with O.G. Barnard's garage on the left and Woodward & Woodward's saleyard on the right; standing at the gate of the cattle market is Jim Barton, who used to be responsible for cleaning the saleyard. A Suffolk Iron Foundry lorry is collecting mangle rollers stored in the former brewery-cum-waterworks. (Geoff Clarke)

*Following pages:* A view from the church tower in the 1950s looking towards the station, with a down train about to pass over the level crossing. The former brewery can be seen on the left, and in the middle of the picture is the Co-operative Hall, on the far side of the river. Just to the right of the station, on the far side of the railway tracks, is the timberyard of the Stowmarket Timber Company. (Ivan Codd)

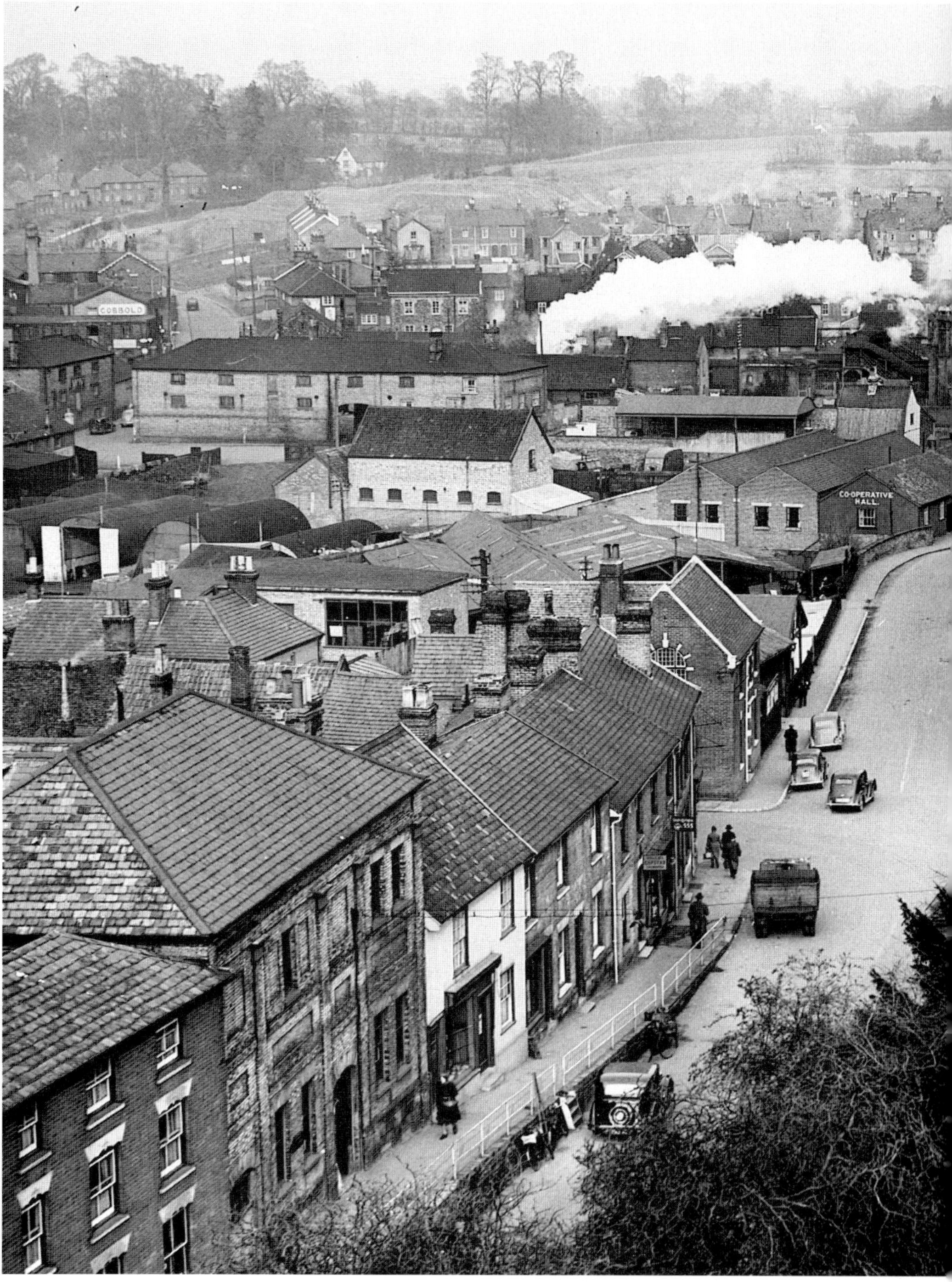
COBBOLD
CO-OPERATIVE HALL

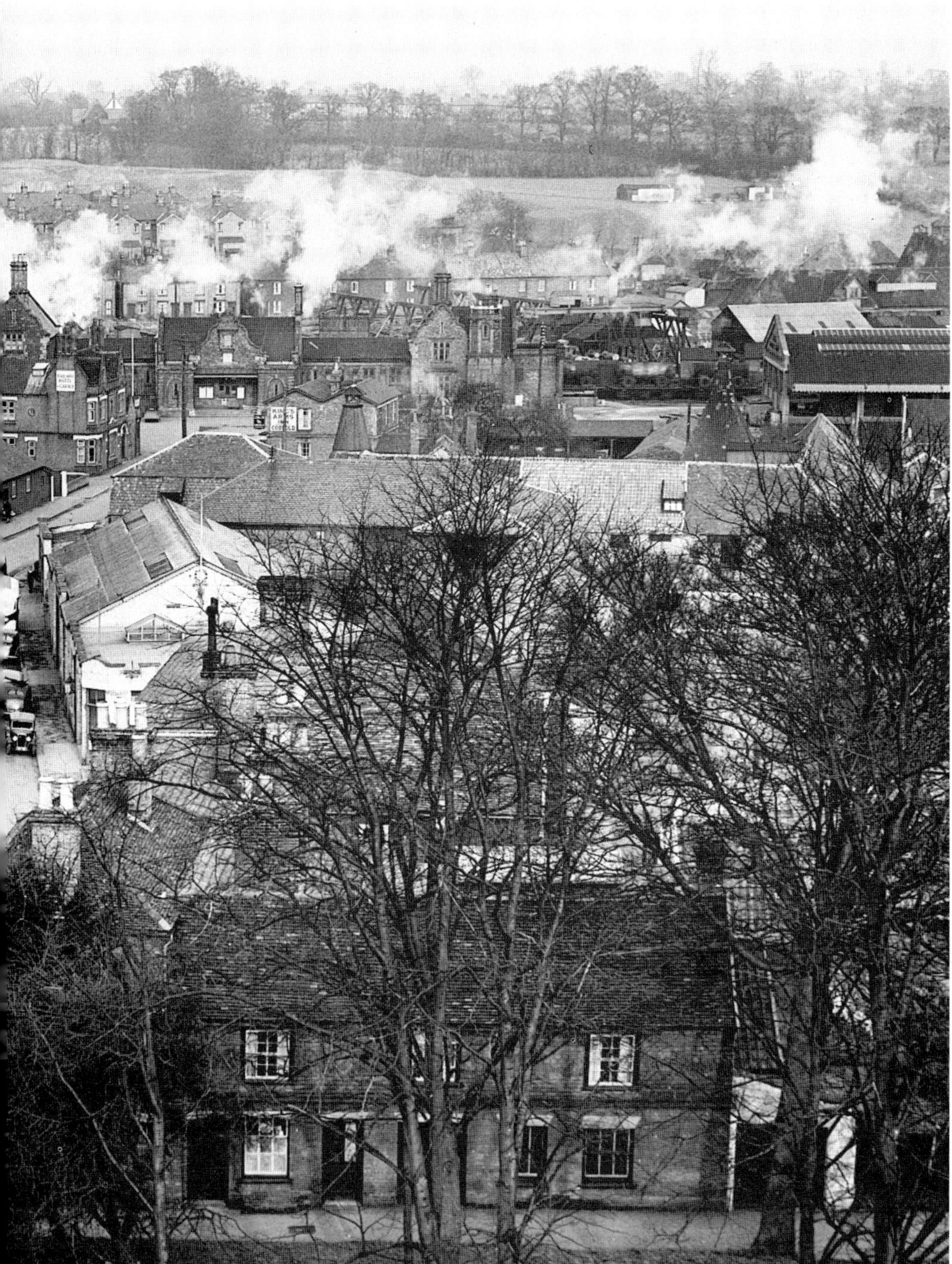

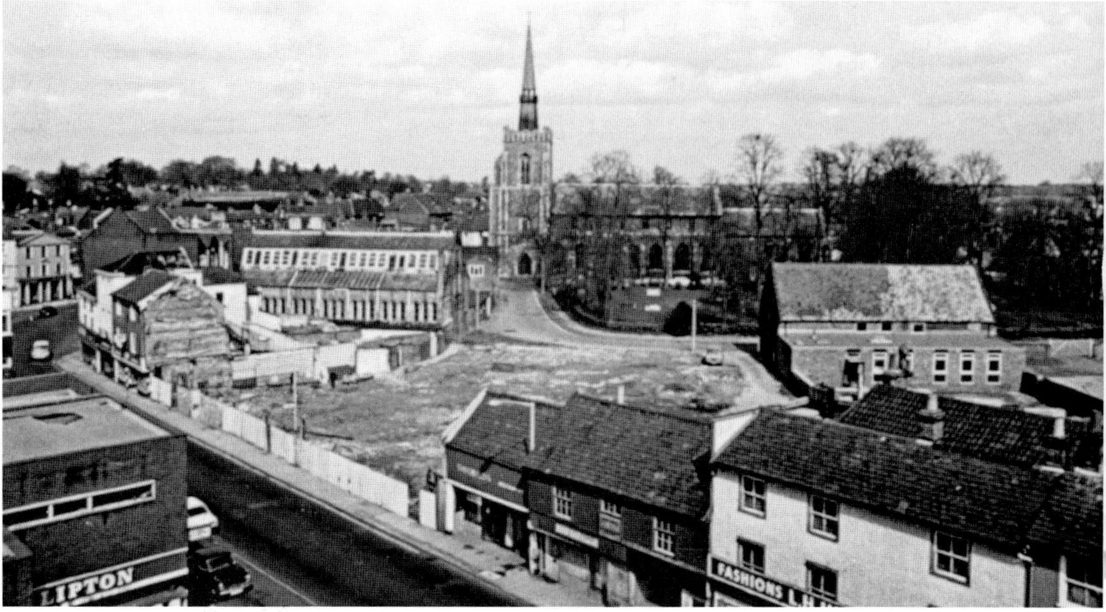


Less than two years after the demolition of Turner's premises, shops on the opposite side of Ipswich Street are also torn down, in April 1972, providing this glimpse of the parish church and of the glass-roofed Corn Exchange, which had closed in 1966. (Ivan Codd)

# BRITAIN IN OLD PHOTOGRAPHS



### ALDERNEY

Alderney: A Second Selection, *B Bonnard*

### BEDFORDSHIRE

Bedfordshire at Work, *N Lutt*

### BERKSHIRE

Maidenhead, *M Hayles & D Hedges*
Around Maidenhead, *M Hayles & B Hedges*
Reading, *P Southerton*
Reading: A Second Selection, *P Southerton*
Sandhurst and Crowthorne, *K Dancy*
Around Slough, *J Hunter & K Hunter*
Around Thatcham, *P Allen*
Around Windsor, *B Hedges*

### BUCKINGHAMSHIRE

Buckingham and District, *R Cook*
High Wycombe, *R Goodearl*
Around Stony Stratford, *A Lambert*

### CHESHIRE

Cheshire Railways, *M Hitches*
Chester, *S Nichols*

### CLWYD

Clwyd Railways, *M Hitches*

### CLYDESDALE

Clydesdale, *Lesmahagow Parish Historical Association*

### CORNWALL

Cornish Coast, *T Bowden*
Falmouth, *P Gilson*
Lower Fal, *P Gilson*
Around Padstow, *M McCarthy*
Around Penzance, *J Holmes*
Penzance and Newlyn, *J Holmes*
Around Truro, *A Lyne*
Upper Fal, *P Gilson*

### CUMBERLAND

Cockermouth and District, *J Bernard Bradbury*
Keswick and the Central Lakes, *J Marsh*
Around Penrith, *F Boyd*
Around Whitehaven, *H Fancy*

### DERBYSHIRE

Derby, *D Buxton*
Around Matlock, *D Barton*

### DEVON

Colyton and Seaton, *T Gosling*
Dawlish and Teignmouth, *G Gosling*
Devon Aerodromes, *K Saunders*
Exeter, *P Thomas*
Exmouth and Budleigh Salterton, *T Gosling*
From Haldon to Mid-Dartmoor, *T Hall*
Honiton and the Otter Valley, *J Yallop*
Around Kingsbridge, *K Tanner*
Around Seaton and Sidmouth, *T Gosling*
Seaton, Axminster and Lyme Regis, *T Gosling*

### DORSET

Around Blandford Forum, *B Cox*
Bournemouth, *M Colman*
Bridport and the Bride Valley, *J Burrell & S Humphries*
Dorchester, *T Gosling*
Around Gillingham, *P Crocker*

### DURHAM

Darlington, *G Flynn*
Darlington: A Second Selection, *G Flynn*
Durham People, *M Richardson*
Houghton-le-Spring and Hetton-le-Hole, *K Richardson*
Houghton-le-Spring and Hetton-le-Hole: A Second Selection, *K Richardson*
Sunderland, *S Miller & B Bell*
Teesdale, *D Coggins*
Teesdale: A Second Selection, *P Raine*
Weardale, *J Crosby*
Weardale: A Second Selection, *J Crosby*

### DYFED

Aberystwyth and North Ceredigion, *Dyfed Cultural Services Dept*
Haverfordwest, *Dyfed Cultural Services Dept*
Upper Tywi Valley, *Dyfed Cultural Services Dept*

### ESSEX

Around Grays, *B Evans*

### GLOUCESTERSHIRE

Along the Avon from Stratford to Tewkesbury, *J Jeremiah*
Cheltenham: A Second Selection, *R Whiting*
Cheltenham at War, *P Gill*
Cirencester, *J Welsford*
Around Cirencester, *E Cuss & P Griffiths*
Forest, The, *D Mullin*
Gloucester, *J Voyce*
Around Gloucester, *A Sutton*
Gloucester: From the Walwin Collection, *J Voyce*
North Cotswolds, *D Viner*
Severn Vale, *A Sutton*
Stonehouse to Painswick, *A Sutton*
Stroud and the Five Valleys, *S Gardiner & L Padin*
Stroud and the Five Valleys: A Second Selection, *S Gardiner & L Padin*
Stroud's Golden Valley, *S Gardiner & L Padin*
Stroudwater and Thames & Severn Canals, *E Cuss & S Gardiner*
Stroudwater and Thames & Severn Canals: A Second Selection, *E Cuss & S Gardiner*
Tewkesbury and the Vale of Gloucester, *C Hilton*
Thornbury to Berkeley, *J Hudson*
Uley, Dursley and Cam, *A Sutton*
Wotton-under-Edge to Chipping Sodbury, *A Sutton*

### GWYNEDD

Anglesey, *M Hitches*
Gwynedd Railways, *M Hitches*
Around Llandudno, *M Hitches*
Vale of Conwy, *M Hitches*

### HAMPSHIRE

Gosport, *J Sadden*
Portsmouth, *P Rogers & D Francis*

### HEREFORDSHIRE

Herefordshire, *A Sandford*

### HERTFORDSHIRE

Barnet, *I Norrie*
Hitchin, *A Fleck*
St Albans, *S Mullins*
Stevenage, *M Appleton*

### ISLE OF MAN

The Tourist Trophy, *B Snelling*

### ISLE OF WIGHT

Newport, *D Parr*
Around Ryde, *D Parr*

### JERSEY

Jersey: A Third Selection, *R Lemprière*

### KENT

Bexley, *M Scott*
Broadstairs and St Peter's, *J Whyman*
Bromley, Keston and Hayes, *M Scott*
Canterbury: A Second Selection, *D Butler*
Chatham and Gillingham, *P MacDougall*
Chatham Dockyard, *P MacDougall*
Deal, *J Broady*
Early Broadstairs and St Peter's, *B Wootton*
East Kent at War, *D Collyer*
Eltham, *J Kennett*
Folkestone: A Second Selection, *A Taylor & E Rooney*
Goudhurst to Tenterden, *A Guilmant*
Gravesend, *R Hiscock*
Around Gravesham, *R Hiscock & D Grierson*
Herne Bay, *J Hawkins*
Lympne Airport, *D Collyer*
Maidstone, *I Hales*
Margate, *R Clements*
RAF Hawkinge, *R Humphreys*
RAF Manston, *RAF Manston History Club*
RAF Manston: A Second Selection, *RAF Manston History Club*
Ramsgate and Thanet Life, *D Perkins*
Romney Marsh, *E Carpenter*
Sandwich, *C Wanostrocht*
Around Tonbridge, *C Bell*
Tunbridge Wells, *M Rowlands & I Beavis*
Tunbridge Wells: A Second Selection, *M Rowlands & I Beavis*
Around Whitstable, *C Court*
Wingham, Adisham and Littlebourne, *M Crane*

### LANCASHIRE

Around Barrow-in-Furness, *J Garbutt & J Marsh*
Blackpool, *C Rothwell*
Bury, *J Hudson*
Chorley and District, *J Smith*
Fleetwood, *C Rothwell*
Heywood, *J Hudson*
Around Kirkham, *C Rothwell*
Lancashire North of the Sands, *J Garbutt & J Marsh*
Around Lancaster, *S Ashworth*
Lytham St Anne's, *C Rothwell*
North Fylde, *C Rothwell*
Radcliffe, *J Hudson*
Rossendale, *B Moore & N Dunnachie*

### LEICESTERSHIRE

Around Ashby-de-la-Zouch, *K Hillier*
Charnwood Forest, *I Keil, W Humphrey & D Wix*
Leicester, *D Burton*
Leicester: A Second Selection, *D Burton*
Melton Mowbray, *T Hickman*
Around Melton Mowbray, *T Hickman*
River Soar, *D Wix, P Shacklock & I Keil*
Rutland, *T Clough*
Vale of Belvoir, *T Hickman*
Around the Welland Valley, *S Mastoris*

### LINCOLNSHIRE

Grimsby, *J Tierney*
Around Grimsby, *J Tierney*
Grimsby Docks, *J Tierney*
Lincoln, *D Cuppleditch*

Scunthorpe, *D Taylor*
Skegness, *W Kime*
Around Skegness, *W Kime*

## LONDON

Balham and Tooting, *P Loobey*
Crystal Palace, Penge & Anerley, *M Scott*
Greenwich and Woolwich, *K Clark*
Hackney: A Second Selection, *D Mander*
Lewisham and Deptford, *J Coulter*
Lewisham and Deptford: A Second Selection, *J Coulter*
Streatham, *P Loobey*
Around Whetstone and North Finchley, *J Heathfield*
Woolwich, *B Evans*

## MONMOUTHSHIRE

Chepstow and the River Wye, *A Rainsbury*
Monmouth and the River Wye, *Monmouth Museum*

## NORFOLK

Great Yarmouth, *M Teun*
Norwich, *M Colman*
Wymondham and Attleborough, *P Yaxley*

## NORTHAMPTONSHIRE

Around Stony Stratford, *A Lambert*

## NOTTINGHAMSHIRE

Arnold and Bestwood, *M Spick*
Arnold and Bestwood: A Second Selection, *M Spick*
Changing Face of Nottingham, *G Oldfield*
Mansfield, *Old Mansfield Society*
Around Newark, *T Warner*
Nottingham: 1944–1974, *D Whitworth*
Sherwood Forest, *D Ottewell*
Victorian Nottingham, *M Payne*

## OXFORDSHIRE

Around Abingdon, *P Horn*
Banburyshire, *M Barnett & S Gosling*
Burford, *A Jewell*
Around Didcot and the Hagbournes, *B Lingham*
Garsington, *M Gunther*
Around Henley-on-Thames, *S Ellis*
Oxford: The University, *J Rhodes*
Thame to Watlington, *N Hood*
Around Wallingford, *D Beasley*
Witney, *T Worley*
Around Witney, *C Mitchell*
Witney District, *T Worley*
Around Woodstock, *J Bond*

## POWYS

Brecon, *Brecknock Museum*
Welshpool, *E Bredsdorff*

## SHROPSHIRE

Shrewsbury, *D Trumper*
Whitchurch to Market Drayton, *M Morris*

## SOMERSET

Bath, *J Hudson*
Bridgwater and the River Parrett, *R Fitzhugh*
Bristol, *D Moorcroft & N Campbell-Sharp*
Changing Face of Keynsham,
*B Lowe & M Whitehead*
Chard and Ilminster, *G Gosling & F Huddy*
Crewkerne and the Ham Stone Villages,
*G Gosling & F Huddy*
Around Keynsham and Saltford, *B Lowe & T Brown*
Midsomer Norton and Radstock, *C Howell*
Somerton, Ilchester and Langport, *G Gosling & F Huddy*
Taunton, *N Chipchase*
Around Taunton, *N Chipchase*
Wells, *C Howell*
Weston-Super-Mare, *S Poole*
Around Weston-Super-Mare, *S Poole*
West Somerset Villages, *K Houghton & L Thomas*

## STAFFORDSHIRE

Aldridge, *J Farrow*
Bilston, *E Rees*
Black Country Transport: Aviation, *A Brew*
Around Burton upon Trent, *G Sowerby & R Farman*
Bushbury, *A Chatwin, M Mills & E Rees*
Around Cannock, *M Mills & S Belcher*
Around Leek, *R Poole*
Lichfield, *H Clayton & K Simmons*
Around Pattingham and Wombourne, *M Griffiths, P Leigh & M Mills*
Around Rugeley, *T Randall & J Anslow*
Smethwick, *J Maddison*
Stafford, *J Anslow & T Randall*
Around Stafford, *J Anslow & T Randall*
Stoke-on-Trent, *I Lawley*
Around Tamworth, *R Sulima*
Around Tettenhall and Codsall, *M Mills*
Tipton, Wednesbury and Darlaston, *R Pearson*
Walsall, *D Gilbert & M Lewis*
Wednesbury, *I Bott*
West Bromwich, *R Pearson*

## SUFFOLK

Ipswich: A Second Selection, *D Kindred*
Around Ipswich, *D Kindred*
Around Mildenhall, *C Dring*
Southwold to Aldeburgh, *H Phelps*
Around Woodbridge, *H Phelps*

## SURREY

Cheam and Belmont, *P Berry*
Croydon, *S Bligh*
Dorking and District, *K Harding*
Around Dorking, *A Jackson*
Around Epsom, *P Berry*
Farnham: A Second Selection, *J Parratt*
Around Haslemere and Hindhead, *T Winter & G Collyer*
Richmond, *Richmond Local History Society*
Sutton, *P Berry*

## SUSSEX

Arundel and the Arun Valley, *J Godfrey*
Bishopstone and Seaford, *P Pople & P Berry*
Brighton and Hove, *J Middleton*
Brighton and Hove: A Second Selection, *J Middleton*
Around Crawley, *M Goldsmith*
Hastings, *P Haines*
Hastings: A Second Selection, *P Haines*
Around Haywards Heath, *J Middleton*
Around Heathfield, *A Gillet & B Russell*
Around Heathfield: A Second Selection,
*A Gillet & B Russell*
High Weald, *B Harwood*
High Weald: A Second Selection, *B Harwood*
Horsham and District, *T Wales*
Lewes, *J Middleton*
RAF Tangmere, *A Saunders*
Around Rye, *A Dickinson*
Around Worthing, *S White*

## WARWICKSHIRE

Along the Avon from Stratford to Tewkesbury, *J Jeremiah*
Bedworth, *J Burton*
Coventry, *D McGrory*
Around Coventry, *D McGrory*
Nuneaton, *S Clews & S Vaughan*
Around Royal Leamington Spa, *J Cameron*
Around Royal Leamington Spa: A Second Selection,
*J Cameron*
Around Warwick, *R Booth*

## WESTMORLAND

Eden Valley, *J Marsh*
Kendal, *M & P Duff*
South Westmorland Villages, *J Marsh*
Westmorland Lakes, *J Marsh*

## WILTSHIRE

Around Amesbury, *P Daniels*
Chippenham and Lacock, *A Wilson & M Wilson*
Around Corsham and Box, *A Wilson & M Wilson*
Around Devizes, *D Buxton*
Around Highworth, *G Tanner*
Around Highworth and Faringdon, *G Tanner*
Around Malmesbury, *A Wilson*
Marlborough: A Second Selection, *P Colman*
Around Melksham,
*Melksham and District Historical Association*
Nadder Valley, *R. Sawyer*
Salisbury, *P Saunders*
Salisbury: A Second Selection, *P Daniels*
Salisbury: A Third Selection, *P Daniels*
Around Salisbury, *P Daniels*
Swindon: A Third Selection, *The Swindon Society*
Swindon: A Fourth Selection, *The Swindon Society*
Trowbridge, *M Marshman*
Around Wilton, *P Daniels*
Around Wootton Bassett, Cricklade and Purton, *T Sharp*

## WORCESTERSHIRE

Evesham to Bredon, *F Archer*
Around Malvern, *K Smith*
Around Pershore, *M Dowty*
Redditch and the Needle District, *R Saunders*
Redditch: A Second Selection, *R Saunders*
Around Tenbury Wells, *D Green*
Worcester, *M Dowty*
Around Worcester, *R Jones*
Worcester in a Day, *M Dowty*
Worcestershire at Work, *R Jones*

## YORKSHIRE

Huddersfield: A Second Selection, *H Wheeler*
Huddersfield: A Third Selection, *H Wheeler*
Leeds Road and Rail, *R Vickers*
Pontefract, *R van Riel*
Scarborough, *D Coggins*
Scarborough's War Years, *R Percy*
Skipton and the Dales, *Friends of the Craven Museum*
Around Skipton-in-Craven, *Friends of the Craven Museum*
Yorkshire Wolds, *I & M Sumner*